UNPUBLISHED Bo-FRAGMENTS IN TRANSLITERATION II

UNPUBLISHED Bo-FRAGMENTS IN TRANSLITERATION II

(Bo 6151–Bo 9535)

OĞUZ SOYSAL and BAŞAK YILDIZ GÜLŞEN

CHICAGO HITTITE DICTIONARY SUPPLEMENTS • 3
THE ORIENTAL INSTITUTE OF THE UNIVERSITY OF CHICAGO
CHICAGO • ILLINOIS

ISSN: 0081-7554
LCCN: 2018946127
ISBN-13: 978-1-61491-044-2

The Oriental Institute, Chicago
Chicago Hittite Dictionary Supplements 3

Published 2019. Printed in the United States of America.
Printed by Ace Graphics Inc, Illinois USA.

Series Editors
Charissa Johnson, Leslie Schramer, and Thomas G. Urban
with the assistance of Emily Smith

Cover Illustration
Middle Hittite treaty between Taḫurwaili, the king of Ḫatti
and Eḫeya, the king of Kizzuwatna (KBo 28.108 + Bo 9490)

This paper meets the requirements
of ANSI / NISO Z39.48-1984
(Permanence of Paper)

In Memoriam

Prof. Dr. Şerafettin Turan (1925–2015)

and

Gürbüz Yıldız (1943–2016)

TABLE OF CONTENTS

FOREWORD

The present volume continues the systematic edition of the unpublished Bo-Texts deposited in the Museum of Ancient Anatolian Civilizations in Ankara. The results which were yielded in the first installment, *Unpublished Bo-Fragments in Transliteration I (Bo 9536–9736)* (CHDS 2, published 2015), and the positive reactions of our colleagues encouraged us to produce another volume that is presented as CHDS 3 in this monograph, with the title *Unpublished Bo-Fragments in Transliteration II (Bo 6151–Bo 9535).*

In June 2012, when CHDS 2 was still in preparation, Başak Yıldız Gülşen, the curator of the Ankara Museum, proposed a collaboration for editing of the fragments in the number range of Bo 8695 to Bo 9535. Ms. Yıldız Gülşen has the publication rights of these 171 pieces, which are similar in size to the overlapping fragments Bo 9536–Bo 9736 already edited by Soysal in the previous volume. After our agreement on this cooperation, the digital pictures of the fragments were taken in December 2012. The restoration work in the museum and consequently insufficient light conditions, however, forced us to retake the pictures of some tablets again in June 2014 for a better result. Meanwhile, the transliterations of the texts in question were prepared, whereby a number of joins and duplicates were noticed. The first results are now found at the *Konkordanz der hethitischen Keilschrifttafeln* (http://www.hethport.uni-wuerzburg.de/hetkonk/) under their relevant text categories, and in two related articles: "A New Join to the Mita-Text (Bo 8742) and a Duplicate of the Zannanza-Affair (Bo 8757)" and "Further Joins from the Boğazköy-Tablets," published in the French journal *NABU* 2014/4, pp. 145–48 and *NABU* 2015/3, pp. 113–17, respectively. The following eleven direct joins were made during the period July 2014–April 2015:

Bo 8696 + KUB 56.43

Bo 8710 + IBoT 1.22 + KUB 20.60

Bo 8742 + KUB 23.72 +

Bo 8752 + Bo 9615 + KUB 41.2 + KBo 52.27

Bo 8796 + VS 28.30

Bo 9441 + KBo 3.18 + 19 + 17

Bo 9449 + Bo 4422 + KUB 39.104

Bo 9514 + Bo 3251

Bo 9516 + KUB 17.24

Bo 9518 + Bo 4744 + KUB 26.1a

Bo 9526 + KBo 6.10 + KBo 6.20

At the time the work on the fragments in question was in progress, the following direct joins had already been discovered by other scholars, as indicated at the *Konkordanz der hethitischen Keilschrifttafeln*:

Bo 8704 + Bo 4395 + KUB 45.67 (D. Groddek)

Bo 8752 + (Bo 9615 +) KUB 41.2 + KBo 52.27 (J. L. Miller)

(Bo 9441 +) Bo 7303 + KBo 3.19 (J. Lorenz)

Bo 9490 + KBo 28.108 (F. Fuscagni)

Bo 9511 + KBo 3.38 (F. Fuscagni)

After the aforementioned direct joins were found or suggested, based mainly on the work with the lexical files in Chicago, the fragments in question were physically glued by the museum staff in Ankara, and rephotographed by us in June 2015 for this publication. In cases where pertinent fragments were dispersed in different museums, we received again helpful technical support from the Akademie der Wissenschaften und der Literatur Mainz (Kommission für den Alten Orient) for generating the joins through image processing using the old black & white tablet photos which are in the possession of the Akademie. They are the following texts:

Bo 6810 + KUB 44.16 + IBoT 3.69

Bo 8710 + IBoT 1.22 + KUB 20.60

Bo 8742 + KUB 23.72 +

Bo 8796 + VS 28.30

Bo 9441 + KBo 3.18 + 19 + 17 + Bo 7303

Bo 9511 + KBo 3.38

Bo 9516 + KUB 17.24

Bo 9518 + Bo 4744 + KUB 26.1a

Bo 9582 + KUB 36.2d

Bo 9614 + KUB 33.38

Bo 9630 + KUB 9.32 +

Bo 9650 + KUB 8.51

Bo 9705 + Bo 8282 + KUB 15.1

As usual, the fragments dealt with here are mostly of religious nature that have significance especially for rituals and festivals. A few fragments are additions to important historical compositions: Bo 8742 (CTH 146), Bo 8757 (CTH 40), Bo 9441 (CTH 311.2.B), Bo 9466 (CTH 3.2), Bo 9490 (CTH 29.A), Bo 9504 (CTH 215), and Bo 9511 (CTH 3.1.B). The discovery of the fragments Bo 7103 (see below) of the *BĒL MADGALTI*-Instructions (CTH 261), Bo 9518 of the LÚ.SAG-Instructions (CTH 255.2.E) and Bo 9526 of the Hittite Laws (CTH 292.II.b.A) is worth mentioning as well. The non-Hittite Bo 9520 (CTH 819), a Sumerian literary text naming "Enki, the king of the Abzu" represents a further text variety.

Ms. Yıldız Gülşen has another group of unpublished Bo-fragments from the former share of Sedat Alp that were divided up among the young scholars after his passing away. We decided to include them here in order to enrich the content of CHDS 3. These extras are twenty small-to-medium-size pieces and only a limited selection in the number range of Bo 6000 to Bo 8000:

Bo 6151

Bo 6207

Bo 6238

Bo 6271

Bo 6370

Bo 6570

Bo 6788

Bo 6810

Bo 6827

Bo 6909

Bo 6978

Bo 7050

Bo 7103

Bo 7284

Bo 7317

Bo 7444

Bo 7833

Bo 7937

Bo 8029

Bo 8084

The tentative transliterations of some of them were once utilized by Alp in his book *Beiträge zur Erforschung des hethitischen Tempels* (1983) for discussions on ^{É}*ḫalentuwa-*. The majority of the texts belong to the religious genres (festivals, rituals, cult inventories, vows, mythological compostions); the only exception is Bo 7103, an instruction fragment (CTH 261). From this group one direct join was discovered in May 2015 as part of Bo 6810 + KUB 44.16 + IBoT 3.69.

For all technical issues, refer to the "Foreword" of CHDS 2, p. xi, which would concern and cover everything here as well. It should be additionaly pointed out, however, that we used this time centimetric scales on the photos of some "extra" texts as they consist of 10 lines or more. Thus they are of cosiderably larger size than our regular Bo-fragments.

This volume contains two appendices for the convenience of readers: Appendix 1 "Addenda and Corrigenda to CHDS 2" aims to update the data of Bo 9536–Bo 9736 after their publication, taking additionally discovered joins and duplicates into consideration. All newly joined Bo-fragments were photographed in December 2015 and included here. The composite images are again by courtesy of the Akademie der Wissenschaften und der Literatur Mainz (Kommission für den Alten Orient). Appendix 2 "Concordance of Bo-Texts and CHDS 2–3" lists and numbers all Bo-fragments edited in two volumes of this series in order to locate them easier as they are cited at the *Konkordanz der hethitischen Keilschrifttafeln*. For further remarks see the pertinent sections.

The research of Soysal was supported by a financial grant from the Oriental Institute of the University of Chicago that made it possible for him to travel to Turkey in December 2015. He would like to express his sincere thanks to Gil Stein and Theo van den Hout for their interest in, and their support of his research on the unpublished Bo-texts in the last five years. Soysal and Yıldız Gülşen are grateful to the director of the Museum of Ancient Anatolian Civilizations, Enver Sağır, the deputy director, Emel Yurttagül, and the curators İsmet Aykut, Mine Çifçi, Şerife Yılmaz, Filiz Akman, and Selda Delioğlu for their constant assistance. Furthermore, the authors are deeply indebted to Francesco Fuscagni and Gabrielle Stivala (both Mainz, Germany) for the image processing of the joins as mentioned above, Gül Demirayak (Ankara, Turkey) for her permisson to utilize the unpublished piece Bo 3396, and Thomas Urban, Charissa Johnson, Leslie Schramer, Rebecca Cain, and Emily Smith who made the publication of this book possible. Gary Beckman (Ann Arbor, MI) made helpful suggestions regarding interpretation of some problematic signs and words; let us thank him for his kind support.

Finally, for the information of readers it should be remembered that some of our Turkish colleagues have preferred a different process to publish the Bo-texts in their custody, as İlknur Taş (DBH 43, 2014) and Rukiye Akdoğan (DBH 46, 2016) did for Bo 8264–Bo 8485 and Bo 4658–Bo 5000, respectively. They further plan to provide the cuneiform copies of these fragments in separate publications.

Let us consider this volume as the last publication of a small-budget project and hope to bring out more cuneiform material from Boğazköy in the context of more extensive collabrations in the near future.

Oğuz Soysal
January 15, 2016, Chicago

LIST OF ABBREVIATIONS

TEXTS, AUTHORS, LITERATURE

AAA	*Annals of Archaeology and Anthropology*. Liverpool
ABoT	Ankara Arkeoloji Müzesinde bulunan Boğazköy Tabletleri
AMMY	*Anadolu Medeniyetleri Müzesi Yıllığı*. Ankara
Anatolica	*Annuaire International pour les Civilisations de l'Asie Anterieure*. Institut Historique et Archeologique Neerlandais a Istanbul. Leiden
AoF	*Altorientalische Forschungen*. Berlin
Aramazd	*Armenian Journal of Near Eastern Studies*. Yerevan
AS	Assyriological Studies. Chicago
AS 25	McMahon, Gregory. *The Hittite State Cult of the Tutelary Deities*. 1991
Belleten	Belleten. *Revue publiée par la Société d'histoire turque / Türk Tarih Kurumu*. Ankara
BGH	Richter, Thomas. *Bibliographisches Glossar des Hurritischen*. Wiesbaden, 2012
Bo	Inventory numbers of Boğazköy tablets excavated 1906–1912
CAD	The Assyrian Dictionary of the Oriental Institute of the University of Chicago. Chicago
CHD	The Hittite Dictionary of the Oriental Institute of the University of Chicago. Chicago
CHDS	Chicago Hittite Dictionary Supplements. Chicago
CHDS 2	Soysal, Oğuz. *Unpublished Bo-Fragments in Transliteration I (Bo 9536–Bo 9736)*. 2015
ChS	Corpus der hurritischen Sprachdenkmäler. Roma
ChS I/3–2	Wegner, Ilse. *Hurritische Opferlisten aus hethitischen Festbeschreibungen. Teil II: Texte für Teššub, Ḫebat und weitere Gottheiten*. 2002
CLL	Melchert, Harold C. *Cuneiform Luvian Lexicon*. Chapel Hill, 1993
CTH	Laroche, Emmanuel. *Catalogue des textes hittites*. Paris, 1971
DBH	Dresdner Beiträge zur Hethitologie. Dresden — Wiesbaden
DBH 6	Groddek, Detlev, Albertine Hagenbuchner, and Inge Hoffmann. *Hethitische Texte in Transkription: VS NF 12*. 2002
DBH 13	Groddek, Detlev. *Hethitische Texte in Transkription: KUB 20*. 2004
DBH 14	Groddek, Detlev. *Hethitische Texte in Transkription: KUB 59*. 2004
DBH 20	Groddek, Detlev. *Hethitische Texte in Transkription: KUB 60*. 2006
DBH 23	Groddek, Detlev. *Hethitische Texte in Transkription: IBoT 4*. 2007
DBH 35	*Hethitologie in Dresden. Textbearbeitungen, Arbeiten zur Forschungs- und Schriftgeschichte*. 2011
DBH 41	Asan, Ali Naci. *Der Mythos vom erzürnten Gott. Ein philologischer Beitrag zum religionshistorischen Verständnis des Telipinu-Mythos und verwandter Texte*. 2014
DBH 43	Taş, İlknur. *Hethitische Texte in Transkription: Bo 8264–Bo 8485*. 2014
DLL	Laroche, Emmanuel. *Dictionnaire de la langue louvite*. Paris, 1959
DŠ	Güterbock, Hans G. "The Deeds of Šuppiluliuma as Told by his Son, Muršili II." *JCS* 10: 41ff., 59ff., 75ff., 1956
Eothen	Eothen. Florence
Eothen 11	*Anatolia antica. Studi in memoria di Fiorella Imparati*. 2002
FHG	Fragments hittites de Genève
FHL	Fragments hittites du Louvre
Flora	Ertem, Hayri. *Boğazköy metinlerine göre Hititler devri Anadolu'sunun Florası*. Ankara, 1974

FsHoffner	*Hittite Studies in Honor of Harry A. Hoffner Jr. on the Occasion of His 65th Birthday.* Winona Lake, 2003
GestaSupp	del Monte, Giuseppe F. *Le gesta di Suppiluliuma.* Pisa, 2009
GLH	Laroche, Emmanuel. *Glossaire de la langue hourrite.* Paris, 1978-1979
HbOr	Handbuch der Orientalistik. Leiden
HHB I	Schuster, Hans-Siegfried. *Die ḫattisch-hethitischen Bilinguen. I. Einleitung, Texte und Kommentar.* Teil 1. Leiden, 1974
HDA	von Schuler, Einar. *Hethitische Dienstanweisungen für höhere Hof- und Staatsbeamte.* Graz, 1957
HED	Puhvel, Jaan. *Hittite Etymological Dictionary.* Berlin — New York
HEG	Tischler, Johann. *Hethitisches etymologisches Glossar.* Innsbruck
HFAC	Beckman, Gary, and Harry A. Hoffner. "Hittite Fragments in American Collections." *JCS* 37:1ff., 1985
HG	Friedrich, Johannes. *Die hethitischen Gesetze.* Leiden, 1959
HHT	Riemschneider, Kaspar Klaus. *Hurritische und hethitische Texte.* Munich, 1974
HPMM	Hethitologie Portal Mainz — Materialien. Wiesbaden
HPMM 6	Fuscagni, Francesco. *Hethitische unveröffentlichte Texte aus den Jahren 1906-1912 in der Sekundärliteratur.* 2007
HS	*Historische Sprachforschung.* Göttingen Zürich
HT	*Hittite Texts in the Cuneiform Character in the British Museum.* London 1920
HW^2	Friedrich, Johannes, Annelies Kammenhuber, et alii. *Hethitisches Wörterbuch. Zweite, völlig neubearbeitete Auflage auf der Grundlage der edierten hethitischen Texte.* Heidelberg
HZL	Rüster, Christel, and Erich Neu. *Hethitisches Zeichenlexikon. Inventar und Interpretation der Keilschriftzeichen aus den Boğazköy-Texten.* StBot Beiheft 2. Wiesbaden, 1989
IBoT	Istanbul Arkeoloji Müzelerinde Bulunan Boğazköy Tabletleri
IF	*Indogermanische Forschungen. Zeitschrift für Indogermanistik und allgemeine Sprachwissenschaft.* Straßburg — Berlin
IJDL	*International Journal of Diachronic Linguistics and Linguistic Reconstruction.* München.
JAOS	*Journal of the American Oriental Society.* Ann Arbor
JCS	*Journal of Cuneiform Studies.* New Haven
KBo	Keilschrifttexte aus Boghazköi. Leipzig — Berlin
KN	Haas, Volkert. *Der Kult von Nerik. Ein Beitrag zur hethitischen Religionsgeschichte.* Studia Pohl 4. Roma, 1970
Konkordanz	Košak, Silvin. *Konkordanz der hethitischen Keilschrifttafeln* http://www.hethport.uni-wuerzburg.de/hetkonk/
KUB	Keilschrifturkunden aus Boghazköi. Berlin
KuT	Edition numbers of Kuşaklı tablets
LH	Hoffner, Harry A. *The Laws of the Hittites. A Critical Edition.* Leiden - New York - Köln, 1997
MIO	*Mitteilungen des Instituts für Orientforschung.* Berlin
Murš. I	Soysal, Oğuz. Muršili I. Eine historische Studie. Inaugural-Dissertation zur Erlangung der Doktorwürde der Philosophischen Fakultät I der Julius-Maximilians-Universität zu Würzburg 1989. Würzburg, 1994
NABU	*Nouvelles Assyriologiques Brèves et Utilitaires.* Paris
OLZ	*Orientalistische Literaturzeitung.* Leipzig - Berlin
Onomasticon I	van Gessel, Ben H. L. *Onomasticon of the Hittite Pantheon.* Part I. HbOr, Abt. I, Bd. 33. Leiden — New York — Boston — Köln, 1998
OrAnt	Oriens Antiquus. Rivista del Centro per le antichità e la storia dell'arte del Vicino Oriente. Roma
NH	Laroche, Emmanuel. *Les Noms des Hittites.* Paris, 1966
Nuntarrijašḫa	Nakamura, Mitsuo. *Das hethitische* nuntarrijašḫa-*Fest.* Leiden, 2002
Royal Hittite Instructions	Miller, Jared L. *Royal Hittite Instructions and Related Administrative Texts.* Atlanta, 2013
RŠ	Inventory numbers of Ras Šamra tablets

Samuha	Lebrun, René. *Samuha, foyer religieux de l'empire hittite*. Louvain-la-Neuve, 1976
SMEA	Studi Micenei ed Egeo-Anatolici. Roma.
StBoT	Studien zu den Boğazköy-Texten. Wiesbaden
StBoT 22	Oettinger, Norbert. *Die Militärischen Eide der Hethiter*. 1976
StBoT 27	Singer, Itamar. *The Hittite* KI.LAM *Festival*. Part One. 1983
StBoT 37	Klinger, Jörg. *Untersuchungen zur Rekonstruktion der hattischen Kultschicht*. 1996
StBoT 50	Popko, Maciej. *Arinna. Eine heilige Stadt der Hethiter*. 2009
StMed	Studia Mediterranea. Pavia.
StMed 14	Daddi, Franca Pecchioli. *Il vincolo per i governatori di provincia*. 2003
SV I	Friedrich, Johannes. *Staatsverträge des Ḫatti-Reiches in hethitischer Sprache I*. Mitteilungen der Vorderasiatisch-ägyptischen Gesellschaft 31/1. Leipzig, 1926
Tempel	Alp, Sedat. *Beiträge zur Erforschung des hethitischen Tempels, Kultanlagen im Lichte der Keilschrifttexte*. Ankara, 1983
THeth	Texte der Hethiter. Heidelberg
THeth 21	Popko, Maciej. *Zippalanda: Ein Kultzentrum im hethitischen Kleinasien*. 1994
THeth 22	Yoshida, Daisuke. *Untersuchungen zu den Sonnengottheiten bei den Hethitern: Schwurgötterliste, helfende Gottheit, Feste*. 1996
THeth 26	Taggar-Cohen, Ada. *Hittite Priesthood*. 2006
VBoT	Verstreute Boghazköi-Texte. Marburg, 1930
Votive	J. de Roos, Hittite Votive Texts. Istanbul, 2007
VS	*Vorderasiatische Schriftdenkmäler der Staatlichen Museen zu Berlin*
ZA	*Zeitschrift für Assyriologie und Vorderasiatische Archäologie*. Leipzig — Berlin — New York

GENERAL

abl.	ablative	MS	Middle Script
acc.	accusative	Murš.	Muršili
adj.	adjective	Muw.	Muwatalli
all.	allative	n.	note
cf.	*confer*, compare	N/A	no information available
coloph.	colophon	neut.	neuter (gender)
com.	common (gender)	NH	New Hittite
dat.	dative	nom.	nominative
dupl.	duplicate	NS	New Script
e. g.	*exempli gratia*, for example	obv.	obverse
eras.	erasure	OH	Old Hittite
etc.	*et cetera*, and so forth	OS	Old Script
ENS	Early New Script	part.	participle
gen.	genitive	pl.	plural
Hurr.	Hurrian	pre-NS	Pre-New Script
ibid.	*ibidem*, in the same place	pres.	present
imp.	imperative	pret.	preterite
inst.	instrumental	rev.	reverse
iter.	iterative	rt. col.	right column
LMS	Late Middle Script	rt. e.	right edge
LNH	Late New Hittite	sg.	singular
LNS	Late New Script	subst.	substantive
loc.	locative	sup.	supine
lt. col.	left column	Šupp.	Šuppiluliuma
lt. e.	left edge	u. e.	upper edge
Luw.	Luwian / luwoid	unkn.	unknown
MH	Middle Hittite	voc.	Vocative
mid.	middle (voice)	*	unattested, hypothetical form
mng.	meaning	†	ghost word

UNPUBLISHED Bo-FRAGMENTS IN TRANSLITERATION II (Bo 6151–Bo 9535)

1. Bo 6151

Description: Festival.
CTH: 670 "*Fragments divers.*"
Dating and Script: LNS.
Remarks: One-sided fragment from the left column of a tablet.
Measurements: 2.6 × 6.3 × 1.6 cm.
Bibliography: I. Singer, StBoT 27 (1983) 110; F. Fuscagni, HPMM 6 (2007) 134 (bibliography).

Bo 6151

Left column

§ 1' 1' *ir-ḫa-a*$^{?}$*-u-u̯]a-an-zi ti-i̯ạ-zi*

2' I-*ŠU*$^{?}$ *ir-ḫa-a*$^{?}$*]-iz-zi* ^{d}*Ḫa-ra-at-š[i-in*$^{?}$]

---

§ 2' 3' .G]AL.GAL-*i̯a-kán*[1] ^{É}*ar-ki-u̯i*$_5$*-i̯a*[2]

4' (-)*a]n-da* ^{LÚ}*ḪA-ZA-NU*[3]

5' [4]] *ḫa-an-da-an* *ḫar-zi*

(broken off)

Text-critical notes: [1] On the use of logographic plural GAL.GAL see CHD Š /1 (2002) 93. In the present context the most appropriate possibility seems to be [$^{LÚ.MEŠ}$SANGA.G]AL.GAL.[2] This attestation is cited by I. Singer, StBot 27, 110. [3] Rare spelling for the common form ^{LÚ}*ḪA-ZA-AN-NU*; also attested in the Middle Hittite letter from Kuşaklı KuT 49 obv. 2. [4] To be restored with *ka-ru-ú*; cf. IBoT 3.1 obv. 16' and KBo 27.42 II 32.

2. Bo 6207

Description: Festival.

CTH: 635 "*Fragments de fêtes de Zippalanda et du mont Daha.*"

Dating and Script: OH/NS.

Remarks: Two-sided fragment from the left (obv. III) and right (rev. IV) portions (with edges) of a tablet. Obv. III lines 1'–4' are parallel to KBo 44.170:5'–8'.

Measurements: 5.9 × 5.8 × 2.8 cm.

Bibliography: S. Alp, *Tempel* (1983) 306–07; M. Popko, THeth 21 (1994) 276–79; F. Fuscagni, HPMM 6 (2007) 136–37 (transliteration and bibliography)

Bo 6207 obv. III

6207 rev. IV

Bo 6207 rev. IV (right edge)

Bo 6207 obv. III

6207 rev. IV

Obverse III

§ 1' 1' [LUGAL-*uš-ká*]*n*$^{?1)}$ ^{É}*ḫa le-en-tu-u̯*[*a-aš*]

2' [*an-d*]*a* *pa-iz-zi*

3' [^{LÚ}S]ANGA-*ma* ^{LÚ}*ta-az-ze-el-l*[*i-iš*]

4' ⸢*I*⸣-*NA* É ^{d}UTU *pa-a-an-zi*

---

§ 2' 5' MUNUS.LUGAL-*ma* $^{\text{NA}_4}$*ḫu-u-u̯a-ši*

6' *pí-ra-an* *ti-i̯a-zi*

7' ta ^{d}*Ḫa-ra-at-ši ir-ḫ*[*a-a*$^{?}$*-iz-zi*]

8' ⸤G⸥IŠ.^{d}INANNA.TUR $^{\text{LÚ.MEŠ}}$*ḫal-li-i̯a-r*[*e-e*$^{?}$*-eš*]

9' [S]ÌR-*RU* ^{LÚ}ALAN.ZU$_{9}$ *me-ma-*[*a*$^{?}$*-i*]

10' ^{LÚ}*ki-i-ta-aš* *ḫal-za-a-i*

11' LÚ ^{d}U-*ma* MUNUS ^{d}U ⸢*x*⸣

12' [*ḫa-l*]*u-kán* *tar-ni-iš-kán-zi*$^{2)}$

(broken off)

Reverse IV

§ 1' 1'] ⸢*x-x-iš*(-)*x*⸣$^{3)}$(-)[

2' [*ta*]*-aš*$^{4)}$ *UŠ-KE-EN*

---

§ 2' 3' [MUNUS.L]UGAL-*aš* *IT-TI* $^{\text{NA}_4}$ZI.KỊN

4' [*ú-i*]*z-zi* ^{LÚ}SANGA

5' [^{LÚ}*t*]*a-az-ze-el-li-iš*

6' [*ták-n*]*a-aš* ^{d}UTU-*aš* *pár-na-aš* *pí-ra-an*

7' [LUGAL-*i-k*]*án*$^{?5)}$ *me-na-aḫ-ḫa-an-da*

8' [*ti-a*]*n-zi* ^{LÚ}SAGI.A LUGAL-*i*

9' [*a-ku-u̯*]*a-an-na* *pa-a-i*

10' [^{LÚ}SA]GI.A DINGIR-LIM-*ma*

11' ^{LÚ}*t*]⸤*a-az-z*⸥*e-el-li*

12']-*x̣*$^{6)}$

(broken off)

Text-critical notes: $^{1)}$ Restoration with the particle =*kan* is due to space in the broken part and following KBo 44.170:5'. $^{2)}$ For the verbal form *tarniškanzi* cf. LÚ ^{d}IŠKỤR [MUNUS$^{?}$] ^{d}IŠ[KUR$^{?}$ *ḫa-l*]*u-kạ́n tar-ni-iš-ká*[*n-zi*] in KBo 11.49 VI 4' (CTH 592.2.II$^{?}$.1.A). $^{3)}$ M. Popko, THeth 21, 278, reads *x x x x x ḫal-x*, which does not help much for interpretation of rev. IV 1'. $^{4)}$ The sign is not "*ni*", but "*aš*", thus M. Popko's restoration [DINGIR-*LIM-n*]*i* is no longer tenable. $^{5)}$ The tentative restoration is our suggestion. $^{6)}$ With M. Popko one reads possibly [. . .-*E*]*N*. This word, however, is not to be interpreted as [*UŠ-KE-E*]*N* if M. Popko's restoration [*A-NA* ^{LÚ}*t*]*a-az-ze-el-li* for line 11' should be adopted here.

3. Bo 6238

Description: Vow.
CTH: 590 "*Fragments de songes et d'ex-voto.*"
Dating and Script: Ḫatt. III/NS.
Remarks: One-sided, slightly abraded fragment.
Measurements: 5.4 × 7.2 × 2.4 cm.
Bibliography: F. Fuscagni, HPMM 6 (2007) 137 (bibliography).

Bo 6238

Bo 6238

§ 1' 1']-x̣ x̣-x̣$^{?}$(-)[
2' *ki*$^{?}$]-*nu-na* x̣$^{?}$-[

---

§ 2' 3'](-)x̣(-)*ÚR*$^{?}$-*P̣Ạ*$^{?}$-*LỤ-Ụ*[1] *A-NẠ*(?)[
4']-*ẹš*$^{?}$ *iš-tạ-mạ-aš-š*[*u*$^{?}$-*un*$^{?}$
5']-*ạn-zi ku-iš-ki* x̣-[
6']-x̣ *me-mi-iš-ki-ši nu-ṷạ*-x̣-[
7' .Ḫ]I.A *ma-ni-in-ku-ṷa-nu-ut*[2] *nu-ṷ*[*a*-
8']-*tạ-ni-in-ti*[3] *kị-nu-na-i̯a-ṷa-zạ* [
9' -*e*]*š*$^{?}$ *kụ-ị-e-ẹš nu-ṷa-at-ta a-pu-u-ụn* [
10']-x̣$^{?}$(-)x̣-*ṷa*-x̣ *e-eš-ti* [

---

§ 3' 11']-x̣-*ṷa-rạ-an* ^{m}UR.MẠḪ.LÚ-*iš*[4] *ú-ịt nụ-ṷa*(-)x̣-[
12' -*ṷ*]*a*$^{?}$ *kụ-ịt* SAG.DỤ-*za pí-iḫ-ḫu-un nu-ṷa-mu-za a-ši me-m*[*i-an*]
13'] *pí-iḫ-ḫu-un-ṷa-aš-ši Ú-UL ku-it-ki ki-nu-na-ṷa*
14' *ku-it*]-*ki te-pu pí-an-du nụ-ṷa-rạ-at A-NA* ^{d}*Al-la-a*⸢*n*⸣-[*ni*$^{?}$[5]]
15'](-)x̣$^{?}$-*i̯ạ*$^{?}$-*aš-ṷa-kạ́n ḫa-az-zi-ṷi*$_{5}$ *ẹ-eš-šu-u-an te-eḫ-ḫị*
16'](-)x̣-x̣ IGI.ḪI.A-*ṷa le-e ṷa-aḫ-nu-ši*

---

§ 4' 17']-⌞*x-p*⌟*a*$^{?}$ *I-MỤR*[6] *ma-an-ni-in-nị-uš-ṷa-mu k*⌞*u-i-e*⌟-*e*[*š*]
18']-⌞*x*⌟ *A-NA* ^{GIŠ}BANŠUR *ki-i̯a-ạn*-[*te*$^{?}$-*eš*$^{?}$
19']⌞^{LÚ}⌟*ṬE*$_{4}$-*MA-ŠU*(?)(-)⌞*x*(-)*x*⌟(-)[
20' (traces)
(broken off)

Text-critical notes: [1] To relate to Akkadian $^{(GIŠ)}$*ḪURPALÛ* 'mace' ? [2] This form is already quoted by E. Neu, IF 85 (1980) 82. [3] Here is expected an acephalic Luwian predicate in pres. pl. 3, perhaps [*ti-ṷa*]-*ta-ni-in-ti*; cf. *ti-ṷa-da-ni-in-ti* in KBo 12.89 III 9'. [4] ^{m}UR.MAḪ-LÚ-*iš* appears also in some related texts e.g., KUB 15.5+ II 52' (CTH 583), KUB 15.30 III 4' (CTH 590) and KUB 48.118 I 14' (CTH 584.7). [5] Cf. *A-NA* ^{d}*Al-la-ni* in KUB 15.11+ II 5, 12 (CTH 584.3). [6] To be restored as [*Ù-TU*$_{4}$ MUNUS.LUGAL *I-NA* ^{URU}*Ka-t*]⌞*a-pa*⌟$^{?}$ Cf. KUB 15.12 I 7', 11' (CTH 590).

4. Bo 6271

Description: Festival.

CTH: 617 "*AN.TAḪ.ŠUM*^{sar}*. 32*^{e} *jour:* ^{d}*KAL de Taurisa.*"

Dating and Script: OH/LNS.

Remarks: One-sided fragment that is largely from the right column (with edge) of a tablet.

Measurements: 5.5 × 6.0 × 1.7 cm.

Bibliography: S. Alp, Tempel (1983) 306 (transliteration of lines 6'–7' only); F. Fuscagni, HPMM 6 (2007) 138 (partial transliteration and bibliography).

Bo 6271

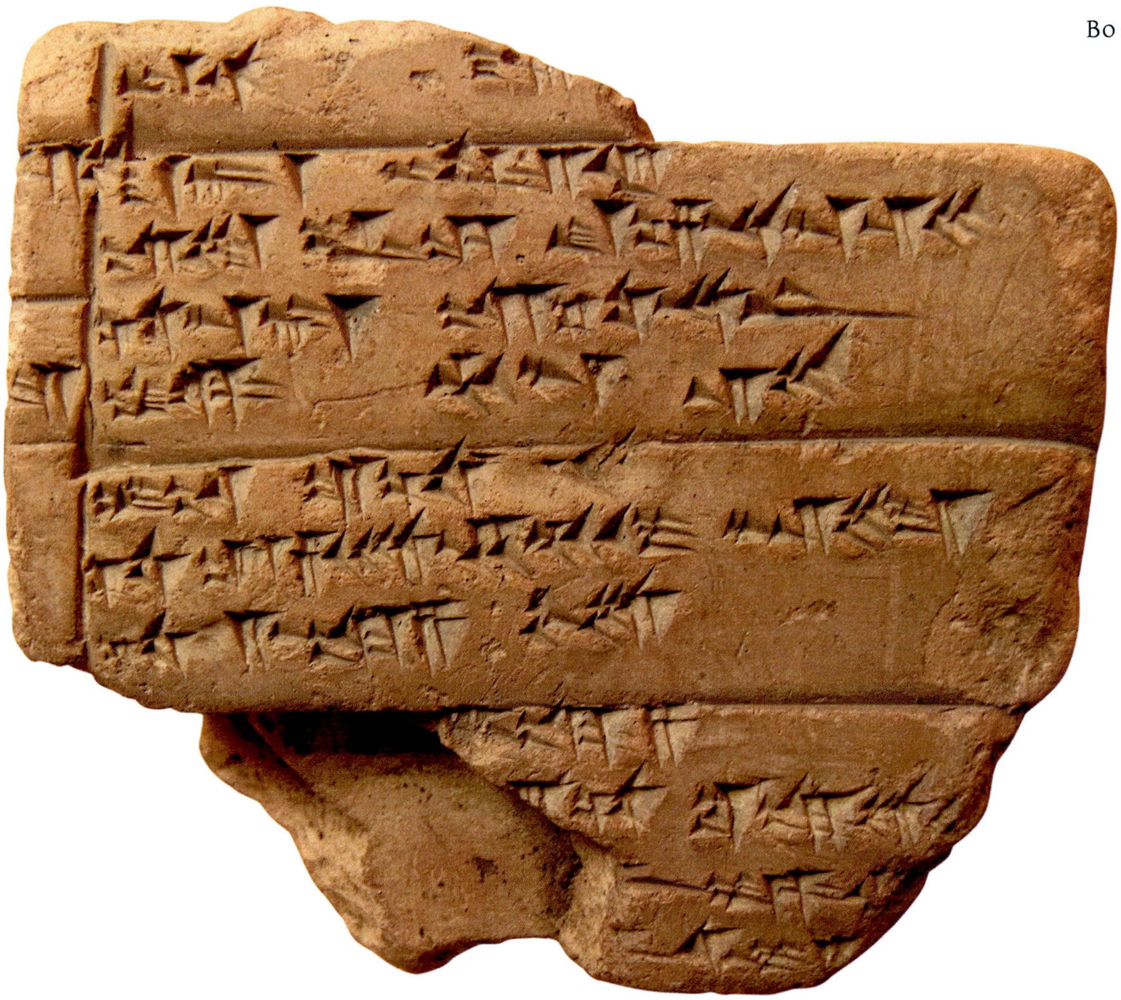

Bo 6271

Left column

§ 1' . . .

---

§ 2' 1']-x̣$^{?}$-*zi*

2' . . .

---

§ 3' 3' . . .

4' -*i̯*]*a*

---

§ 4' . . .

(broken off)

Right column

§ 1' 1' *QA-TAM* *d*⸢*a-a-i*$^{?}$⸣ [

---

§ 2' 2' *ták-kán BI-IB-RU*

3' *IŠ-TU* GẸŠTIN.KU$_7$ *šu-un-na-an-zi*

4' *ta-an-kán iš-ta-na-ni*

5' EGIR-*pa ti-an- zi*

---

§ 2' 6' LUGAL-*uš e*$^{!}$-*ša* ⸢x⸥

7' *ta* ^{É}*ḫa-le-en-tu-u-i ḫal-zi-i̯a*

8' *tạ a-aš-ka-za šal-li*

---

§ 2' 9' [LUGAL-*uš* GUB$^{?}$-*aš*[1)]] *ạ-ạš-ka-za*

10' [^{d}LAMMA ^{URU}*Ta-ú-r*]⸤*i*⸥-*ša*

^{TÚL}*Ka-li-i*[*m-ma-an*[2)]]

11' [*e-ku-zi* GIŠ.^{d}INANNA.GA]L SÌR-*R*[*U*[3)]]

12' ^{d}]*Ạ-ạš-ši-i̯ạ*-[*za*$^{?}$[4)]

(broken off)

Text-critical notes: [1)] Or: TUŠ-*aš*. [2)] This divine spring is interchangeable with ^{d}Kalimma in KUB 2.8 V 14', 19'. [3)] For the reconstruction of the lines 9'–11' see KUB 2.8 V 12'-15' (CTH 617.1); cf. also KBo 13.176 obv. 1'–4' (CTH 617.3). [4)] Alternatively [^{d}]*Ạ-ạš-ši-i̯ạ*-[*zi*] as it appears in KBo 13.176 obv. 4'.

5. Bo 6370

Description: Mythological.
CTH: 323 "*Disparition et retour du Soleil (mugawar).*"
Dating and Script: NS.
Remarks: Two-sided, lightly abraded fragment. The text between II 9"–10" and III 1–6 is similar to KUB 33.68 II 9–16 (CTH 332.3.A).
Measurements: 5.2 × 6.1 × 2.0 cm.
Bibliography: N/A.

Bo 6370 obv. (II$^?$)

Bo 6370 rev. (III$^?$)

Bo 6370 obv. (II$^?$)

Bo 6370 rev. (III?)

Bo 6370 rev. III? (right edge)

Obverse (II$^{?}$)

§ 1' 1'–4' (illegible signs)

5' *LI-I*]*M*(?) NUMUN-*a*[*n*(?)

6'$^{?}$ . . .

---

§ 2' 7" -*e*]*ṣ̌*$^{?}$

8"]-*x̣ nam-m*[*a*(-)

9" *ma-aḫ-ḫ*]*ạ*$^{?}$*-ạn dụ-ụạ-ạ*[*r-né-e*$^{?}$*-ez-z*]*i*$^{?}$ [

10" [*nu pár-aš-te-ḫ*]*ụ*(?)*-uš ạr-ḫạ x̣-x̣-x̣-ši*$^{?}$*-ị*$^{?}$(-)[1)][

(bottom of the tablet)

Reverse (III$^{?}$)

§ 1 1 [. . .$^{?}$ *kar-di-ị*]*ạ*(?)*-at-ta ar-ḫa dạ-an-z*[*i*

2 [. . .$^{?}$ *zi-ga*] ^{ḍ}UTU-*uš* ḪUL-*lu ut-tar ạr-ḫạ* [*pé-eš-ši-ịa*]

3 [*nu-za a-aš-šu*] *ụd-da-a-ạr* *da-a*

---

§ 2 4 [^{GIŠ}GEŠTIN.È.A] *mạ-ạḫ-ḫa-an* GEŠTIN-*ŠU kar-dị-ịt ḫar-zi na-x̣-x̣*$^{?}$(-)*x̣*$^{?}$*-x̣*$^{?}$

5 *Ú-UL ku-i*]*š-kị da-a-ị* LUGAL-*ụš-ša*$^{?}$*-ạz* MUNUS.LUGAL-*aš-x̣*$^{?}$

6](-)*x̣-x̣ du-uš-ga-ra-at-ta-an*

7 *ḫa*]*r*$^{?}$*-zi nu-uš-ma-aš-ta ạr-ḫạ kụ-ịš-k*[*i*(?)

---

§ 3 8 [^{GIŠ}*ṢÉ-ER-TU*$_{4}$ *ma-aḫ-ḫa-an*] Ị̀-*ŠU* ŠÀ-*ịt ḫar-zi x̣*-[

9 ḪUL$^{?}$]-*lụ ḫạ-lu-kán ḫar-zị* [

10]-⌞*x ḫa*⌟*-tu-kán* ⌞*x*⌟-[

(broken off)

Text-critical note: [1)] The sign remnants do not permit the verbal form *pé-eš-ši-i-e-ez-zi* as it appears in KUB 33.68 II 10. Or read *ịš-ḫụ-u-ụạ*$^{?}$*-ị* ?

6. Bo 6570

Description: Festival.

CTH: 626 "*Fête de la 'hâte' (nuntarriyashas).*"

Dating and Script: OH/LNS.

Remarks: One-sided fragment with two partially preserved columns of the obverse.

Bo 6570 II lines 1'–22' duplicate KBo 30.77 IV 12'–28' (CTH 626.Tg30.III) from where the restorations are adopted.

Measurements: 10.4 × 9.2 × 2.6 cm.

Bibliography: S. Alp, *Tempel* (1983) 65–66 (transliteration and translation); M. Nakamura, Nuntarrijašḫa (2002) 263 (text-critical apparatus); F. Fuscagni, HPMM 6 (2007) 144–45 (transliteration and bibliography).

Bo 6570 obv. I and II

Bo 6570 obv. I and II

Bo 6570. Left: obv. I; middle: obv. II (right edge); right: rev. III (right edge)

Obverse I

§ 1' 1'](-)⌜*x*⌝(-)[ ]-⌜*a*⌝*n*?-*zi̯*

2']-*x̤*?-*zi*

3' . . .?

---

§ 2' 4'' K]AŠ?.GEŠTIN

5'' -*z*]*i*

---

§ 3' 6'' -*i̯*]*a*?-*zi*

7'']-*x̤*?

(broken off)

Obverse II

§ 1' 1' [GIŠ.^{d}(INANNA.GAL SÌR-*RU* I NINDA.GUR$_4$.RA) *pár-ši-i̯*]⌜*a*⌝[1)]

---

§ 2' 2' [DINGIR]-*LUM-ša-m*⌜*a-aš-k*⌝*án du-uš-kán-zi*

3' GU̇NNI-*an-kán ḫu-u-u̯a-i̯a-an- zi*

4' *kat-ta-an* ⌜*iš-ḫu-u-u̯a-u-u̯a-aš* GAM-*an*⌝ *iš-ḫu-u-u̯a-an-zi*

---

§ 3' 5' LUGAL-*uš* GUB-*aš* ^{d}U *ŠA-ME-E* I-*ŠU e̩-ku-zi*

6' ^{LÚ}NAR ^{URU}*Ka-ne̩-eš* SÌR-*RU* KI.II[2)]

---

§ 4' 7' LU̇GAL-*uš* $^{\text{URU(!)}}$*ḫa-le-en-tu-u-u̯a-aš*[3)]

8' *ar-ḫa pa- iz- zi*

9' ^{KUŠ}NÍG.BÀR *ḫal-zi-i̯a*

10' [(*t*)]*a ḫa-at-kán-zi* ⌜*x*⌟ *iš-pa-an-ti*[4)]

11' [(*t*)]*a ap-pa-a- i*[5)]

---

§ 5' 12' $^{\text{EZE̩N}_4}$*nu̩-un-tar-aš-ḫa-aš* ⌜ ⌟

13' $^{\text{EZEN}_4}$*ze̩-e-ni-i̯a-aš-kán*

14' [6)] $^{\text{EZEN}_4}$*nu̩-u̩n-tar-aš-ḫa-aš* ⌜ ⌟ *ḫa-an-ta-an-za*[7)]

15' *nu ku-i̩t-pát* NINDA.KU$_7$ ^{DUG}*ḫal-u̯a-tal-la* LÀL

16' ^{DUG}ḪAB.ḪAB GÚ.GÍD.DA GEŠTIN

17' *Ú-UL e-eš- zi*

---

§ 6' 18' [(^{m})]⌞*Ḫa*⌟-*at-tu-ši*-DINGIR-*LIM-iš* LUGAL.GAL

19' [(*da-a*)]- *iš*

---

§ 7' 20' [(*ma-a-an-kán*)] MU.ḪI.A[8] *ša-ku-u̯[(a-an-d)]a*[?9)]*-ri-i̯a-an-zi*
21' [(*Ú-UL-an-kán*)] *ḫa-˻p˼u-ša-an-[(z)]i*

---

§ 8' 22' [*m*(*a-a-an* LUGAL-*uš A-NA*)] ᵈI[(B ᴱ)ZEN₄AN.TAḪ.ŠUMˢᴬᴿ][10)]
(broken off)

Reverse III

(Only a few signs remain on the right edge)

§ 1' 1'] KI.II
2' . . .
3'] *an-dur-za* KI.II
4' ...
5'-7'? (illegible signs)
8'' KI].II(?)
(broken off)

Text-critical notes: [1)] Or: KI.⸢II⸣ like in line 6'. [2)] KBo 30.77 IV 16' writes it out: I NINDA.GUR$_4$.RA *pár-*[*ši-i̯a*]. [3)] KBo 30.77 IV 17' has correct form ᴱ*ḫa-le-*°. [4)] KBo 30.77 IV 18': GE[$_6$*-an-ti*]. [5)] In KBo 30.77 IV 19' this sentence is written in a separate paragraph. [6)] KBo 30.77 IV 21' inserts *A-NA*. [7)] KBo 30.77 IV 21': *ḫa-a-an-da-*°. [8)] KBo 30.77 IV 25': MU.KAM.ḪI.A. [9)] It is difficult to decide if the broken sign is *da* or *ta*. [10)] For restoration of the festival designation cf. IBoT 1.3 I 1–2 (CTH 614).

7. Bo 6788

Description: Festival.

CTH: 625 "*Fragments de l'AN.TAḪ.ŠUM^{sar}?*"

Dating and Script: LNS.

Remarks: Two-sided fragment from the top (obv. I) and bottom part (rev. IV) of a tablet.

Measurements: 3.4 × 4.3 × 2.2 cm.

Bibliography: S. Alp, Tempel (1983) 306–307 (transliteration and translation); F. Fuscagni, HPMM 6 (2007) 151 (transliteration and bibliography).

Bo 6788 obv. I

Bo 6788 rev. IV

Obverse I

§ 1 1 *mạ-ạ-an pár-ku-i* EZE[N$_4$[1)]
i-i̯a-an-zi

2 ^{d}*Zi-it-ḫa-ri-i̯a-a*[*n pa-ra-a*(?)[2)]

3 *ú-da-an-zi ku-i*[*t*(-)[3)]

4 *I-NA* É.DU$_{10}$.⸢Ú⸣[S.SA *pa-iz-zi*(?)

5 $^{É?}$*ḫa-l*[*e-en*$^?$*-tu*$^?$-

6 *ạ*$^?$*-nị-*⸢*i̯a*⸣-[*at-ta*

(broken off)

Reverse IV (Colophon)

1 DUB.[x.KAM

2 AŠ É(.)[

3 *nu šal-li* [*a-še-eš-šar*

(bottom of the tablet)

Text-critical notes: 1) On the issue of the usage of *parkui* (sg. nom-acc. neut.) with common gender EZEN (cf. *pár-ku-in* EZEN in KBo 24.93 IV 6) see CHD P/2 (1995) 165 f. 2) Cf. VS 28.1 obv. 6' (CTH 604.G). 3) Perhaps *ku-i*[*t-ma-an*]. The reading *ku-i-*[*ta*(-) . . .] by S. Alp, Tempel 306, is unlikely.

8. Bo 6810 + KUB 44.16 + IBoT 3.69

Description: Festival.

CTH: 682.1.C *"Fête de 'tous les dieux KAL'"* ?

Dating and Script: NS.

Remarks: Bo 6810 is a one-sided fragment, and lines 1'–11' directly join KUB 44.16 + IBoT 3.69 II 16'–26'. Duplicate is KBo 22.189 II 8–15 (CTH 682.1.E) from where the restorations are taken.

The assignment of KUB 44.16 + IBoT 3.69+ to CTH 682 is based on the condition that KUB 44.16 + IBoT 3.69+ V 1' ff. duplicates KUB 2.1 II 22' ff. (CTH: 682.1.A) as G. McMahon, AS 25 (1991) 84 states. However, KUB 44.16 + IBoT 3.69+ obverse (I–III) and reverse (IV–VI) may contain two different festival texts. The frequent mention of NIN.DINGIR, one of the key figures of the descriptions in the fragments above (II 17' ff.), makes it conceivable that Bo 6810 + KUB 44.16 + IBoT 3.69 II belongs either to CTH 649 *"Fragments de fêtes nommant la NIN.DINGIR"* or CTH 738 *"Fêtes de la divinité Tetešḫabi"* as well.

Measurements: 6.7 × 4.5 × 2.5 cm.

Bibliography: G. McMahon, AS 25, 88–89 (text edition of KUB 44.16 + IBoT 3.69 without Bo 6810).

Bo 6810 + KUB 44.16 obv. II

Bo 6810

Bo 6810 + IBoT 3.69 obv. II (composite image)

Obverse II

(Line numbers of Bo 6810 in parentheses)

§ 10' . . .

16' (= 1') [*nu*$^{?}$] LỤGAL-*uš Ị-NẠ* ⌜É ^{d}LAMM⌝A[1)] *pa-iz-zi*

---

§ 11' 17' (= 2') [(*ḫa-a*)]*n-te-ez*$^{!}$*-zum-ni*[2)] NIN.DING[(I)]R-*aš*

18' (= 3') [(UGULA ^{L})]$^{Ú.MEŠ}$*ḫa-pị́-i̯a-aš* DUMU.Ẹ́.[(GA)]L ^{É}*ḫi-lam-ni*

19' (= 4') [*ka-r*]*u-ú*[3)] *a-ra-an-t*[*a*[4)]]

---

§ 12' 20' (= 5') [(NIN)].DINGIR-*aš*[5)] LUGAL-*i ḫi-in-<ik->zi*$^{!}$[6)] [*n*]*am-ma-aš* ^{É}*ḫi-i-li-i̯a-aš*

21' (= 6') [*ar*$^{?}$]-*ta*[7)] LUGAL-*uš* ^{É}*ḫi-i-l*[(*i*)] *ti-i̯a-zi*[8)]

---

§ 13' 22' (= 7') [(DUMU)].Ẹ́.GAL *ME-E QA-TI pẹ́-*⌞*e*⌟*-da-i*

23' (= 8') [(LUGAL-*u*)]*š QA-TI-ŠU a-ar-rị* [(GA)]L.DUMU.MEŠ[9)].É.GAL GADA-*an*

24' (= 9') [(*pa-a*)]-⌞*i*⌟ LỤGAL-*uš QA-TI*[10)]*-ŠU a-a*[(*n*)]*-ši*[11)]

---

§ 14' 25' (= 10') [*na-aš-t*]*a*(?)[12)] LUGAL-*uš* ⌞^{d}LAMMA$^{?}$⌟(-)[. . .-*z*]*i*

26' (= 11')]⌞*x x*⌟[-*z*]*i*

(Bo 6810 breaks here off; text continues in IBoT 3.69+ II 27' ff.)

Text-critical notes: [1)] KBo 22.189 II 8: ^{d}*I-na-ra-aš pár-na.* [2)] KBo 22.189 II 8: *ḫa-an-te-ez-zi-zum-ni*. Thus, correct the reading *ḫa-an-te-ez-zi* KASKAL-*NI* by G. McMahon, AS 25, 88. [3)] Omitted in KBo 22.189 II 11. [4)] KBo 22.189 II 11: *-da*. After this, no paragraph divider is drawn. [5)] KBo 22.189 II 11 omits *-aš*. [6)] KBo 22.189 II 11: *ḫi-ik-zi*. [7)] Whole sentence is omitted in KBo 22.189 II 12. [8)] KBo 22.189 II 12: *ti-i-e-zi*. After this, no paragraph divider is drawn. [9)] KBo 22.189 II 14 omits MEŠ. [10)] KBo 22.189 II 15: *QA-TE*^{MEŠ}*-ŠU*. [11)] KBo 22.189 II 15-16 add: ⌞NIN.DINGIR⌟ / ⌞^{É}*ḫi-i-li*⌟ [*ti-i-e-zi*(?)]. [12)] In the broken part there is space for 2–3 signs. For restoration with *na-aš-ta* cf. KUB 44.16 + IBoT 3.69 II 9'.

9. Bo 6827

Description: Ritual or festival.
CTH: 470 "*Fragments de rituels*" or 670 "*Fragments divers.*"
Dating and Script: MS.
Remarks: One-sided fragment from the right portion (close to the edge) of a tablet.
Measurements: 4.3 × 4.4 × 1.5 cm.
Bibliography: H. Otten, ZA 71 (1981) 143 n. 20; I. Singer, StBoT 27 (1983) 110 n. 65.

Bo 6827

Bo 6827

§ 1' 1'] ⸢I$^{?}$ MUNUS$^{?}$ *na-aš-ta*⸣[
2' *p*]⸢*í*⸣-*ra-ạn ạr-ḫ̮a*
3' ^{GI}]^{Š}MÁ *an-ku*$^{?}$ *Ú-UL-ma-a*[*z*$^{?}$(-)...$^{?}$]
4']-*x̣ ú-ẹ-eš*[1] *pa-ra-a* ⸢*x*⸣ [
5']- *aš*$^{?}$ [2]

---

§ 2' 5']-*x̤* ^{É}*ar-ga-i-ú-ta*[3]
6' ^{GIŠ}*ú*]-*ị-du-le-e-eš*[4]
7'] I-*e-da-ni* ^{GIŠ}*ú*-⸤*i-du-l*⸥[*i-i̭a*$^{?}$ ...$^{?}$]
8' -*i̭*]*a-aš a*⸤*r-ta*$^{?}$*-ri*$^{?}$⸥ [

---

§ 3' 9' (traces)
(broken off)

Text-critical notes: [1] For usage of personal pronoun *weš* "we" in a ritual text see e.g., KBo 17.1 + I 21' // KBo 17.3 + I 16' (both OS). [2] Alternatively read "*nị*" as the final sign of a predicate (pres. pl. 1.) in *-wani* / *-weni.* [3] The spelling of the word exhibits a sign inversion for the correct °-*ú-i*-°. This with *-ta* extended form (a Hurro-Luwoid pl. nom.-acc. neut. ?) of (^{É})*argawi-* / (^{É})*arkiwi-* is seen also as ^{É}*ar-ki-ú-i-ta* in KUB 39.97+ obv. 2. The attestation in Bo 6827 is cited already by H. Otten, ZA 71, 143 n. 20 and I. Singer, StBot 27, 110 n. 65. [4] On (^{GIŠ})*widuli-* "fence, partition, screen ?" see R. Akdoğan — O. Soysal, AMMY 2002 (2003) 175–76 with anterior bibliography.

10. Bo 6909

Description: Festival.

CTH: 670 "*Fragments divers.*"

Dating and Script: NS.

Remarks: Two-sided fragment with top (obv.$^{?}$) and bottom (rev.$^{?}$) part of a tablet. The text has a distinct Hattian background (especially through the divine designations in obv.$^{?}$ 1–6) and cult features ([$^{\text{LÚ.MEŠ}}$*ḫ*]*apēš* in obv.$^{?}$ 1, ^{GIŠ}*kurakki ḫūek-* in obv.$^{?}$ 11 and the unique spelling ^{GIŠ}SAG.KUL-*aš* GIŠ-*r*[*ui*] in rev.$^{?}$ 5') which would better fit either CTH 649 or CTH 738.

Measurements: 6.6 × 6.2 × 3.4 cm.

Bibliography: N/A.

Bo 6909 obv.$^{?}$

Bo 6909 rev.$^{?}$

Bo 6909 obv.?

Bo 6909 rev.?

Obverse?

§ 1 1 $^{\text{LÚ.MEŠ}}$*ḫ]a-pé-e-eš* ^{d}*Zi-i⌞t-ḫa⌟-[ri-i̯a(-)*

2 ^{d}*Kam]-pí-pu-it-ti* ^{d}*Z[i-*

3 ^{d}*K]a-tạḫ-ḫa* ^{d}*Zi-it-ḫ[a-ri-i̯a*

4 *-i̯]a?-zi* ^{d}*Ḫa-pa-an-tạ-l[i-i̯a*

5 ^{d}*Ḫ]a-ša-am-mi-li* *Ù A-NẠ* [

6 ^{d}*W]a$_a$-še-ez-zi-li-i̯a* *ši-pa-[an-*

---

§ 2 7]*-šạ* DINGIR-*LAM* ^{GIŠ}ZAG.GAR.RA(-)[

8] *da-an-zi* *na-an-ša-a[n*

9]*-x̣?-zi nu ḫu-u-ke-eš-šar* [

10 *iš-t]a-na-ni* *pí-ra-an ti-a[n-zi*

11]*-ma* ^{GIŠ}*ku-ra-ak-ki ḫu-u-ká[n?-zi?* [1)]

12 *me-n]a-aḫ-ḫa-an-da-kạ́n* *ku-iš* ^{GIŠ}*k[u-ra-ak-ki-iš*[2)]

(broken off)

Reverse?

§ 1' 1' [. . .? *A-NA* ^{d}*Ḫa-ša]-am-me-lị*[3)][

2'] I NINDA *LA-AB-KU-m[a?*]

3' [*ḫar-za*]-⌜*z*⌝*u-ta* ⌜*x*⌟ *i-i̯a-an-* *z*⌜*i*⌝ [

---

§ 2' 4' [*ḫa-aš*]*-šị-i* I-*ŠU* ^{GIŠ}DAG-*ti* I-*ŠU* [

5' ⌜^{G}⌝^{IŠ}AB-*i̯a* I-*ŠU* ^{GIŠ}SAG.KUL-*aš* GIŠ-*r[u*[4)]*-i* I-*ŠU*]

6' *nam-ma ḫa-aš-ši-i* *ta-pu-uš-za* [

7' I-*ŠU* *da-a-i*

---

§ 3' 8' *še-er-ra-aš-ša-an* ^{UZU}NÍG.GI⌞G⌟(./-)[

9' ⌞*x-x-x*(?)⌟ *zi-i⌞k-ki⌟-[iz?-zi*

(bottom of the tablet)

Text-critical notes: [1)] For the phrase "to slaughter (an animal) at the pillar / column" see KUB 58.61 I 19' (CTH 649): [*ku-r*]*a-ak-ki* GÙB-*la-az ḫu-u-kán-z*[*i*] [2)] A sg. nom. com. form *ku-ra-ak-ki-iš* is known only from RŠ 25.421 obv. 28'. [3)] For lines 1'-3' cf. similar IBoT 3.1 rev. 46'-47'. [4)] Beside ^{GIŠ}SAG.KUL-*aš* GIŠ-*i* in KBo 21.98 II 19' (CTH 738.I.15.A) this is a rare spelling for common *ḫattalwaš* GIŠ-(*ru*)*i* "to / for the door bolt."

11. Bo 6978

Description: Ritual.

CTH: 448 "*Rituels à la déesse solaire de la terre.*"

Dating and Script: NS.

Remarks: Bo 6978 is a one-sided fragment written in an elegant script. Its lines 6'–14' duplicate KUB 60.161 III 2'–9' (CTH 448.2.1.4.A; NS) and another unpublished fragment Bo 4469:2'–8', from where the restorations are adopted.

Measurements: 6.4 × 6.1 × 1.8 cm.

Bibliography: D. Groddek, DBH 20 (2006) 177; S. Görke (ed.), hethiter.net/: CTH 448.2.1.4 (Expl. A, 17.02.2012). Both are text editions of KUB 60.161 without Bo 6978 and Bo 4469.

Bo 6978

Bo 6978

§ 1' 1']-x̣-x̣ *a-šẹ-*⌜*ša*⌝-[*an*?-*zi*?$^{1)}$

2' *ar*?]-*ḫạ* $^{TÚG?}$GADA.GAL *ḫu-i*⌜*t-ti-x*⌝-[

3'](.)x̣$^{2)}$ ẠD.KID ^{LÚ}DUGUD ZAG-*na-za ti-*[*i̯a-an-zi*

4'] Ị DỤG.GẸŠTIN$^{!?}$-*mạ-ạš-ši* GÙB-*la-za t*[*i-i̯a-an-zi*

5' -*š*]*a*?-*an* IX NINDA.ÉRIN.MEŠ X-*iš* I ^{NINDA}*u̯a-g*[*e*?-*eš*?-*šar*

6']-x̣ I NINDA.GÚG I *ŠA-A-TI ki-it-t*[*a*-(*ri*)$^{3)}$

7' ZAG-*n*]*a-zạ ti-i̯ạ-an-zi* I DUG.GEŠTIN-*ma-aš-ši* [G(ÙB-*la-za ti-a*)*n-zi*]

8' [(KA.GAG.A.NAG-*m*)]*ạ-aš-ši pí-ra-an ar-ta-ri*$^{4)}$ *pí-ra-*[*an-*. . . (I GA.KIN.AG I *EM-Ṣ*)*Ú* $^{5)}$ . . .?]

---

§ 2' 9' [. . .]-x̣ *da-a-an pé-e-da*<-*an*>$^{6)}$ II *ŠA-A-T*[(*Ù ḫar-ki k*)*ap-pa-a-ni*)]

10' [II *ŠA*]-*Ạ-TÙ kap-pa-a-ni* GE$_6$! II *ŠA-A-T*[(*Ù A-ZA-AN-NU* ḪÁD.DU.A)$^{7)}$]

11' [(II *Š*)]*A-A-TÙ* ŠE.GIŠ.Ì II *ŠA-A-TÙ* ^{GIŠ}*IN-*[(*BU an-da im-mi-i̯a-an-ta*)]

12' [(XXX *ḫur-l*)]*a*$^{8)}$-*ti-iš ti-i̯a-ti-ịš*?$^{9)}$ *ku-ga-ni-ẹ-*[(*e*)*š*?$^{10)}$ *š*(*A* BA.BA.ZA)]

13' [(I *PA*)] ZÌ.DA *še-ep-pí-it-t*[(*a-aš*)] Ị *PA* ZÌ.D[A *ḫar-š*(*a-ni-li-i̯a-aš*$^{11)}$ I *PA* ZÌ.DA ŠE)]

14' [(I *P*)*A* Z]Ì.DA *pa-ra-a-aš-ši-i̯*[(*a-an-na-aš*)$^{12)}$] ⌞*x-x-x*?⌟ [$^{13)}$

15']⌞*x-x-x-x*⌟[

(broken off)

Text-critical notes: $^{1)}$ Cf. KUB 60.161 II 46''. $^{2)}$ Perhaps to restore as [. . .-*kán I-NA* ^{GIŠ}BANŠU]R; cf. KBo 48.71:14' // KUB 40.110 rev.6': [(*n*)]*a-an-kán I-NA* ^{GIŠ}BANŠUR ^{LÚ}DUGUD *ti-en-zi*. $^{3)}$ KUB 60.161 III 2': GAR-*ri*. $^{4)}$ KUB 60.161 III 4': GAR-*ri*. $^{5)}$ Restoration is after KUB 60.161 III 5'. For space reasons the placement of these words at the beginning of the line 9' seems unlikely. $^{6)}$ KUB 60.161 III 5': *pé-e-da-aš-ša-an*. $^{7)}$ Restoration follows Bo 4469:3' where the garden plant designation [*A-ZA*]-*AN-NU* unexpectedly has no post determinative ^{SAR}. $^{8)}$ The sign in KUB 60.161 III 9' is clearly "*la*" not "*at*". Both sign forms can be easily compared and differentiated in ***la-at**-ti-in* in the same text II 36''. The word *ḫur-la-ti-iš* is a hapax of unknown meaning; here appears to be one of three ingredients (*ḫurlatiš*, *tiyatiš*, *kuganeš*) of BA.BA.ZA "porridge". $^{9)}$ Already cited by H. Ertem, Flora (1974) 143 and J. Tischler, HEG III/10 (1994) 370. This hapax possibly goes back to the Akkadian *TĪYATU* "asafoetida", hence the Hittitized form of it, if the reading of the last sign "*iš*" is correct. $^{10)}$ This word, a hapax of unknown meaning, denotes one of three ingredients of BA.BA.ZA "porridge" and it is preserved in the duplicates always partially: *ku-ga-nị-*[. . .] (Bo 4469:5') and [. . .]-⌞*ga*⌟-*ni-e*[*š*?] (KUB 60.161 III 9'). $^{11)}$ For restoration see I *PA* ZÌ.DA *ḫar-ša-ni-i-li-i̯a-aš* in KUB 35.142 IV 12'. $^{12)}$ ZÌ.DA *parāššiyannaš* (written as one word) means "flour of sprouting (grain)" for which cf. ŠE *parā šiyannaš* in KBo 5.2 I 38 and incomplete in KBo 5.5 I 10'. CHD Š/3 (2013) 344: "grain of sprouting" (i.e., either "sprouting grain" or "seed grain ready for sprouting"). $^{13)}$ Bo 4469:8' has for this spot I *PA* ZỊZ? *zẹ-ẹ-na-a*[*n-ta-aš*].

12. Bo 7050

Description: Festival.

CTH: 594.N "*Au printemps, à Tippuwa.*"

Dating and Script: OH/NS.

Remarks: One-sided fragment with two columns. Lines 1'–13' of the left column duplicate IBoT 4.64 obv. 1'–11' (CTH 594.K) and KBo 13.224:1'–7' (CTH 594.G) from where the restorations are adopted.

Measurements: 6.9 × 6.2 × 1.3 cm.

Bibliography: D. Groddek, DBH 23 (2007) 49–50 (to IBoT 4.64).

Bo 7050

Bo 7050

Left column

§ 1' . . .

———

§ 2'
1' -(*tu-ḫi-i̯*)]*a-aš*[1)]*-ma̩-kán*
2' (EGIR)]-*an* *ar-ḫa*
3' [. . .? *pé-e-*(*ḫu-te-ez-z*)]*i* *ta̩-aš pa-iz-z*⌜*i*⌝
4' [DUMU.MEŠ.(É.GAL[2)] ^{NINDA}*ša-r*)]*a-am-ma̩* *ti-an-zi̩*

———

§ 3'
5' [(*ta n*)*am-m*(*a* L)]Ú ^{GIŠ}GIDRU *pí-ra-an*
6' [(*ḫu-u-u̯a-a-i ta* ^{L})]$^{\text{Ú.MEŠ}}$ŠU.GI
7' [($^{\text{LÚ.MEŠ}}$*Ú-BA-RÙ-TIM*)] $^{\text{LÚ.MEŠ}}$DUGUD
8' [($^{\text{MUNUS.MEŠ}}$[3)]ŠU.GI-*i̯a*)] *a-ša-a-ši*

———

§ 4'
9' [(TU$_7$.ḪI.A *ták-ša-an*)] *šar-ra-at-ta-ri*
10' [(GAL *ME-ŠE-TI$_4$*[4)] *te-ez*)]*-zi* *a-še-eš-ni*
11' [(*ta-a*[5)]*-u̯a-al la-a*)]*-ḫu-u̯a-a*[6)]*-an-du*

———

§ 5'
12' [*nu*? (GIM-*an-ma* TU$_7$.ḪI.A *t*)]*a-ru-up-ta-ri*
13' [*nu*? ($^{\text{LÚ.MEŠ}}$MUḪALDIM ^{GIŠ}*ki-iš-te*)]-⌞*m*⌟*u-uš*
14' -*z*]⌞*i*?⌟
(broken off)

Right column

§ 1' . . .

———

§ 2'
1' ^{LÚ}ŠU̩.G[I(-)
2' *na-an*(-)[
3' DUMU.É.G[AL(-)
4' *pa-a-i̩* [
5' *a-x̩-*[
(broken off)

Text-critical notes: [1)] ^{MUNUS}*zintuḫiyaš* or GAL $^{\text{MUNUS.MEŠ}}$*zintuḫiyaš* ? Based on the signs [. . .*-i̯*]*a-aš-ma-* in Bo 7050 the handcopy [. . .]*-tu-ḫi-i̯a*(-)*tar*!-[. . .] in the duplicate IBoT 4.64 obv. 1' is now dubious. Correct also the restoration *tar-*[*kum-mi-*. . .] by M. Popko apud D. Groddek, DBH 23 (2007) 49. [2)] Thus, correct the reading [. . .]-⌜*ú-u̯a*⌝ by D. Groddek, DBH 23, 49. [3)] KBo 13.224:2' omits MEŠ. [4)] KBo 13.224:4' has [GA]L $^{\text{LÚ.MEŠ}}$*ME-ŠE-TI$_4$*. [5)] KBo 13.224:5' omits *-a-*. [6)] IBoT 4.64 obv. 11' omits *-a-*.

13. Bo 7103

Description: Instruction.

CTH: 261 *"Instructions aux chefs de postes (bêl madgalti)."*

Dating and Script: Arn. I / NS.

Remarks: Bo 7103 is a one-sided fragment from the right portion of a tablet (reverse III), its lines 7'–16' are duplicate to KBo 50.280b + KUB 40.56 + KUB 31.88 + III 7'–17' (CTH 261.I.A; Arn. I / MS), KUB 13.2+ III 1–7 (CTH 261.I.B; Arn. I / NS) and KBo 53.255 III 9'–15' (CTH 261.I.F; Arn. I / NS), from which the restorations are adopted. The placement of the restored words, either at the end of a line or at the beginning of the next one, is approximate and may vary.

Measurements: 6.1 × 3.1 × 1.0 cm.

Bibliography: E. von Schuler, HDA (1957) 46–47; F. P. Daddi, StMed 14 (2003) 142–47; J. L. Miller, Royal Hittite Instructions (2013) 226–29 (all are text editions without Bo 7103).

Bo 7103 rev. III

Bo 7103 rev. III

Reverse III

§ 1' 1'-2' (traces)

---

§ 2' 3'[1]]-x̣-an
4' G]$^{\text{⌜IŠ}}$T⌝IR
5' GI]$^{\text{Š.ḪUR}}$gul-za-tar[2]
6']- du̩[3]

---

§ 3' 7' [(A-NA ^{GIŠ}TIR.ḪI.A-i̯)a[4] . . .]-a? [5] ^{GIŠ}ḲỊRI$_6$.GẸŠTIN-x̣? [6]
[na-a(ḫ-š)a-r(a-az) [7])]
8' [(ki-it-ta-r)u . . .? (ŠÀ URU-L)]IM-i̯ạ-kán[8] an-nạ-ạl-[li[9](-). . .?]
9' [($^{\text{NA}_4}$ḫu-u̯a-š)i (ku-i)t(?)[10] . . .? (EGI)]R-ạn-ma-at Ú-U[(L kap-pu-u-u̯a-an
ki-nu-na-at-za)]
10' [(EGIR-an kap-pu-u-u̯a-an-du[11] na-at ša-ra-a)] ti-ịt-tạ-nụ-[(an-du)]
11' [(nam-ma-aš-ši ka-ru-ú-li-i̯a-az ku-it SISKUR)[12]] ḳi-it-ta-at[13] [
12' [(na-at-ši pí-i̯a-an-du[14] URU-ri-i̯a-aš-ša-a)]n? ku-e PÚ.MEŠ[15] [
13' [(EGIR-an nu-uš-ša-an A-NA PÚ SÍSKUR)] ḳi-it-ta-ri[16] [
14' [(na-at-ši e-eš-ša-an-du[17] a-ar-aš-k)]án-du[18] ku-e-da-ni-ma [(A-NA PÚ)]
15' [(SÍSKUR NU.GÁL na-at-kán ša-ra)]-ạ? a-ar-aš-kán-d[(u)[19]]
16' [(an-da-at-kán le-e IGI-u̯a)]-⌞an?-ta?-ri?-nu-u⌟š-kán-[(zi)[20]
17']⌞x⌟[
(broken off)

Text-critical notes: [1] As the words in the lines 3'–5' would indicate, the content of this paragraph is not available in any of other exemplars. The lines 7'–8' contain the text which is left out in the beginning of KUB 13.2+ III in a blank paragraph. This context is partially available also in KBo 50.280b + KUB 40.56 + KUB 31.88 + III 7'–9' and KBo 53.255 III 8'–9'; cf. F. P. Daddi, StMed 14, 142 n. 361. [2] The attestation $^{\text{GIŠ.ḪUR}}$gulzatar "wooden tablet" is cited already by F. Starke, StBoT 31 (1990) 457, however, with the different line number. [3] It is not certain if this word can be restored as [. . . (i-i̯a-an)]-du following KBo 50.280b + III 7' and KUB 13.2+ II 46'. [4] See KBo 53.255 III 8'. [5] To be restored as [^{GIŠ}MÚ.SAR.ḪI].A ? [6] Thus, the source and reason for a reading [šu]-up-pé-eš-na-aš in this place posited by J. L. Miller, Royal Hittite Instructions, 226 is now dubious. [7] After KBo 50.280b + KUB 40.56 + III 8'. [8] Duplicate restoration follows KBo 53.255 III 9'. J. L. Miller, Royal Hittite Instructions, 228 omits ŠÀ. [9] KBo 53.255 III 9' has likewise an-n[a-. . .], while KUB 31.88 + KUB 40.56 + III 9' uses the synonym ka-ru-ú-i-l[i]. [10] Uncertain restoration is taken from KUB 31.88 + III 9'; cf. J. L. Miller, Royal Hittite Instructions, 228. [11] Restored after KUB 31.88 + KUB 40.56 + III 11'. KUB 13.2+ III 1 has kap-pu-u-u̯a-at-te$_9$-en. [12] Restored after KUB 13.2+ III 2–3. KUB 31.88 + KUB 40.56 + III 12': [nu-u]š-ši ka-ru-ú-i-li-i̯a-az ku-it SÍSKUR and KBo 53.255 III 11': nu-uš-ši-kán ka-r[u-. . .]. [13] Omitted in KUB 13.2+ III 3 and KUB 31.88 + KUB 40.56 + III 12'. [14] Restored after KUB 13.2+ III 3. KUB 31.88 + KUB 40.56 + III 13': [e-eš]-ša-an-du. KBo 53.255 III 12': pé-eš-kán-d[u]. [15] KUB 31.88 + KUB 40.56 + III 13': A-NA URU-LIM-i̯a-aš-ša-an ku-e PÚ.ḪI.A. [16] KUB 31.88 + KUB 40.56 + III 14': [nu k]e?-e-da-ni A-NA TÚL SÍS[K]UR e-eš-zi. KBo 53.255 III 12': [17] KUB 31.88 + KUB 40.56 + III 14': ši-pa-an-za-kán-du. [18] KUB 13.2+ III 5: ar-aš-kán-du. [19] KUB 13.2+ III 6-7: na-at-kán ša-ra-a im-ma / ar-aš-kán-du. [20] KUB 31.88 + KUB 40.56 + III 17': [n]a-at-kán an-da le-e IGI-u̯a-an-da-ri-iš-ki-iz-zi.

14. Bo 7284

Description: Festival.
CTH: 666 "*Culte de Arinna.*"
Dating and Script: OH/LNS.
Remarks: One-sided fragment from the right or middle column of a tablet.
Measurements: 6.5 × 7.1 × 2.2 cm.
Bibliography: S. Alp, Tempel (1983) 103 (transliteration and translation of the lines 4'–7'); F. Fuscagni, HPMM 6 (2007) 162; M. Popko, StBoT 50 (2009) 57 (transliteration and translation of the lines 1'–5').

Bo 7284

Bo 7284

Left column

(A few illegible signs)

Right column

§ 1' 1' [*ta-r*]*u-up-ta-r*[*i*?
2' [. . .?](-)x *ir-ḫa-a*1)-*an-*⌜*z*⌝[*i*?
3' [*i*]*r-ḫa-a-iz-zi* ⌜dZe-en-tu-ḫi-x?⌝(-)[. . .? 2)]

---

§ 2' 4' LUGAL-*uš-kán IŠ-TU* É dZe-e[*n-tu-ḫi-ia ú-iz-zi*]
5' *ta-aš I-NA* É*ḫa-le-en-tu-ua pa-iz-zi* x?(-)[
6' *ták-kán* BAL-*an-ti nam-ma-kán A-NA* É(.)[3)
7' *ḫu-u-ma-an-da-aš* SISKUR *an-da tar-na-a-an-z*[*i*

6' LUGAL-*uš* É*aš-ta-tu-ú-i*4) *ti-ia-zi* [
7' VIII ⌜x⌟ (eras.?) *ME*? SILA$_4$-*kán an-da ŠA* LÚKAŠ$_4$.E [
8' *ŠA* LÚALAM.ZU$_9$ DUG*ḫu-up-pár* NINDA.GUR$_4$.R[A(./-)
9' *šu-up-pa-e-eš* LÚSANGA.ḪI.A *e-ša-an-d*[*a*(-)
(broken off)

Text-critical notes: 1) M. Popko, StBoT 50, 57 erroneously reads *ir-ḫa-u-*. 2) For lines 3'–4' see KBo 41.94 I 8'–9' (CTH 666). 3) S. Alp, Tempel 103 restores as É.[MEŠ DINGIR.MEŠ]. 4) Note that this word, designating a (cultic) building or section (M. Popko, StBoT 50, 12, suggests, however, "a military facility, barracks"), appears here for the first time with a determinative.

15. Bo 7317

Description: Festival.
CTH: 670 *"Fragments divers."*
Dating and Script: NS.
Remarks: One-sided fragment written in an elegant script.
Measurements: 4.0 × 5.5 × 0.8 cm.
Bibliography: N/A.

Bo 7317

Bo 7317

§ 1' 1']-*x̣ kạt-t⸢a-an(?)⸣*
2'] *še-er ki-it-ta x̤*$^{?}$(-)[

---

§ 2' 3' *Š*]*A*$^{?}$ DINGIR-*LIM A-NA* TÚG.ḪI.A *še-er k⸢i-it*$^{?}$⸣-[*ta*$^{?}$
4' *še-e*]*r ki-it-ta ma-aḫ-ḫa-an-ma-ká*[*n*
5' ^{NA_4}*ḫ*]*u-u̯ạ-ši-i̯a-az kat-ta ú-iz-z*[*i*
6' -*i̯*]*a-ạn-zạ nụ* ^{d}UTU-*ŠI a-ar-t*[*a*(-)
7']-˻*x* ^{d}*Ḫ*˼*a-pa-an-ta-li-i̯*[*a*$^{?}$ [1)]
8' *UŠ-K*]˻*E*˼-*EN* ^{LÚ}SANGA KU[R$^{?}$-
9'](-)*x̣-tạ-r*[*i*(-)
10']˻*x*$^{?}$-*x x*˼[
(broken off)

Text-critical note: [1)] Or to read: -*ta-li-i-i*[*n*] ?

16. Bo 7444

Description: N/A.
CTH: 832 *"Fragments en langue hittite de nature inconnue."*
Dating and Script: OH?/NS.
Remarks: One-sided small fragment from the left portion (with edge) of a tablet.
Measurements: 3.2 × 2.1 × 0.9 cm.
Bibliography: N/A.

Bo 7444

§ 1' 1' ⌜*ḫa-a*⌝(?)-[
2' *ta-aš-t*[*a*?(-)

---

§ 2' 3' LUGAL-*u̯a-aš* [
4' LÚ.MEŠDUGUD(-)[
5' MỤNUSAMA.DIN[GIR-*LIM*
6' LÚ.MEŠẸ.[1)

---

§ 3' 7' ⌞*x-x*⌟ [
(broken off)

Text-critical note: 1) Read and interpret LÚ.MEŠSỊM[UG.A] or LÚ.MEŠẸ-[*PIŠ* . . .] ?

17. Bo 7833

Description: Ritual.
CTH: 470 "*Fragments de rituels.*"
Dating and Script: MH/ENS.
Remarks: Double-sided fragment from the right portion (with top and bottom) of a tablet. Reverse III 14'–15' are duplicate of, or parallel to HFAC 33:2'–3'.
Measurements: 9.1 × 8.3 × 2.8 cm.
Bibliography: S. Košak, hethiter.net/: hetkonk (v. 1.91).

Bo 7833 obv. II

Bo 7833 rev. III

Bo 7833 obv. II

Bo 7833 rev. III (right edge)

Bo 7833 rev. III

Bo 7833 rev. III (right edge)

Bo 7833 (right edge; signs from obv. II)

Obverse II

§ 1 1]-*x̣-ma-kán x̣*-[
2 *n*]*u*$^?$*-kán an-tu-uḫ-ša̱-a̱n* ŠỤM-⸢*ŠU*$^?$⸣ [
3]-*ṃa̱-an-te-eš* NAM.LÚ.Ụ$_{19}$.LU-*i̯a an-da̱ x̣-x̣-x̣*$^?$ [
4 ^{DUG}*KU*]-*KỤ-UB ú-i-te-na-aš* ^{MUNUS}ŠỤ.GI *an-da* ỤRU$^?$(-)[

---

§ 2 5 ^{MUNUS}ŠU.G]I *ḫi-lam-ni an-da* ^{d}UTU-*i-kán me-na̱*$^?$-[*aḫ*$^?$*-ḫa*$^?$*-an*$^?$*-da*$^?$
6 *d*]*a-a-i̯ nu-uš-ša-an A-NA* I ^{GIŠ}BA̱N[ŠUR
7] NỊNDA.GUR$_4$.RA.GÍD.DA *ŠA* 1/2 *UP-NI da-a-i̯*$^?$[
8]-*x̣-ma da-a̱-i̯ nam-ma-aš-ša-an x̣-x̣*$^?$*-x̣*(-)[
9]-*i̯ na̱-an-za-an la-at-ta-al-lị*(-)[[1)]
10 -*z*]*i A-NA* I ^{GIŠ}BANŠUR-*ma-aš-ša-an x̣*$^?$-[
11]-*x̣ da-a-i na-a̱n-za-an ŠA QA-TỊ* [
12]-*x̣-ša ŠA QA-TỊ* ^{d}UTU-*i pí-ra-an da̱-a̱-i̯* [. . .$^?$]

---

§ 3 13 -*z*]*i nu-uš-ša̱-an* ^{MUNUS}ŠU.GI *la-at-ta-al-l*[*i*(-)
14 E]GIR-*pa da-a-i nu* GEŠTIN *ši-pa-an-ti* [
15 *ka-a-š*]*a-u̯a in-na-ra-u̯a-an uk-tu-u-ri* $^{d?}$[
16 -*t*]*u$_4$-me-en nu-kán an-tu-uḫ-ša-an* ŠUM-*x̣*(-)[
17 *n*]*a*$^?$*-at zi-ik* ^{d}UTU-*uš* EGIR-*an ša̱*$^?$-[

---

§ 4 18]⸤*nu-uš-ša*⸥*-an ka-la-ak-tar* ⸤*x-x*⸥(-)[
19]-⸤*x* G⸥A.KU$_7$-*i̯a*(-)⸤*x*⸥(-)[
(broken off)

Obverse II (right edge)

1’]-*an-ti-eš*(-)[. . .$^?$]
2’ -*š*]*a*$^?$*-an*
3’-4’ . . .
5’]-*ša̱-a̱n-zị*
6’ . . .
7’]-*ị*

Reverse III

§ 1’ 1’-2’ (traces)

---

§ 2’ 3’ *m*]*e*$^?$*-mị-ị̯š-ki-iz-zi ŠA* PÚ ^{d}*x̣*(./-)[
4’]-*x̣-a̱n-te-eš šu-me-eš az-zi-ik-k*[*i*$^?$*-it*$^?$*-tén*
5’]-*x̣*$^?$*-eš e-eš-tén na-aš-ta an-tu-uḫ-ša*-[

6' *-t]a-u̯ạ-za-kán u̯a-ar-ap-zi* [. . .?]

7']-*x̣ ạr-ḫạ pa-iz-zi* U_4.I.KAM *QA-TI* [

---

§ 3' 8' [*ma-a-an*(?) . . .? *l*]*ụ-u̯k-kat-ta nu* ^{MUNUS}ŠU.GI NINDA.Ì.E.DẸ.Ạ III ^{DUG}*KU-KỤ-U*[*B*]$^{\text{ḪI.A}}$-*i̯*[*a*]

9']-*i nu-uš-ša-an* III PÚ.ḪI.A *ku-e iš-pa-an-tạ-*[*a*]*z*

10']-*x̣-aš ạ-pé-ẹ-da-aš A-NA* III PÚ.ḪI.A *pa-iz-zi* [2]

11']-*x̣-ịz-zị-i̯ạ IŠ-TU* I PÚ I ^{DUG}*KU-KU-UB šu-un-na-ị*

12']-*mạ-kán Ạ-NA* PÚ.ḪI.Ạ *an-da pé-eš-ši-iš-ki-iz-zi*[3] [4]

---

§ 4' 13' *-a*]*n*? *ḫa-an-te-ẹz-zi pal-ši ku-e-ez IŠ-TU* PỤ́ *u̯a-a-tar* [*ḫ*]*a-a-ni*

14' *ki-i*]*š-ša-an te-ez-zi ka-a-ša-u̯a in-na-ra-u̯a-aš* ^{d}LẠMMA-*aš*

15' EGIR-*p*]*a*[5] *dạ-aḫ-ḫu-ụn nu A-NA* EN.SÍSKUR *in-na-ra-u̯a-an ẹ-ẹš-du*

16']-*x̣* PÚ-*i-ma-kán ạn-da ki-iš-ša-an me-ma-i ki-i-mạ-u̯ạ* [6]

17' *-a*]*n*? PÚ *uk-t*⌞*u*⌟-[*u-ri nu-u̯a-r*]⌞*a*⌟*-at-kán Ú-UL ḫ*⌞*a-a-x*⌟(-)[. . .] [7]

18' EN.S]ÍSKUR-*i̯ạ x̣*? [. . . DUMU.MEŠ-Š]⌞*U*?⌟ DỤMU.DỤMU.⌞MEŠ-Š⌟[*U*? . . .]-*x̣*

19' *QA-TAM*]-*MẠ u*[*k-tu-u-re-eš*?] *x̣*?-*x̣*? [

(bottom of the tablet)

Text-critical notes: [1] Uncertain if the word is complete in this form (likewise in II 13), which is a hapax and denoting a substance or implement used by the Old Woman in the course of the ritual. [2] One sign from obv. II rt. e. 7'. [3] For this spelling see KBo 9.106 II 52 (MH/NS). [4] Three signs from obv. II rt. e. 5'. [5] Restoration follows HFAC 33:3'. [6] Two signs from obv. II rt. e. 2'. [7] Three signs from obv. II rt. e. 1'.

18. Bo 7937

Description: Festival.

CTH: 668 "*Culte de Ḫanḫana.*"

Dating and Script: OS.

Remarks: One-sided fragment from the left portion (with edge) of a tablet. Its lines 2'–15' duplicate KUB 53.25 obv. 4'–13' + Bo 4053 obv. 1'–7' (NS) from where the restorations are taken. Bo 7937 may belong to the same tablet together with other fragments KUB 54.50, KUB 60.41 and HHT 73 (= Bo 5478) which are written likewise in Old Script; see D. Groddek, DBH 20 (2006) 41.

Measurements: 5.4 × 6.2 × 1.6 cm.

Bibliography: S. Alp, Tempel (1983) 234–35 (transliteration and translation of lines 3'–14'); H. Freydank, OLZ 80 (1985) 251 (corrections to the edition of S. Alp after collations of Bo 7937); D. Yoshida, THeth 22 (1996) 225 (transliteration of lines 3'–10'); F. Fuscagni, HPMM 6 (2007) 168–69 (with anterior bibliography).

Bo 7937

Bo 7937

§ 1' 1' (traces)

2' [(*ḫa-at-tal-u̯*)]*a-aš*[1] GIŠ-*i x̣*-[

---

§ 2' 3' [(^{LÚ}GUDU$_{12}$ ^{UZ})]$^{⌈U⌉}$NỊ́G.GỊG DUMU-*lị ạ*$^{?}$-*šạ-a*[*n*$^{?}$-[2]

4' [[3] (^{UZU}NÍG.G)]IG *ẹ-za-az-zi* ^{LÚ}GUDU$_{12}$ IZ[I$^{?}$ [4]-. . . DUMU-*li* (*pa-a-i* DUMU-*aš*) . . .]

5' [[5] *ir*]-*ḫạ-ịz-zị* ^{LÚ}SAGI GAL-*ri* DUMU-[(*li pa*)-*a-i* DUMU-*aš*

6' ⌈^{d}⌉ỊŠKUR ^{d}ỤTU ^{d}*Ka-ạt-tạḫ-ḫi-in* ^{d}*x̣*-[[6]

7' ^{d}*Ḫa-ša-am-mi-ú-un* ^{d}*Te-li-pí-nụ-un* [

8' ^{d}IŠKUR ^{URU}*A-ri*[7]-*ḫa-az-zi-i̯a* ^{d}*Ka-pạ*$^{?}$-[

9' ^{d}*ZA-BA$_{4}$-BA$_{4}$* ^{d}LAMMA ^{d}*Šu-šu-ma-aḫ-ḫ*[*i-in*

---

§ 3' 10' *na-aš-tạ* DUMU-*aš* ^{É}*ḫạ-le-en-ti-u-az pa-i*[*z-zi*

11' *ar-za-na-aš pár-na pa-iz-zị* LÚ.MEŠ ^{URU}*Ta-a-x̣*-[

12' II $^{LÚ.MEŠ}$*ḫa-a-pẹ́-ẹ-eš pé-e-rạ-ạn ḫ*⌞*u-i̯*⌟[*a-an-zi* . . . (*gal-gal-tu*)-*u*$^{?}$-*ri*]

13' EGIR-*an u̯a-al-ḫạ-an-ni-an-*⌞*zi*⌟[. . . (GÍR.ḪI.A-*ŠU-NU*) . . . (Ù I UDU)]

14' ^{LÚ}AGRIG$^{!}$ ^{URU}*Ḫạ-an-ḫa-na d*⌞*a*⌟-[*a-i*

---

§ 4' 15' DỤMU-*aš ạr-za-nạ-aš* Ẹ́-[

16' ⌞*x*⌟-*x̣-x̣*$^{?}$-*kạ́n*$^{?}$ *pí-ị*$^{?}$-[

17' (traces)

(broken off)

Text-critical notes: [1] One expects here the OH spelling *ḫa-at-ta-lu-u̯a-aš* as seen in HHT 73 I 10'. [2] Perhaps reads *ạ*$^{?}$-*šạ-a*[*n*$^{?}$-*da-aš*]. The second sign is clearly "*ša*" and this does not permit the reading *ạ-tạ-a*[*n*-. . .] as often suggested in previous studies. [3] Contra S. Alp, Tempel 234, there is no space for DUMU-*aš* in this lacuna. [4] For syntactical reasons the clause-linking conjunction *n*[*e*-. . .] (i. e., *nu-e*) is excluded. [5] Nothing missing. [6] One expects here the divine name ^{d}Uruntemu / ^{d}Urunzimu etc. as it appears in an incomplete form ^{d}*Ú-ru*-[. . .] in the duplicate KUB 53.25 obv. 9'. [7] D. Yoshida, THeth 22, 225 reads ^{URU}*A-tal-*° which would seemingly be supported by an Old Hittite occurrence ^{URU}*A-ta-al-ḫa-az-zi*-[. . .] in KBo 13.175 obv. 4.

19. Bo 8029

Description: Cult inventory.
CTH: 530 "*Fragments divers.*"
Dating and Script: NH/LNS.
Remarks: One-sided fragment.
Measurements: 3.6 × 4.7 × 1.8 cm.
Bibliography: N/A.

Bo 8029

Bo 8029

§ 1' 1' -*i*]*r*? ⸢*x*-*x̣*⸣(-)[

2']-*an-zi du-ụš-x̣-x̣*-[[1)]

---

§ 2' 3' -*i̯*]*a-an-ma lu-kat-ti x̣*-[

4']-*x̣* I ^{GIŠ}*ša-i̯a-an*[2)] *i-i̯*[*a-an*?-*zi*

5' -*a*]*t A-NA* DINGIR-*LIM iš-ki-š*[*a*(-)

6']-*x̣* GU$_{4}$.MEŠ UDU.ḪI.A *a-pí-i̯a š*[*e*?-

7']⸤E⸥GIR-*pa* ḪUR.SAG-*i pí-tén-*[*zi*

---

§ 3' 8' *Š*]*A* AN.BAR GAL $^{\text{LÚ.MEŠ}}$UKU.UŠ[3)] [

9'](-)⸤*x-x-i̯a*⸥ *kat-ta-an ti-i̯*[*a-*

10' (traces)

(broken off)

Text-critical notes: [1)] It is difficult to determine if here the verbal *dušk-* "to rejoice" or nominal *duškarat-* "entertainment" is present; syntactically compare GÉŠPU *ḫulḫuliya teškanzi duškiškanzi* (KUB 25.23 I 22') versus DINGIR-LUM *kililanzi dušgarattaš* [. . .] (KUB 38.26 obv. 19'). The visible sign traces rather suggest *du-ụš-kạ*$_{4}$-*r*[*a-*. . .]. [2)] This attestation is hitherto a hapax. [3)] For ^{LÚ}UKU.UŠ "heavy-armed soldier" in a context of cult inventory see KUB 56.39 II 27'.

20. Bo 8084

Description: Cult inventory.

CTH: 530 "*Fragments divers.*"

Dating and Script: NH/LNS.

Remarks: One-sided fragment. If the suggested personal name in line 3' is correct, this fragment may be assigned precisely to CTH 518 "*Culte de Pirwa: recensements*"; see note 2 below.

Measurements: 3.6 × 2.6 × 0.5 cm.

Bibliography: S. Alp, Tempel (1983) 308–09 (transliteration and translation of lines 2'–8'); H. Freydank, OLZ 80 (1985) 251 (corrections to the edition of S. Alp after collations of Bo 8084); F. Fuscagni, HPMM 6 (2007) 172 (with anterior bibliography).

Bo 8084

§ 1' 1' -*z*]⌜*i*⌝ *a*[*n*$^{?}$-

2'](./-)x̣(.)DINGIR-*LIM*[1)] *ḫa-a*[*n-da-an*$^{?}$*-zi*

3' -*l*]*a*$^{?}$*-an-pát* $^{m.d}$AMAṚ.[UTU.LÚ(?)(-)[2)]

4'] XXX NAM.RA SUM-*a*[*n-zi*

---

§ 2' 5' K]Ù.BABBAR DÙ-*an-zi* x̣-[

6'] BÁN ZÍZ ^{DUG}*ḫar-ši* *š*[*u-un-na-an-zi*

7' -*z*]*i-la-kán*[3)] *ta-lu-gạ*$^{?}$[4)]-[

---

§ 3' 8']⌞^{É}*ḫ*⌟*a-le-en-du-ṷa-aš* [

9' [. . .?]

(broken off)

Text-critical notes: 1) S. Alp, Tempel 308 suggests É?.DINGIR-*LIM*. 2) S. Alp's reading $^{m.d}$*Pí*-[*ir-ṷa*?] is unlikely; see H. Freydank, OLZ 80, 251. The proper name $^{m.d}$AMAR.UTU.LÚ (= Šanda-ziti) posited here is attested in the inventory text IBoT 2.131 rev. 24, 26 (CTH 518.1.A) and its unpublished duplicate Bo 3245:7' (CTH 518.1.B). 3) Thus, as per H. Freydank contra S. Alp's reading ŠE?-*at-kán*. 4) This is to be preferred over the reading *ta-lu-ša*-[. . .] by S. Alp which would not correspond with any Hittite lemma known.

21. Bo 8695

Description: Ritual or festival.
CTH: 470 "*Fragments de rituels*" or 670 "*Fragments divers.*"
Dating and Script: (E)NS.
Remarks: One-sided fragment written in a neat script.
The suggested devine features ⸢^{d}*Ḫe*⸣[*pat*] (line 1') and [^{d}]*Āpi* (line 6') would refer to a religious text from the Kizzuwatnan milieu; cf. *Konkordanz*: CTH 500.486.
Measurements: 2.5 × 3.4 × 0.6 cm.
Bibliography: N/A.

Bo 8695

§ 1'	1'	]⸢*x* ^{d}*Ḫé*⸣-[*pát*(?)
	2'	]-⸢*a*⸣*z*[1] *pa-ra-a*[2] *ú-iz-z*[*i*$^{?}$
	3'	Š]Ạ$^{?}$ ^{d}U ^{É}*ḫi-lam-x̣*(-)[[3]
	4'	]-*x̣-zi na-aš-ta x̣*$^{?}$-[
	5'	] *ạ*$^{?}$-*u̯a-an kat-ta* [
	6'	]-⸤*a*$^{?}$⸥-*pí*[4] *ši-pa-a*⸤*n-t*⸥[*i*$^{?}$
	(broken off)	

Text-critical notes: [1] Perhaps [^{É}*ḫi-lam-na*]-⸢*a*⸣*z*; cf. line 3' [2] This word exhibits here the ligature writing -*ra+a*; cf. also *kat-ta* in line 5'. [3] For the phrase ŠA ^{d}U / ^{d}IŠKUR ^{É}*ḫilamni* (*anda*) see e.g., KBo 44.98+ III 5' (CTH 475.Tf02.A), KUB 41.48 III 14' (CTH 705.1). The form of the sign "É" here is unique and should be added to Chr. Rüster — E. Neu, HZL (1989) no. 199 [4] To be restored [*A-NA* ^{d}*A*]-⸤*a*⸥-*pí* ?

22. Bo 8696 + KUB 56.43

Description: Festival.
CTH: 626 *"Fête de la 'hâte' (nuntarriyashas)."*
Dating and Script: OH$^?$/NS.
Remarks: Bo 8696 is a one-sided fragment, and its lines 1'–5' directly join KUB 56.43 obv.$^?$ III 7'–11'.
Measurements: 4.0 × 2.3 × 1.1 cm.
Bibliography: A. Taggar-Cohen, THeth 26 (2006) 314 (to KUB 56.43).

Bo 8696

Bo 8696 + KUB 56.43 obv.? III

Bo 8696 + KUB 56.43 obv.? III rt. edge

Obverse? III

(Line numbers of Bo 8696 are in parentheses)

§ 2' . . .

———

§ 3' 7' (= 1') LUGAL-*uš* GUB-*aš* ᵈ*Ṭe*-[*li*]-*pí-nu*(-)[. . .?]

8' (= 2') *e-ku-zi* GIŠ.ᵈIN[ANNA.G]AL[1)]

9' (= 3') LÚ.MEŠ*ḫal-li-i̯a-re-e*[*š* S]ÌR-*R*[*U*[2)]]

10' (= 4') LÚ*pạl-u̯ạ-tal-la-aš pạl-u̯a-a-i̯z-z*⸢*i*⸣

---

§ 4' 11' (= 5') LÚ GIŠBANŠUR NINDA*zi-i*⸤*p-p*⸥*u-lạ-aš-ši-in*[3)] *da-a-i̯*

(Bo 8696 breaks here off; text continues in KUB 56.43 obv.? III 12' ff.)

Text-critical notes: [1)] After this direct join, correct the reading GIŠ.ᵈI[NANNA GAL/TUR] by A. Taggar-Cohen, THeth 26, 314 [2)] Thus, correct the restoration [*u̯a-al-ḫa-an-zi*] by A. Taggar-Cohen, *ibid.* 314 [3)] Thus, correct the reading NINDA*zi-i*[*p*?-*l*]*a-aš-ši-in* by A. Taggar-Cohen, *ibid.* 314.

23. Bo 8697

Description: N/A.
CTH: 832 “*Fragments en langue hittite de nature inconnue.*”
Dating and Script: NS.
Remarks: One-sided fragment that is too small to determine its genre.
Measurements: 3.0 × 2,6 × 0.6 cm.
Bibliography: N/A.

Bo 8697

§ 1’ 1’](.)*x̤*$^{?}$(.)MAŠ[1] KI.GAG[2][
2’]-*lụ*$^{?}$-*la-an-x̣*(-)[

---

§ 2’ 3’]-*u̯a ŠA x̤*$^{?}$(./-)[
4’]-*x̣-an-zi* [
(broken off)

Text-critical notes: [1] Alternatively read “BAR”. [2] The sign combination “KI.GAG” reads SUR_7 (Akk. *bērūtu* / *bīrūtu*) “mound”; see Chr. Rüster — E. Neu, HZL (1989) under no. 313 “Anhöhe”. Only available occurrence from Boğazköy is KUB 6.7+ IV 9’.

24. Bo 8698

Description: Cult inventory or festival.
CTH: 530 or 670 "*Fragments divers.*"
Dating and Script: LNS.
Remarks: Small fragment from the right portion (with edge) of a tablet.
Measurements: 3.4 × 2.2 × 0.9 cm.
Bibliography: N/A.

Bo 8698

Bo 8698 other side

§ 1' 1' -*a*]⌈*n-zi*(?)⌉ *x̤*?

2']-*x̣*

3'] *ḫal-za*!-*a-i*

4' dZ]*A-BA*₄-*BA*₄ *ti-an-z*[*i*]

5' *pé*]-⌈*e*⌉*š-kán-zi*

6' (eras.?)

7']-*x̣-p*[*í*?-

(broken off)

Other side

§ 1' 1' *u*]*š*?-*ši-i̯*⌈*a-an-x̤*?⌉

(broken off)

25. Bo 8699

Description: Ritual? or festival.
CTH: 470 "*Fragments de rituels*" or 670 "*Fragments divers.*"
Dating and Script: NS.
Remarks: One-sided small fragment from the left column of a tablet.
Measurements: 3.4 × 3.2 × 1.4 cm.
Bibliography: N/A.

Bo 8699

Left column

§ 1'	1'	(traces?)
	2'	]-*x̣-ụš ku-i*[*t*?-*ta*?]
	3'	G]U$_4$![1)].MEŠ UDU.[ḪI?.A?(-). . .?]
	4'	]-*ạ*?
	5'	*d*]*a-an-zi*
	6'	]-*zị*
	7'	(eras.)
	8'	(traces)
	(broken off)	

Text-critical note: [1)] The sign seems to be written with a broken vertical.

26. Bo 8701

Description: Festival.
CTH: 670 “*Fragments divers.*”
Dating and Script: LNS.
Remarks: One-sided small fragment.
Measurements: 3.4 × 3.8 × 1.0 cm.
Bibliography: N/A.

Bo 8701

§ 1’	1’	]⌜SÌR-*RU*(?)⌝ [
§ 2	2’	[. . . ^{d}. . . *x*]-*ŠU e-ku-z*[*i*
	3’	]-*x̣* [
	4’	]-*x̣*$^{?}$(-) *x̣*(-)[
§ 3’	5’	K]AŠ$^{?}$ [
	6’	-*z*]*i*$^{?}$ [

(broken off)

27. Bo 8703

Description: N/A.
CTH: 832 "*Fragments en langue hittite de nature inconnue.*"
Dating and Script: N/A.
Remarks: One-sided, moderately abraded fragment that is too small to classify.
Measurements: 3.2 × 3.2 × 0.8 cm.
Bibliography: N/A.

Bo 8703

§ 1' . . .

———

§ 2' 1' (illegible signs)
2' -*r*]*a*-*ạl*(?)-[
3'] ⌜*i*-*da*?-*x̣*[1)]⌝(-) *x̣*-[

---

§ 3' 4' -*p*]*í*-*lị*-*ịš*(-)*šị*-*i̯*[*a*(-)[2)]
5']-*x̣*-*ši*[3)] *up*-*pí*-*x̣*-[

---

§ 4' 6']⸤*x x*⸥[
(broken off)

Text-critical notes: [1)] The sign looks like rather "*la*" than "*lu*". [2)] Possibly belongs to a proper name; e.g., [m]Kišnapili (NH 589), [m]Piyapili (NH 984). [3)] To restore and read [*A-NA* / *MA-ḪAR* [d]U]TU-*ŠI* ? Thus, the text is perhaps of historical or instructive nature.

28. Bo 8704 + Bo 4395 + KUB 45.67

Description: Ritual or festival.

CTH: 706 "*Fragments de fêtes (ou de rituels) pour Tešub et Ḫebat.*"

Dating and Script: NS.

Remarks: Bo 8704 is a one-sided fragment, and lines 2'–7' directly join Bo 4395 + KUB 45.67 I 1'–6'.

Measurements: 2.4 × 3.4 × 0.9 cm.

Bibliography: I. Wegner, ChS I/3-2 (2002) 133–134 (to KUB 45.67); D. Groddek, IJDL 2 (2005) 19 (on the joins Bo 8704 + Bo 4395 + KUB 45.67) http://www.hethport.uni-wuerzburg.de/hetskiz/sk.php?f=Bo%203805

Bo 8704 + Bo 4395 + KUB 45.67 obv. I

Bo 8704 (detail)

Obverse I

§ 1' 1' (traces)

2' *ᵈPí-te*?*-e*[*n-ḫi*[1)] T]⌜UŠ⌝-*aš e-ku-zi* [I NINDA.SIG *pár-ši-i̯a*]

3' *na-at-ša-an* EGIR-*pa* <*A-NA*> ZAG.GAR.R[A *da-a-i*]

---

§ 2' 4' EGIR-*pa*?*-ma ᵈA-dam-ma ᵈKu-pa-p*[*a ᵈḪa-šu-un-tar-ḫi*]

5' TUŠ-*aš e-ku-zi* I NINDA.SIG *pár-ši-i̯*[*a na-at-ša-an* EGIR-*pa*]

6' *A-NA* ZAG.[G]AR.RA *da-a-i* [

---

§ 3' 7' EGIR-*an-da-ma* ⸤DINGIR.MEŠ-*na*⸥ [*at-t*]⸤*a*⸥-[*ni-u̯iᵢ-na ᵈḪé-pát-u̯iᵢ-na*[1)]]

(Bo 8704 breaks here off; text continues in Bo 4395 + KUB 45.67 I 7' ff.)

Text-critical note: [1)] For the sequence of the divine list from ᵈPitenḫi to ᵈḪepatwiᵢna see e.g., KBo 45.254 I 10'–14' (CTH 706.II).

29. Bo 8706

Description: Festival.
CTH: 670 "*Fragments divers.*"
Dating and Script: NS.
Remarks: Double-sided fragment from the left portion (with edge) of a tablet.
Measurements: 4.3 × 2.5 × 4.2 cm.
Bibliography: N/A.

Bo 8706 obv.$^{?}$

Bo 8706 rev.$^{?}$

Obverse$^{?}$

§ 1' 1' (traces)
2' *ḫu-u-el-pị́*(-)[
3' I ^{DUG}*ḫa-n*[*i*$^{?}$-
4' I ^{DUG}*ḫar-š*[*i*$^{?}$(-)
5' I ^{DUG}*ḫa-x̣*$^{?}$-[

---

§ 2' 6' LUGAL-*uš*(-)[

7' *ma-ni-*[

8' *šạ*$^{?}$(-)x̣$^{?}$(-)[

(broken off)

Reverse$^{?}$

§ 1' 1' $^{\text{L}\ulcorner\text{Ú?}\urcorner}$x̣$^{?}$[

2' *a-ra-*[

---

§ 2' 3' LUGAL-[*uš*(-)

4' III x̣(./-)[

5' $^{\text{ḍ?}}$*Ma-*[

6' AN.TẠḪ̣.[ŠUM^{SAR} [1)]

7' $^{\text{LÚ.MEŠ}}$x̣$^{?}$(.)[

8' (illegible signs)

(broken off)

Text-critical note: [1)] If this reading is correct, the lemma AN.TAḪ.ŠUM^{SAR} would be decisive for the text genre (CTH 625 ?).

30. Bo 8707

Description: N/A.
CTH: 832 *"Fragments en langue hittite de nature inconnue."*
Dating and Script: NS.
Remarks: One-sided fragment from the left portion (with edge) of a tablet that is too small to classify.
Measurements: 3.2 × 1.8 × 2.2 cm.
Bibliography: N/A.

Bo 8707

§ 1' 1' *ạ*?-[
2' É?(./-)[
3' *an-x̣*(-)[1)

§ 2' 4' *A-NA* [
5' ḪUR.SAG-x̣(-)1)[
6' 𒀸 *ḫụ*-[
7' I x̣(./-)[1)
(broken off)

Text-critical note: 1) Or to be read as a proper name.

31. Bo 8708

Description: Festival.
CTH: 647 "*Fragments de fêtes présidées par un "fils"* (DUMU-*as*)" ?
Dating and Script: (L)NS.
Remarks: Double-sided small fragment that belongs to the lower (obv.[?]) and upper (rev.[?]) portion (with edge) of a tablet.
Measurements: 2.6 × 4.1 × 2.9 cm.
Bibliography: N/A.

Bo 8708 obv.[?]

Bo 8708 rev.[?]

Obverse$^{?}$, left column

§ 1' 1']-⸢*x-i̯a*⸣
2' . . .

---

§ 2' 3' *-a]n*$^{?}$*-ta-ạz*
4']-*x̣* BAL-*ti*

(bottom of the tablet)

Obverse$^{?}$, right column

§ 1' 1' *ạ-x̣*(-)[
2' ^{d}*T*[*e*$^{?}$-1)
3' *šu-up*2)*-p*[*a*(-)

(bottom of the tablet)

Reverse$^{?}$, left column

§ 1 1 . . .
2]-*x̣-zi*

---

§ 2 3 ^{URU}*N*]*e-ri-ik*5)
4]-*x̣*
(broken off)

Reverse$^{?}$, right column

§ 1' 1' XI$^{?}$ [

---

§ 2' 2' DUMU3)*-aš* G[UB$^{?}$*-aš*4) ^{d} . . . *e-ku-zi*
(broken off)

Text-critical notes: 1) This divine name may refer to ^{d}Telipinu. 2) A distorted sign form written together with "*pa*". 3) A distorted sign form that looks like rather an "*i*". 4) Cf. KBo 39.83 rev. 2' and VS 28.13 III 16". 5) Probably to ^{d}IŠKUR / ^{d}U ^{URU}Nerik.

32. Bo 8709

Description: N/A.
CTH: 832 "*Fragments en langue hittite de nature inconnue.*"
Dating and Script: (L)NS.
Remarks: One-sided fragment.
Measurements: 3.1 × 4.2 × 1.3 cm.
Bibliography: N/A.

Bo 8709

§ 1' 1']⸢*x*⸣[

2'](-)*x̣-an-ni*?(-)[

3']⸢GIŠ⸣.ḪI.A-*ru*[1)] *ḫu̯-u̯-m*[*a-an-da*?

4'] ⸢*ku*⸣-*i̯t* GIŠ-*ru* [

5'] *ḫu-u-ma-an-pát* GIŠ-*ru*(-)*x̣*?(-)[

6']-*ta-nu-uš-* *ki*[2)] [

---

§ 2' 7']⸤*x*?-*x-x* GIŠ⸥TIR.MEŠ? [

(broken off)

Text-critical notes: [1)] For this plural spelling see KUB 17.10+ I 16'. [2)] If this predicate is an iter. imp. sg. 2 form (e.g., of *ištantanušk-*, **kištanušk-* and *tittanušk-*) it could be decisive for the text genre of the present fragment (instructions concerning woods and forest ?).

33. Bo 8710 + IBoT 1.22 + KUB 20.60

Description: Festival.

CTH: 656.4 *"Fêtes 'mixtes': chants en hatti, hourrite, kanisien, etc."*

Dating and Script: LNS.

Remarks: Bo 8710 is a one-sided fragment, and lines 1'–4' directly join IBoT 1.22 + KUB 20.60:11'–14'.

Measurements: 4.5 × 2.2 × 1.7 cm.

Bibliography: R. Lebrun, Samuha (1976) 183–184 (to KUB 20.60 +); D. Groddek, DBH 13 (2004) 108 (to KUB 20.60 +) http://www.hethport.uni-wuerzburg.de/hetskiz/sk.php?f=Bo%20469

Bo 8710

IBoT 1.22 + Bo 8710 + (composite image)

Right column

(Line numbers of Bo 8710 are in parentheses)

§ 3' . . .

---

§ 4' 11' (= 1') [L]ỤGAL-*uš* GỤB-*aš* ^{d}U KARAŠ *e-kụ-z*[*i*]

12' (= 2') [G]IŠ.^{d}INANNA.GAL SÌR-*RU* I NINDA.GUR$_4$.RA *pạ́r-ši-i̯ạ*

---

§ 5' 13' (= 3') [LU]GẠL-*uš* GUB-*aš* ṾII ^{d}U.Ḫ̣I.A ^{d}Ụ *pí-ḫa-aš-ša-š*[*i-iš*[1)]]

14' (= 4') ^{d}U *ŠA-ME-E* ^{d}Ụ *mụ-u̯a-tal-la-ḫi-ta-aš*[2)]

(Bo 8710 breaks here off; text continues in IBoT 1.22 + KUB 20.60:15'ff.)

Text-critical notes: [1-2)] After the join this divine name is now complete and improves the readings by R. Lebrun, Samuha 183-184 and D. Groddek, DBH 13, 108. Also, revise the occurrence in CHD 3/3 (1986) 317.

34. Bo 8712

Description: Festival.
CTH: 670 "*Fragments divers.*"
Dating and Script: (L)NS.
Remarks: One-sided tiny fragment.
Measurements: 3.3 × 3.2 × 1.6 cm.
Bibliography: N/A.

Bo 8712

§ 1' 1']-*x̣ ḫạ-aš-ši-i* [
2' *pár-š*]*ụ*?-*ụl-li da-ạ-*[*i*]
3' (traces)
(broken off)

35. Bo 8713

Description: N/A.
CTH: 832 "*Fragments en langue hittite de nature inconnue.*"
Dating and Script: LNS.
Remarks: One-sided fragment from the right portion (with edge) of a tablet that is too small to classify.
Measurements: 3.8 × 2.2 × 1.3 cm.
Bibliography: N/A.

Bo 8713

Bo 8713 edge

§ 1' 1']-*x̣-rạ-a*⌜*n-x*⌝(-)[
2' -*a*]*n*$^{?}$ *ku-e-u*[*š*$^{?}$(-)
3'] SỊSKUR[1)].⌜MEŠ$^{?}$⌟ (eras.) [
4' (-)*a*]*n*$^{?}$-*da*
5']-*x̣ an-da*
6']-*x̣-n*[*a*$^{?}$(-)
(broken off)

Text-critical note: [1)] Or to be read [. . . .G]AZ ?

36. Bo 8714

Description: N/A
CTH: 832 “*Fragments en langue hittite de nature inconnue.*”
Dating and Script: N/A.
Remarks: One-sided tiny fragment that possibly belongs to the colophon of a tablet.
Measurements: 3.7 × 2.9 × 1.4 cm.
Bibliography: N/A.

Bo 8714

Colophon$^{?}$

§ 1’ 1’] DỤB.IV.[KAM(?)
2’ *ṬU*]*P*$^{?}$-*PU* *x̤*$^{?}$ [
3’] *Ạ-NA* [
(broken off)

37. Bo 8716

Description: Cult inventory.
CTH: 530 "*Fragments divers.*"
Dating and Script: NH/LNS.
Remarks: One-sided fragment.
Measurements: 3.9 × 1.9 × 0.8 cm.
Bibliography: N/A.

Bo 8716

§ 1' 1' *u̯]a-ạr-šu-l[i*[1)]
2' *ša*$^{?}$*-r]a-a pa-a-a[n-zi*

§ 2' 3' $^{\text{ḪUR.SAG}}$*Ḫ̮]a-a-ḫ̮a-a-i̯[a(-)*[2)]

§ 3' 4']-*x̣* III ^{GIŠ}GIDRU(-/.)*x̣*(-)[
5' -*a*]*n*$^{?}$*-ma*(-) GUB$^{?}$ [3)][
6' *ke*$^{?}$]*-ẹ-da-n*[*i*$^{?}$
7'](-)*x̣-in-x̣*(-)[
8']⌞*x*⌟[
(broken off)

Text-critical notes: [1)] For the cultic term *waršuli akuwanzi* / NAG-(*an*)*zi* in cult inventories see KBo 26.151 I 6' (CTH 522); KUB 17.35 I 33', IV 32 (CTH 525.2); etc. [2)] This line appears to be written as a separate paragraph although no paragraph stroke is visible. The mountain name Ḫ̮aḫ̮aya is attested exclusively in cult inventories, e.g., KBo 26.191:16' (CTH 530); KBo 34.106 I 2 (CTH 509.6); KUB 25.22 III 2, 17 (CTH 524.2); KUB 54.98:12' (CTH 530 [*Konkordanz*: CTH 678]). [3)] The sign looks like "*du*", but also "*at*$^{!}$", so that the reading [GIM-*a*]*n-ma-at*$^{!}$ is conceivable.

38. Bo 8717

Description: N/A.
CTH: 831 "*Fragments en langue inconnue ou indéterminée.*"
Dating and Script: NS.
Remarks: One-sided fragment that is too small to classify.
Despite the affiliation to CTH 790 "*Fragments de rituels et conjurations hourro-hittites*" at the *Konkordanz*, there is no clear evidence that this fragment may be a Hurrian ritual / conjuration. All incomplete words could be Hattian as well.
Measurements: 3.3 × 2.6 × 1.1 cm.
Bibliography: N/A.

Bo 8717

§ 1'	1'	]⌜*x-x*⌝[
	2'	](-)*x̣-e-eš-x̤*$^{?}$(-)[
§ 2'	3'	]-*x̣-pí ša-ạ*-[
	4'	](-)*x̣-u̯u*$_{u}$*-uš-x̣*(-)[
	5'	](-)*na-at-x̤*(-)[
	6'	](-)*x̣-i-en*(-)[
	7'	](-)⌞*x̣-ka*$^{?}$⌟(-)[

(broken off)

39. Bo 8718

Description: Ritual or festival.
CTH: 470 "*Fragments de rituels*" or 670 "*Fragments divers.*"
Dating and Script: NS.
Remarks: One-sided small fragment with two columns.
Measurements: 2.2 × 2.9 × 0.8 cm.
Bibliography: N/A.

Bo 8718

Left column

§ 1'	1'	GIŠ]-*rụ*(?)-*ị*
	2'	] x̣?
	3'	]-*tạ*
	4'	]-*pạ́r*?
	(broken off)	

Right column

§ 1'	1'	GẸŠTIN(-/.)[
	2'	*nam-m*[*a*(-)
	3'	*IŠ-T*[*U*
	4'	*na-a*[*n*(-)
	(broken off)	

40. Bo 8719

Doscription: N/A.
CTH: 832 "*Fragments en langue hittite de nature inconnue.*"
Dating and Script: ENS.
Remarks: One-sided fragment that is too small to classify.
Measurements: 4.8 × 4.8 × 1.0 cm.
Bibliography: N/A.

Bo 8719

§ 1'	1'	](-)*x̣-x̣*?(-)*tạ-mụ-x̣-x̣*(-)[
	2'	-*n*]*ạ*? *ti-i̯a-az-z*[*i*
	3'	.G]I [

(broken off)

41. Bo 8720

Description: Festival.
CTH: 670 "*Fragments divers.*"
Dating and Script: NS.
Remarks: One-sided fragment with two columns.
Measurements: 3.5 × 3.2 × 1.2 cm.
Bibliography: N/A.

Bo 8720

Left column

§ 1'	1'	]-*x̤*
	2'	*pár-ši-i̯*]*a*
§ 2'	3'	-*i̯*]*a-zi*
	4'	. . .
	5'	(-)*d*]*a-an-zi*
	6'	]-⌞*x*?-*zi*⌟
	7'	]-⌞*x*⌟
		(broken off)

Right column

§ 1'	1'	⌜*x*? *x x x*⌝[
	2'	$^{\text{LÚ.MEŠ}}$ḪÚB.B[I
§ 2'	3'	LUGAL MUNUS.LUGAL(-)*x̣*(-)[. . . *a-ku-u̯a-an-zi*]
	4'	GIŠ.^{d}INANNA.G[AL? . . .? SÌR-*RU*
	5'	^{LÚ}ẠLA[N?.ZU$_9$ *me-ma-i*(?) ^{LÚ}*pal-u̯a-tal-la-aš*]
	6'	*pạl-u̯*[*a-a*?-*iz-zi*
§ 3'	7'	^{LÚ}*x̣*(-/.)[
	8'	(traces)
		(broken off)

42. Bo 8721

Description: Oracle.
CTH: 582 "*Fragments d'oracles.*"
Dating and Script: NS.
Remarks: One-sided fragment.
The context here is strongly reminiscent of IBoT 4.48 obv. 1'–5'. According to their identical ductus, both fragments belong rather to same tablet than are duplicates.
Measurements: 4.6 × 4.0 × 0.7 cm.
Bibliography: D. Groddek, DBH 23 (2007) 35 (to IBoT 4.48).

Bo 8721

§ 1' . . .

———

§ 2' 1' ANŠE$^{?}$].KỤR.RA(.)[1)][

2'](-)*x̣̣*$^{?}$-*u̯ạ-kán* ŠÀ *x̣*(-/.)[

3'] ỤRU$^{?}$-*LUM-ma-u̯a x̣*(-/.)[

4'](-)*x̣-i̯a-u̯a*[2)] *Ú-UL a-x̣-*[

5' *A-N*]*A* ^{d}*Pí-ir-u̯a* [

6']-⌞*tar-r*⌟[*i*(-)[3)]

(broken off)

Text-critical notes: [1)] For this logogram and the following context cf. IBoT 4.48 obv. 2' ff. (CTH 582). [2)] To read [. . . .Ḫ̮I].Ạ-*i̯a-u̯a* ? Cf. IBoT 4.48 obv. 2': [ANŠE$^{?}$.KU]R.RA.MEŠ-*i̯a-u̯a* ⌜*Ú*⌝-[*UL*]. [3)] Perhaps belongs to the word *maršaštarri-* "desecration"; cf. IBoT 4.48 obv. 4'–5'.

43. Bo 8722

Description: Festival.
CTH: 670 "*Fragments divers.*"
Dating and Script: NS.
Remarks: One-sided fragment.
Measurements: 3.6 × 2.5 × 0.6 cm.
Bibliography: N/A.

Bo 8722

§ 1' 1']⸢x.M⸣EŠ$^{?}$ [1] $^{\text{L⸢Ú⸣}}$[
2' [^{LÚ}*pal-u̯a*]*-tal-la-aš pal-u̯*[*a-a*$^{?}$*-iz-zi*
3' [^{LÚ}*ki*]*-i̯-ta-aš ḫal-za-a̯-*[*i*]

---

§ 2' 4' [LUGAL MU]NUS.LUGAL *e-ša-a*[*n-ta*$^{?}$]
5' [*A-NA* LU]GAL MUNUS.LUGAL *MẸ-*[*E QA-TI*
6' [DUMU.MEŠ$^{?}$].Ẹ.GAL *x̣*$^{?}$-[
7' [*QA-TI-ŠU-N*]*U a-*[*an-ša-an-zi* [2]
(broken off)

Text-critical notes: [1] For this sign shape see Chr. Rüster — E. Neu, HZL under no. 360 (form 4). [2] Similar hand-washing scenes are found in KBo 30.69 III 5'–9' (CTH 616.Tg28.1) and KBo 49.89+ obv. III 15'–20' (CTH 611.2).

44. Bo 8723

Description: Festival.

CTH: 591.I.b.M "*Fête du mois.*"

Dating and Script: N/A.

Remarks: One-sided tiny fragment that is moderately abraded. Bo 8723 lines 2'–5' are duplicate of, or parallel to, VS 28.29 I 7'–10' (CTH 591.I.b.B), VS 28.30 III 12"–15" (CTH 591.I.b.A), IBoT 2.84+ III 7'–11' (CTH 591.I.b.F) and IBoT 3.51:12'–13' (CTH 591.I.b.D), from where the restorations are adopted. My early assumption that Bo 8723 might be in its lines 2'–4' an indirect join to the other unpublished piece Bo 5825 I 8–10 (CTH 591.I.b.E) turned out to be incorrect after a physical examination in the Ankara Museum in June 2015.

Measurements: 3.3 × 2.7 × 1.0 cm.

Bibliography: J. Klinger, StBoT 37 (1996) 384 (to Bo 5825).

Bo 8723

§ 1' 1' (traces$^{?}$)

2' [(*ta-aš* ^{NINDA}*ta-pár-u̯a*$_{a}$*-šu-i ta-pu-uš-za t*)]*i-i̯ạ-ẓ*[(*i*)]

---

§ 2' 3' [(^{LÚ}UGULA.X $^{\text{LÚ.ME}}$)]^{Š}*ME-ŠE-TỊ*$_{4}$-[(*ma pa-iz-zi*)]

4' [(*na-aš A-NA A-Š*)]*AR* GAL *ME*-[(*ŠE-TI*$_{4}$)]

5' [(*A-NA* $^{\text{LÚ.MEŠ}}$*ME*)]-*ŠẸ-TI*$_{4}$ *kat-t*[(*a-an ti-i̯a-zi*)]

6' (traces)

(broken off)

45. Bo 8724

Description: Festival$^{?}$.
CTH: 670 "*Fragments divers.*"
Dating and Script: N/A.
Remarks: One-sided tiny fragment.
Measurements: 3.3 × 3.2 × 1.1 cm.
Bibliography: N/A.

Bo 8724

§ 1' . . .

——

§ 2' 1' GEŠT]IN$^{?}$

2' -*a*]*n*$^{?}$-*zi*

————————————

§ 3' 3' $^{\text{LÚ.MEŠ?}}$S]AGI.A ⸢$^{\text{d?}}$⸣$^{1)}$[

4' (traces)

(broken off)

Text-critical note: $^{1)}$ Or: [^{LÚ}S]AGI.A-*a*⸢*n*⸣.

46. Bo 8725

Description: N/A.
CTH: 832 "*Fragments en langue hittite de nature inconnue.*"
Dating and Script: OH/NS.
Remarks: One-sided fragment that is too small to classify.
Measurements: 2.9 × 2.7 × 1.3 cm.
Bibliography: N/A.

Bo 8725

§ 1' 1' *ta̤ x̣*-[
2' *ta-aš-x̣*(-)[
3' *ú-u̯*[*a*-

(broken off)

47. Bo 8726

Description: Ritual or festival.
CTH: 500 "*Fragments de rituels (ou de fêtes) du Kizzuwatna*" or 670 "*Fragments divers.*"
Dating and Script: NS.
Remarks: One-sided very thin flake from the left portion (close to edge) of a tablet that is lightly abraded.
Measurements: 3.6 × 4.0 × 0.4 cm.
Bibliography: N/A.

Bo 8726

§ 1' 1' *IŠ-TỤ* ⸢x⸣ (eras.) ^{DUG}DÍLIM.GAL x̣-[
2' *nu-uš-ša-an* NINDA.GUR$_4$.RẠ.[KU$_7$$^?$
3' ^{DUG}*iš-nu-u-ri še-er* [. . .$^?$ *da-a-i*(?)]

---

§ 2' 4' II NINDA.GUR$_4$.RA.KU$_7$ *A-NA* ^{d}[. . . *pár-ši-i̯a*]

---

§ 3' 5' II NINDA.GUR$_4$.RA.KỤ$_7$ *A-NA* ^{d}*Ịš*$^?$-[[1)]
6' [*pá*]⸤*r-š*⸥*i-i̯a* [

---

§ 4' 7' (traces)
(broken off)

Text-critical note: [1)] The keywords ^{DUG}DÍLIM.GAL "bowl" (line 1'), ^{DUG}*išnura-* "kneading trough" (line 3'), and NINDA.GUR$_4$.RA.KU$_7$ "sweet thick bread" (lines 4', 5') are still not sufficient evidence for a Kizzuwatnan cult tradition that is possibly present here. A stronger clue for that, however, would be the divine name ^{d}*Iš*[*ḫara*$^?$] in line 5'.

48. Bo 8727

Description: Cult inventory or festival.

CTH: 530 or 670 "*Fragments divers.*"

Dating and Script: NH/NS.

Remarks: One-sided fragment that is lightly abraded. Bo 8727 lines 2'–4' have strong similarities to KUB 56.56 IV 18–19 (CTH 670.1940), hence both texts may belong to the same composition or even to the same tablet.

Measurements: 3.3 × 3.2 × 1.2 cm.

Bibliography: N/A.

Bo 8727

§ 1' 1' (traces)

2' M]U.I.KẠM[1] *UL-i̯*[*a*(-)

---

§ 2' 3' [*A-NA* EZEN$_4$.ITU.KA]M-*ši*[2] *ŠA* ITU.I.K[AM

4' I *P*]*A* I *UP-NU-i̯a* ZÌ.DẠ[3] [

5']⌞V DUG.KA⌟Š[4] IỊ *ỤP-NỤ x̤*$^{?}$[

6']⌞*x x-x-x*⌟[

(broken off)

Text-critical notes: [1] This is more likely than the reading [. . .] U$_4$.KẠM. [2] Cf. KUB 56.56 IV 18 where it reads *A-NA* EZEN$_4$.ITU.KAM-*ma-aš-ši*. [3] Cf. KUB.56.56 IV 2: I *PA* II *UP-NU* 1/2 *UP-NU-i̯a* ZÌ.DA (thus, not *ku-it* as wrongly copied in the edition volume; see S. Košak, ZA 78 [1988] 149). [4] Cf. KUB.56.56 IV 19.

49. Bo 8729

Description: Mythological or ritual / conjuration with mythology.

CTH: 370 "*Fragments mythologiques*" or 458 "*Fragments de conjurations.*"

Dating and Script: NS.

Remarks: One-sided fragment. The available context concerns a mythological$^{?}$ narrative only; no portion of a possible ritual / incantation is preserved.

Measurements: 2.5 × 3.1 × 1.8 cm.

Bibliography: N/A.

Bo 8729

§ 1'	1'	*la-a*]-⌜*ú*⌝(?) [
	2'	]-*x̣-ma* EZ⌜EN$_4$-*ŠU*⌝
	3'	*ar-ḫ*]*a* *la-a-ú*[1)]
§ 2'	4'	]-*ad-du*[2)] ^{d}*Ḫa-li-pí-i*[*n-nu-*[3)]
	5'	-*u*]*š*$^{?}$-*ša u-un-na-aḫ-ḫ*[*u-un*
	6'	*a*]*r-ḫa da-la-a-aḫ-ḫ*[*u-un*
	7'	](-)*x̣-at da-a na-a*⌜*t*⌝(-)[
	8'	](-)⌞*x̣*$^{?}$-*x* *pé-e*⌟-*da*(-)[

(broken off)

Text-critical notes: [1)] For *ar-ḫa la-a-ú* see KUB 59.54 rev. 5 (CTH 335.21.A), KBo 17.54 I + 8' (CTH 458.1.1.A). [2)] An imperative form or the divine name [^{d}Uriy]addu ? [3)] The spelling of the deity Ḫalipinu with -*nn*- is otherwise unattested.

50. Bo 8730

Description: Treaty / protocol or instruction / oath.

CTH: 212 “Traités (ou protocoles): fragments” or 275 “Fragments de protocoles (ou de traités ?).”

Dating and Script: NS.

Remarks: One-sided small, moderately abraded fragment from the left portion (with edge) of a tablet. For lines 2’–6’ cf. KBo 19.60:22’-24’ (CTH 212.128) and VS 28.126:10’-12’ (CTH 212.155).

Measurements: 2.8 × 2.4 × 2.0 cm.

Bibliography: N/A.

Bo 8730

§ 1’ 1’ (traces)

2’ *ma-ni-ạḫ-x̣-*[[1)]

3’ *nạ-ạš-ta* [

4’ [*ku*]*-it-ki x̣-*[

5’ [*na*$^{?}$]*-ạš-ma* LỤ́(-/.)[

6’ [*ku-i*]*š-kị k*[*u*$^{?}$*-x̣*

7’ [...*-i̯*]*ạ*$^{?}$*-ạz*$^{?}$*-za* [2)] *x̣*$^{?}$(-)[

---

§ 2’ 8’ [*an-da-m*]*ạ-kạ́n*(?) [3)] [

9’ (traces)

(broken off)

Text-critical notes: [1)] This may belong to the noun *maniyaḫḫai-* “administrative district; government”; cf. KBo 19.60:22’, 23’ and VS 28.126:10’, 11’. [2)] Cf. VS 28.126:13’; to be restored as [KUR-*i̯*]*a-az-za* ? [3)] For this tentative restoration see VS 28.126:3’.

51. Bo 8731

Description: N/A.

CTH: 832 "*Fragments en langue hittite de nature inconnue.*"

Dating and Script: NS.

Remarks: One-sided tiny fragment that is too small to classify. Lines 3'–4' clearly refer to the topic of violating the oaths (*lingauš šarra-*).

Measurements: 2.8 × 2.2 × 1.4 cm.

Bibliography: N/A.

Bo 8731

§ 1' 1']-*x̣-i* [

2'](-)*x̣-ul-ụa*[1)] *x̣*-[

3']-*x̣* *li-in-x̣*?-[

4' -*u*]*š*? ⌜x⌟ (eras.) *šar-r*[*a*-

5']-*x̣* *x̣*-[

(broken off)

Text-critical note: [1)] A Hittite word or [. . .] *Ụ́-UL-ụa*.

52. Bo 8732

Description: Ritual or festival.
CTH: 470 "*Fragments de rituels*" or 670 "*Fragments divers.*"
Dating and Script: NS.
Remarks: One-sided fragment from the right portion (with edge) of a tablet.
Measurements: 4.7 × 2.5 × 1.2 cm.
Bibliography: N/A.

Bo 8732

§ 1' 1'](-)⸢*x-x̣-i̯*⸣*a-zị*$^{?}$

---

§ 2' 2'] ^{GIŠ}*ar-m*[*i*$^{?}$-[1]
3' -*n*]*a-aš* ^{GIŠ}DẠG$^{?}$(-)[
4']-*x̣ ḫi-la*[*m*-[2]
5' -*ḫ*]*a*$^{?}$-*an-da x̣*-[
6']-*x̣ ti-en*-[*zi*]

---

§ 3' 7']-*x̣* PÚ-*i*(-)*x̤*$^{?}$(-)[
8'](-)*pạl-ụ́*(?)-[
9' (traces)
(broken off)

Text-critical notes: [1] To be related to the word ^{GIŠ}*armizzi-* "bridge." [2] To be related to the word $^{\text{(É)}}$*ḫilammar* "gate house."

53. Bo 8734

Description: Historical$^{?}$.

CTH: 215 "*Fragments non caractérisés.*"

Dating and Script: NH.

Remarks: One-sided fragment that is too small to classify. Whether a historical text is present here depends on the interpretation of the words in lines 4'–5'; see text-critical notes below.

Measurements: 2.9 × 2.4 × 1.2 cm.

Bibliography: N/A.

Bo 8734

§ 1' 1']-⌜*x̣-ta-an* ^{m}U⌝[R.[1]

2' ^{U}]^{RU}*Ḫa-at-tu-š*[*a*(-)

3' -*e*]*š-ta*[2] *pu-u-ta*[*l*$^{?}$-*li*$^{?}$-[3]

4']-*x̣ šu-ul-l*[*a*-[4]

5' -*z*]*i*$^{?}$-*uš t*[*e*-[5]

6' (traces)

(broken off)

Text-critical notes: [1] So, rather than ⌜I U⌝[R.MAḪ/SAG]; cf. the proper names ^{m}UR.MAḪ(.LÚ), ^{m}UR.SAG etc. [2] Or: [. . . .M]EŠ-*ta*. [3] So, rather than *pu-u-r*[*i*- . . .]; for *putalliya*- "to gird (troops)" in historical context see CHD P/3 (1997) 401 f. [4] Possibly to *šullai-*/*šulliya*- "to quarrel" or *šullatar* "fight." [5] [*tu-uz-z*]*i-uš t*[*e-eḫ-ḫ*°- . . .] "[I] p[lace(d) the troo]ps" ?

54. Bo 8735

Description: Ritual or festival.
CTH: 470 "*Fragments de rituels*" or 670 "*Fragments divers.*"
Dating and Script: NS.
Remarks: One-sided fragment.
Measurements: 2.8 × 4.0 × 1.6 cm.
Bibliography: N/A.

Bo 8735

§ 1' 1']-⸢*ši-i̯*⸣[*a*(?)(-)
2']-*x̣ pạ-a-an-z*[*i*
3' *me*[?1)]]-*ẹ-mi-i̯a-an- zị* [
4']-*x̣ ú-da-an-z*[*i*

---

§ 2' 5'] ⸤*x x* EN.SISKUR⸥(-)[2)][
(broken off)

Text-critical notes: [1)] The plene-spelling *me-e-*° for *memiyanzi* "they speak / recite" is so far unattested; thus to be restored as [*ú*]-*ẹ*- instead ? [2)] Alternatively read ⸤EN.SÍS⸥[KUR(-) . . .].

55. Bo 8736

Description: Festival.
CTH: 670 "*Fragments divers.*"
Dating and Script: N/A.
Remarks: One-sided fragment.
Measurements: 3.8 × 2.2 × 0.9 cm.
Bibliography: N/A.

Bo 8736

§ 1' 1']-⌈*šar*⌉(-)[
2' -*k*]*u*$^{?}$-*ra-a*[*n*-$^{1)}$

---

§ 2' 3' [UGULA$^{?}$ $^{\text{LÚ.M}}$]^{EŠ}MUḪALDIM *A*-[*NA*
4'] III $^{\text{LÚ.MEŠ}}$*x̣*(-/.)[
5']-*x̣* LUGAL-*u*[*š*(-)
. . .$^{?}$
(broken off)

Text-critical note: **1)** Probably to $^{\text{(DUG)}}$*kattakurant*- of which co-attestation with UGULA $^{\text{LÚ.MEŠ}}$MUḪALDIM (here line 3') is known from KUB 2.6 IV 19, KUB 10.28 II 7-9, KUB 11.35 II 26' etc. (all CTH 597-598).

56. Bo 8737

Description: Festival.

CTH: 670 "*Fragments divers.*"

Dating and Script: NS.

Remarks: One-sided fragment from the bottom part (with edge) of a tablet. The preserved passage renders a cultic scene where the king visits the bath house and adorns himself with festive garments, as is known from various festival descriptions (CTH 591, 597, 611, 614, 626, 627 etc.).

Measurements: 2.1 × 3.5 × 0.9 cm.

Bibliography: N/A.

Bo 8737

§ 1' 1' [*ma-a-an l*]*u-uk-kat-ta-*⌜*m*⌝[*a*$^{?}$ ^{É} . . . [1]]

2' [*ḫ̮a-aš-š*]*a-an-zi* ^{KUŠ}NÍG.B[ÀR-*aš-ta uš-ši-i̯a-an-zi*]

3' [LUGAL-*uš*] *Ị-NA* É.DU$_{10}$.ÚS.SA [*pa-iz-zi*]

4' [*ta-az*[2]] *ạ-ni-i̯a-at-ta* Ḫ̮ỤB.[BI . . . [3] *da-a-i*]

(bottom of the tablet)

Text-critical notes: [1] One expects here the mention of ^{É}*ḫ̮alentuwa-* (KUB 2.13 I 1 and many other occurrences). [2] Cf. KUB 2.13 I 4. Alternatively restore with *nu-za* (KUB 25.16 I 5). [3] Restoration can further be completed with GUŠKIN (KUB 2.13 I 4) or KUBABBAR (KBo 11.43 I 15).

57. Bo 8738

Description: N/A.
CTH: 832 "*Fragments en langue hittite de nature inconnue.*"
Dating and Script: LNS.
Remarks: One-sided fragment that is too small to classify.
Measurements: 2.5 × 2.5 × 0.9 cm.
Bibliography: N/A.

Bo 8738

§ 1' 1'](-)*x̣-x̣*(-)[
2']-*x̣ ị-kụ̈-ni-mị*(?) [
3' *-t*]*i-ịš ud-d*[*a-*
4']*-ú-ụš du-u̯*[*a*$^?$*-*
5' *-t*]*a*$^?$ *nu-u̯a-ra-*[
6' (traces)
(broken off)

58. Bo 8739

Description: Inventory or ritual.
CTH: 243 "*Inventaires de tissus et de vêtements*" or 470 "*Fragments de rituels.*"
Dating and Script: (E)NS.
Remarks: One-sided fragment. The keywords ^{TÚG}E.ÍB *MAŠLU* and $^{\text{(TÚG)}}$*ḫupita-* would refer more likely to CTH 448.
Measurements: 2.4 × 2.6 × 0.6 cm.
Bibliography: N/A.

Bo 8739

§ 1' 1'](-)⌈*x*(-)*x*-*x*-*x*$^{?}$⌉(-)[
2'] *ŠA* I *x̤*(-)[
3' ^{TÚG}]Ẹ.ÍB *MAŠ-LU* I-[*NU*$^{?}$-*TIM*$^{?}$ [1]
4' -*š*]*a*$^{?}$-*an* I-*NU*-[*TIM*$^{?}$
5' -*š*]⌊*a-a*⌋*n*(?) *ḫu-pí*-[*ta*$^{?}$- [2]
6']-*x̤* *ŠA* *x̤*-[
7']⌊*x* *x*⌋[
(broken off)

Text-critical notes: [1] Cf. KUB 17.18 II 19', 22' (CTH 448.2.1.1.A). [2] Possibly goes back to the lexeme $^{\text{(TÚG)}}$*ḫupita-* (KUB 58.104 II 9' [CTH 448.4.7]: *nu-uš-ša-an ḫu-u-pí-ta-an*; and FHL 17:2'–3' [CTH 448.4.1.c.B]: *nu-u*[*š*$^{?}$-*ša*$^{?}$-*an*$^{?}$ . . .] / ^{TÚG}*ḫu-u-pí-ta-an*).

59. Bo 8741

Description: Ritual or festival.
CTH: 470 "*Fragments de rituels*" or 670 "*Fragments divers.*"
Dating and Script: NS.
Remarks: One-sided fragment.
Measurements: 3.1 × 2.2 × 0.9 cm.
Bibliography: N/A.

Bo 8741

§ 1' 1'](-)*x̣-x̣-x̣*[?](-)[
2']-*x̣*[1)] *ze-e*[*n*[?]-*na*[?]-
3' *pa*[?]-*r*]*a-a ú-u̯*[*a-an-zi*[2)]
4'] [GIŠ]ZA.LAM.GAR(-/.)[
5']-*zi nạ-ạn x̤*(-)[
6' *m*]*e-mi-i̯a-nu-u*[*š*
7' (traces)
(broken off)

Text-critical notes: [1)] Read [. . . -*p*]*í* or [*Ú-U*]*L* ? [2)] Cf. KBo 23.57 I 9'–10'.

60. Bo 8742 + KUB 23.72 +

Description: Historical.
CTH: 146 "*Midas de Pahhuwa.*"
Dating and Script: MH/MS.
Remarks: Bo 8742 is a one-sided fragment, and lines 1'–8' directly join KUB 23.72 rev. 5–12.
Measurements: 2.8 × 2.6 × 1.0 cm.
Bibliography: O. R. Gurney, AAA 28 (1948) 36, 42; A. Kosyan, Aramazd 1 (2006) 76-77, 82; S. Reichmuth, DBH 35 (2011) 115–16, 122–23; O. Soysal, NABU 2014/4, 145–47 (transliteration, translation, and remarks).

Bo 8742

KUB 23.72 + Bo 8742 + rev. (composite image)

Reverse

(Line numbers of Bo 8742 are in parentheses)

§ 1 1-4 . . .

5 (= 1') ⌞*A-NA*⌟ LÚ.MEŠ ^{URU}*Pa-aḫ-ḫu-u̯a-ma ḫạ-ạt-ra-a-nu-un nu ma-a-an pa-a-a*⌜*n-z*⌝*i* LÚ.MEŠ ^{URU}*Pa-aḫ-ḫu-u̯a ḫa-an-da-a-an*$^{!}$(-)*x̣*-$^{1)}$[. . . É ^{m}*Mi-i-ta*]

6 (= 2') [*Q*]⌜*A-DU*⌝ DẠM-*ŠU* DUMU.MUNUS ^{m}*Ú-ša-a-pa* DUMU.MEŠ-*ŠU QA-DU MAR-ŠI-TI-ŠU*$^{2)}$ *QA-DU* SAG.GÉME.ÌR.MEŠ-*ŠU* GU$_{4}$.ḪI.A-*ŠU* UDU.ḪI.A-*Š*[*U MI-IM-MI-ŠU* *ar-nu-an-zi*(?)]

7 (= 3') Ẹ ^{m}*Ḫa-aš-ša-a-na* É ^{m}*Ka-li-mu-na QA-DU* DAM.MEŠ-*ŠU-NU* DUMU.MEŠ-*ŠU-NU* SAG.GÉME.ÌR.MEŠ-*ŠU-NU* GU$_{4}$.ḪI.A-*ŠU-NU* UDU.ḪI.A-*Š*[*U-NU MI-IM-MI-ŠU-NU*]

8 (= 4') *ar-nu-an-zi nu ḫụ-ụ-ma-an pa-ra-a pí-an-zi a-ap-pa* ^{SÍG}*ma-iš-t*⌞*a-a*$^{3)}$*-an ma*⌟*-*⌜*ši-u̯a-an-t*⌝*a-an* *Ú-UL a*[*p-pa-an-zi*]

§ 2 9 (= 5') V SAG.DU.MEŠ-*i̯a* -*ką́n ku-e ŠA* ᵐ*Ú-ša-a-pa I-NA* ᵁᴿᵁ*Pa-aḫ-ḫu-u̯a še-*[*er*] *IT-TI* DUMU.MUNUS-*ŠU nu a-pé-e-i̯*[*a* . . .]

10 (= 6') *ŠA* ᵈUTU-*ŠI-i̯a ku-i-uš* URU.DIDLI.ḪI.A *ḫar-kán-zi* ᵁᴿᵁ*Ḫal-mi-iš-na-an* ᵁᴿᵁ[*Ḫur-l*]*a-an* ᵁᴿᵁ*Pa-aḫ-ḫu-u-ra-an* ᵁᴿᵁ*A-pá*[*r-ḫu-u-la-an* . . . ?]

11 (= 7') *ar-ḫa tar-na-an-zi̥* DU̥MU ᵐ*Ú-šḁ-a-pa-i̯a ap-pa-an-zi na-an pa-*[*r*]*a-a pí-an-zi ma-a-na-aš-kán* ᵁᴿᵁ*Pa-*[*aḫ-ḫu-u̯a-az*? *ar-ḫa*(?) . . .]

12 (= 8') *na-aš ku-u̯a-pí pa-a-an-za na-aš-ša-an*[4] *ku-e-da-ni* URU-*ri* EGIR-*an na-an-ša-an A-NA* ᵈUTU-*ŠI kat-ta u*[*p-pí-an-zi*(?)]

(Bo 8742 breaks here off; text continues in KUB 23.72 + rev. 13ff.)

Text-critical notes: [1] The tablet photo (hethiter.net/: PhotArch N04763) shows rather *ḫa-an-da-a-an*!(-) *m*[*a*?(-) . . .]. [3] The reading *MAR*(not *E*!)-*ŠI-TI-ŠU* "his possessions" is confirmed from the tablet photo (hethiter.net/: PhotArch N04762). [3] Reading with an additional "*a*" due to the sign remnant as seen in the tablet photo (hethiter.net/: PhotArch N04763). [4] This reading is supported by the recent join and confirmed from the tablet photo (hethiter.net/: PhotArch N04762).

61. Bo 8743

Description: Historical or vow / prayer.

CTH: 215 "*Fragments non caractérisés*", 389 "*Fragments de prières*" or 590 "*Fragments de songes et d'ex-voto.*"

Dating and Script: LNS.

Remarks: One-sided fragment. There is no sufficient evidence supporting the historical nature of this fragment (contra *Konkordanz*). The narrative in pres. sg. 1 (voluntative) *wetemi* and *piḫḫi* "I will build, give" would also fit a vow / prayer.

Measurements: 3.9 × 2.7 × 0.7 cm.

Bibliography: N/A.

Bo 8743

§ 1'
1'-2' (traces)
3']-x̤ Ẹ GIR-*pạ* x̤-[
4']-*x̤-i̯ạ Ú-UL m*[*a*?-
5' *i*]*m-mạ ku*![1)]*-u̯a-pí* E[GIR?-
6']-*x̣-zi A-NA* I URU-*L*[*IM*
7']-*kị*? *ú-e-te-mi*[2)] x̤(-)[
8' *p*]*í-iḫ-ḫi nu-mu* I-*an-x̤*?(-)[3)][
9'](-)⌞x̣⌟-*ru*[4)]*-eš-ki-ịt n*[*a*-
10'](-)⌞x̣(-)*an*?*-x* x̣?⌟[
(broken off)

Text-critical notes: [1)] The sign is written as "*te.*" [2)] Cf. *ú-i-te-mi* "I (will) build" in KBo 22.71 II 9' (CTH 378. IV.B). [3)] Alternatively to be interpreted as PN m·d x̤-[. . .]. [4)] For this (late) shape of the sign see Chr. Rüster — E. Neu, HZL under no. 43 (variant 18). The reading of the whole word as ⌞*a*⌟*-ru-eš-ki-it* "he used to prostrate himself" is possible.

62. Bo 8744

Description: N/A.
CTH: 832 "*Fragments en langue hittite de nature inconnue.*"
Dating and Script: N/A.
Remarks: One-sided tiny, abraded fragment from the upper-right portion (with edge) of a tablet.
Measurements: 3.3 × 1.7 × 1.8 cm.
Bibliography: N/A.

Bo 8744

Bo 8744 right edge

§ 1 1]-*x̣*- *x̣*$^{?}$

____

____

§ 2 2 -*z*]*ị*

3 . . .

4]-*x̣*-*zị*

____

§ 3 5 (.)S]ẠG-*nạ*-*x̣*

6]-*x̣* *ẹ*-*ẹš*-*dụ*

7]-*x̣*-[. . .]-⌞*z*⌟[*i*$^{?}$ . . . $^{?}$]

(broken off)

63. Bo 8746

Description: Festival$^{?}$.
CTH: 670 "*Fragments divers.*"
Dating and Script: N/A.
Remarks: One-sided tiny fragment. The preserved lines belong to a list of breads.
Measurements: 2.4 × 2.8 × 1.2 cm.
Bibliography: N/A.

Bo 8746

§ 1' 1' (traces)

---

§ 2' 2' NIND]A$^{?}$.SIG LX⸢X⸣-[*iš*$^{?}$
3' .R]A$^{?}$ NINDA.ZI.SIG[1)] ẋ(.)[
4' . . .$^{?}$

---

§ 4' 5' (traces)
(broken off)

Text-critical note: **1)** NINDA."ZI".SIG is attested only here; cf. NINDA."ZI".ḪAR.ḪAR.

64. Bo 8748

Description: Ritual or festival.
CTH: 470 "*Fragments de rituels*" or 670 "*Fragments divers.*"
Dating and Script: NS.
Remarks: One-sided tiny fragment from the lower left portion (with bottom part) of a tablet.
Measurements: 2.6 × 2.2 × 0.5 cm.
Bibliography: N/A.

Bo 8748

§ 1' 1']-⌜*x*⌝-*x̣*(-)[
2']-⌜*x̣*⌝ DINGIR.MEŠ(-)*za*-*x̣*$^{?}$(-)[
3' -*a*]*n*-*za*[1)] *ki*-*š*[*a*-*ri*
4']-*x̣* BAL-*an*-[*ti*$^{?}$
(bottom of the tablet)

Text-critical note: [1)] Restore [*iš*-*pa*-*a*]*n*-*za* or [GE$_6$-*a*]*n*-*za* (cf. KUB 25.44 II$^{?}$ 25'; KUB 34.125 left col. 11'; etc.)

65. Bo 8749

Description: Cult inventory$^?$.
CTH: 530 "*Fragments divers.*"
Dating and Script: NS.
Remarks: One-sided tiny fragment.
Measurements: 2.4 × 2.7 × 0.8 cm.
Bibliography: N/A.

Bo 8749

§ 1' 1']⸢*x* *x* U$_4$.KAM⸣-*t*[*i*(-)
2'].MEŠ *pé-eš-ká*[*n-zi*
3']-*x̣* DỊNGIR.MEŠ-*aš*(-)[

(broken off)

66. Bo 8750

Description: N/A.
CTH: 832 "*Fragments en langue hittite de nature inconnue.*"
Dating and Script: NS$^{?}$. The script, especially "LÚ" in line 2', reminds one of Bo 9535 (see below).
Remarks: One-sided tiny fragment that is too small to classify.
Measurements: 2.8 × 2.7 × 1.1 cm.
Bibliography: N/A.

Bo 8750

§ 1' 1'](-)⸢*x̤-az*$^{?}$⸣(-)[
2']-*x̤* $^{\text{LÚ.ME}}$[^{Š}
3' -*a*]*n* *x̣-x̣*(-)[
4']-*pí-ịz*$^{?}$-[
5' (traces)
(broken off)

67. Bo 8751

Description: Festival.
CTH: 670 "*Fragments divers.*"
Dating and Script: LNS.
Remarks: A small piece from the inscribed upper edge of a tablet.
Measurements: 1.1 × 3.3 × 1.9 cm.
Bibliography: N/A.

Bo 8751

Upper edge

§ 1 1 ^{N}]^{A_4}*ḫu-u-u̯a-ši-i̯a p*[*í-ra-an*(?)[1)]

2 *A-NA* ^{d}UTU ^{URU}*A-ri*]-⌞*in*⌟-*na ši-ip-*[*pa-an-*

(broken off)

Text-critical note: [1)] Alternatively read *p*[*é-en-ni-i̯a*$^{?}$- . . .]; cf. KUB 32.82 rt. col. 8 and IBoT 2.79:8'–9'.

68. Bo 8752 + Bo 9615 + KUB 41.2 + KBo 52.27

Description: Ritual.

CTH: 402.G *"Rituel de Malli, contre la sorcellerie."*

Dating and Script: MH/NS.

Remarks: Bo 8752 directly joins another unpublished fragment Bo 9615 and KUB 41.2 (NS). See also under Bo 9615 + Bo 8752 + KUB 41.2 + KBo 52.27 (CHDS 2 pp. 82-83). Bo 8752 + Bo 9615 + I 1-3 are duplicate to KBo 11.12 + KBo 10.43 I 1–4 (MS), KBo 12.126 + KBo 12.127 + KUB 24.9 + I 1–3 (NS) and IBoT 2.123 obv. 1'–3' (NS) from where the restorations are taken.

Measurements: 2.1 × 4.3 × 1.8 cm.

Bibliography: O. Soysal, Anatolica 38 (2012) 182-183 (transliteration and remarks).

Konkordanz der hethitischen Keilschrifttafeln

http://www.hethport.uni-wuerzburg.de/hetskiz/sk.php?f=1058/u

Bo 8752

Bo 8752 (top left) + Bo 9615 (top right) +
KUB 41.2 obv. I (KBo 52.27 is not included)

Obverse I

§ 1   1   [*U*(*M-MA* ᶠ*A-al-li-i* MUNUS)¹⁾] ᵁᴿᵁ*Ar-za-u-u̯a*²⁾ *ma-a-an* [(UN-*aš*³⁾) U]Ḫ₇- *an-za*⁴⁾ *na̦-an kiš-an*⁵⁾

        2   [(*a-ni-i̯a-mi* V ALAM)⁶⁾] IM ŠÀ-*BA* II LÚ⁷⁾ *nu* ᴷᵁ[(ˢ*kur-šu-u*)]*š*⁸⁾ *ka̦r-pa-an ḫar-kán-zi*

        3   [(*na-aš-ta an-da* EME)⁹⁾].⌞M⌟EŠ¹⁰⁾ *ki-an-ta-ri*¹¹⁾   [   ]

Text-critical notes: ¹⁾ Restoration after KBo 11.12 + I 1. ²⁾ Duplicate KBo 11.12 + I 1: ᵁᴿᵁ*Ar-za-ui₅*. ³⁾ Restoration follows KBo 12.126 + I 1 and KBo 11.12 + I 1; duplicate KBo 11.12 + I 1: *an-tu-u̯a-ah̬-ha̦-aš*. ⁴⁾ Duplicate KBo 11.12 + I 2: *al-u̯a-an-za-ah̬-ha-an-za*. ⁵⁾ Duplicate KBo 11.12 + I 2: *ki-iš-ša-an*. ⁶⁾ Restoration after KBo 11.12 + I 2-3. ⁷⁾ Duplicate KBo 11.12 + I 3: LÚ.MEŠ. ⁸⁾ Restoration follows IBoT 2.123 obv. 2'; duplicates KBo 12.126 + I 2: ᴷᵁˢ[*kur*]-*ša̦*-[*aš*] and KBo 11.12 + I 3: *kur-šu-uš*. ⁹⁾ Restoration after KBo 11.12 + I 4. ¹⁰⁾ Duplicates KBo 11.12 + I 4: EME.ḪI.A and IBoT 2.123 obv. 3': [E]ME.ḪI.A. ¹¹⁾ IBoT 2.123 obv. 3': *ki-i̯a-an-ta*-[*ri*].

69. Bo 8753

Description: Vow?.
CTH: 590 "*Fragments de songes et d'ex-voto.*" ?
Dating and Script: N/A.
Remarks: One-sided tiny fragment.
Measurements: 3.8 × 3.0 × 1.2 cm.
Bibliography: N/A.

Bo 8753

§ 1' 1']-x̣(-)[

---

§ 2' 2']-x̤? 1/2? 1) ⌜x̣-x̣⌝ ŠI[D-*eš*- 2)

---

§ 3' 3']-x̣-*zi-i* 3) [

4' -*p*]*í*?-*i̯a*-x̣(-)[

5' (traces)

(broken off)

Text-critical notes: 1) The sign is "*pár*, *maš*", less likely "*qa*". 2) This sign is written without determinative, thus it belongs to ŠID-*eššar* (= *kappueššar*) "count(ing)", and not to LÚ/MUNUSSANGA; cf. KUB 15.17+ I 12 (CTH 585.A); KUB 31.53 + 1320/u obv. 10 (CTH 585.G+I) 3) Possibly a PN of foreign origin in the stem form; cf. KUB 31.53 + 1320/u obv. 11 immediately after a paragraph (separated with double strokes) mentioning ŠID-*eš-na-za*.

70. Bo 8754

Description: Festival.
CTH: 670 "*Fragments divers.*"
Dating and Script: (L)NS.
Remarks: One-sided tiny fragment.
Measurements: 1.6 × 4.0 × 1.4 cm.
Bibliography: N/A.

Bo 8754

§ 1'   1'   (traces)

---

§ 2'   2'   ]⌈*pár*⌉-*šị-i̯a*

---

§ 3'   3'   ] IỊ NINDA.GUR$_4$.RA   *pár-š*⌊*i-i̯*⌋[*a*]

(broken off)

71. Bo 8757

Description: Historical.

CTH: 40 "*Actes de Suppiluliuma.*"

Dating and Script: Murš. II / NS.

Remarks: Bo 8757 is a one-sided fragment, and lines 2'–7' duplicate KBo 14.12 + IV 12–19 (CTH 40.IV.1.E_3) from where the restorations are adopted. The placing of the restored words either at the end of a line or at the beginning of the next one is approximate and may slightly vary.

Measurements: 2.9 × 2.1 × 1.0 cm.

Bibliography: H. G. Güterbock, DŠ (1956) 97–98; G. F. del Monte, GestaSupp (2008) 95, 122–23; O. Soysal, NABU 2014/4, 145–47 (transliteration of, and remarks on Bo 8757).

Bo 8757

§ 1' 1' (traces)

2' [LUGAL-*u*(*n-ma-u̯a-ra-an-za-an* *Ú-UL i-i̯*)]*a-a*[(*t-te-ni*) *UM-MA* ^{m}*Ḫ*(*a-a-ni-MA A-NA A-BU-YA*)]

3' [(*BE-LÍ-YA a-pa-a-at-u̯*)]*a Ú-UL* [*a*(*n-ze-el* KUR-*aš te-ep-nu-mar*)][1]

---

§ 2' 4' [DUMU.LUGAL-*u̯a* (*ma*)-*a-a*(*n-na-aš ku-u̯a-p*)]*í e-eš-t*[(*a an-za-a-aš-ma-an-u̯a*) *da*-(*me-e-da-ni* KUR-*e*)]

5' [(*ú-u̯a-u-en ma-a*)]-*an-u̯a-an*[2]-*na-a*[(*š*) *a*(*n-ze-el BE-LÍ ú-e-ki-iš-ki-u-en*)]

6' [*an-za-a-aš-u̯a*) *BE*]-*LÍ-NI*[3] *ku-i*⸤*š*⸥ [(^{m}*Ni-ip-ḫu-ru-ri-i̯a-aš e-eš-ta nu-u̯a-ra-aš*)]

7' [(BA.ÚŠ) DU(MU-*aš-ma-u̯a*)]-*aš-ši* NU.G[(ÁL) . . .]

8'](-)⸤x̣-x̣-x̣⸥(-)[

(broken off)

Text-critical notes: [1] KBo 14.12 + IV has no paragraph stroke after this line. [2] KBo 14.12 + IV 16 omits -*an*-. [3] KBo 14.12 + IV 17 has EN-*NI*.

72. Bo 8758

Description: Festival.
CTH: 670 "*Fragments divers.*"
Dating and Script: LNS.
Remarks: One-sided fragment from the left or middle column of a tablet.
Measurements: 3.1 × 3.9 × 1.2 cm.
Bibliography: N/A.

Bo 8758

Left or middle column

§ 1' 1' $^{L]Ú.⌜ME⌝[Š}$
2' *ḫu-u-ma(?)-a]n-te-eš* ⌜*ú*⌝-[
3' -*a*]*n-ma-kán* GA[L$^{?}$
4' . . .
5' I]⸤G⸥I-*an-dạ* *ti-an-zi*
6' (traces$^{?}$)
(broken off)

73. Bo 8759

Description: Ritual?.
CTH: 470 "*Fragments de rituels.*"
Dating and Script: N/A.
Remarks: One-sided tiny fragment.
Measurements: 2.3 × 2.1 × 1.1 cm.
Bibliography: N/A.

Bo 8759

§ 1' 1'] ⌜*za-p*⌝[*i*?-
2' SÍ]G.GE$_6$ *a*[*n*-[1)]
3' ^{UZU}G]Ú(?)-*iš-ši*[2)] *x*-[

---

§ 2' 4']⌞*x x*⌟[
(broken off)

Text-critical notes: [1)] To *anda ḫulaliya-* "to wrap up" ? Cf. KUB 32.112 IV? 3': [S]ÍG.GE$_6$ *an-da ḫu-u-la-li-ja-a*[*z*-*zi*]. [2)] Cf. KUB 32.112 IV? 4'.

74. Bo 8760

Description: Festival.

CTH: 670 "*Fragments divers.*"

Dating and Script: NS.

Remarks: One-sided fragment. The context is parallel to KUB 10.89 II 7'–11' (CTH 591.III.A); KBo 10.18 rt. col. 19'–23' (CTH 626.Tg06.III.1.C); KBo 30.121 II 2–5 (CTH 670.39); KBo 11.28 II 14'–18', III 3'–6', 12'–15', 21'–24', IV 21'25', 31'–35', IV 42'–46' (CTH 711.A) from where the restorations are taken.

Measurements: 2.2 × 3.4 × 0.9 cm.

Bibliography: N/A.

Bo 8760

§ 1' 1'] ⸢LUGAL⸣-[*i pa-a-i*]

2' [LUGAL-*uš*] *pár-š*⸢*i*⸣-[*i̯a* ^{LÚ}SAGI.A-*kán*]

3' [LUGAL-*i* NINDA].GỤR$_4$.RA ⸢*e-ẹ*⸣[*p-zi*]

4' [*na-an-ká*]*n pa-ra-a pẹ́*-[*e-da-i*]

5' [*pár-aš-n*]⸤*a*⸥-*u-u̯a-aš-kạ́n* [

6' [*ú-iz*]- *z*[*i*]

(broken off)

75. Bo 8761

Description: N/A.
CTH: 832 “*Fragments en langue hittite de nature inconnue.*”
Dating and Script: LNS.
Remarks: One-sided fragment that is too small to classify.
Measurements: 2.8 × 2.0 × 0.7 cm.
Bibliography: N/A.

Bo 8761

§ 1’ 1’]⸢*x* *x*⸣[

2’ ^{URU}K]Á.DINGIR.RA-*x̣*(-)[

3’]-*iš* *nụ* [

4’ -*u*]*l*$^{?}$ *kiš-a*[*n*

5’]-*ạ*$^{?}$ (eras.) *ú-u̯*[*a*$^{?}$-

(broken off)

76. Bo 8762

Description: Ritual?.
CTH: 470 "*Fragments de rituels.*"
Dating and Script: NS.
Remarks: One-sided small fragment from the right column of a tablet.
Measurements: 1.9 × 2.6 × 1.0 cm.
Bibliography: N/A.

Bo 8762

Right column

§ 1' 1' (traces)
2' *ši-pa-a*[*n-*
3' *ḫa-ri-i̯*[*a*?-
4' *na-aš-t*[*a*
5' ⸤*x x*⸥[
(broken off)

77. Bo 8763

Description: N/A.
CTH: 832 "*Fragments en langue hittite de nature inconnue.*"
Dating and Script: MS$^{?}$.
Remarks: One-sided small fragment from the right column of a tablet.
Measurements: 3.0 × 2.3 × 1.4 cm.
Bibliography: N/A.

Bo 8763

Right column

§ 1' 1' (traces)

---

§ 2' 2' *lu-uk-ka*[*t-ti*$^{?}$(-)
3' ^{URU}*Ḫa-a*[*t*$^{?}$-
4' *na-x̣*(-)[
5' ⌞$^{URU?}$⌟[
(broken off)

78. Bo 8764

Description: N/A.
CTH: 832 "*Fragments en langue hittite de nature inconnue.*"
Dating and Script: N/A.
Remarks: One-sided fragment that is too small to classify.
Measurements: 2.1 × 2.7 × 1.0 cm.
Bibliography: N/A.

Bo 8764

§ 1' 1'] ⸢*tar-na-a*?⸣-*ạ̤ḫ̮*?-[
2']⸤I?⸥ *kụ-ug-g*[*ul-la*-[1)]
3' S]AR?.Ḫ̮I.A *x̣-x̣*(-)[
4'](-)*x̣-aš-ša-a*[*n*(-)
5' -*z*]*i*(-)*x̤*?(-)[
(broken off)

Text-critical note: [1)] Cf. KUB 41.7 + II 13', KUB 39.56 I 13'. If this is a ritual / medical text, no PN like ⸤m⸥*Kụ-ug-g*[*ul-li*(-) . . .] (E. Laroche, NH no. 605) can be expected.

79. Bo 8765

Description: N/A.
CTH: 832 "*Fragments en langue hittite de nature inconnue.*"
Dating and Script: LNS.
Remarks: One-sided fragment that is too small to classify.
Measurements: 2.3 × 2.4 × 1.0 cm.
Bibliography: N/A.

Bo 8765

§ 1'	1'	]⌜*x*⌝[
§ 2'	2'	^{m}. . .]-*ị-li-i*[*š*(-)
	3'	^{m}*Ḫi*$^{?}$]-*ị-mu*-DINGIR-*L*[*IM*(-)
	4'	^{U}]^{ZU}NÍG.GI[G
	5'	]-*da* *x̤*$^{?}$(-)[
§ 3'	6'	]⌞ *x x x*$^{?}$ *x*⌟[
		(broken off)

80. Bo 8766

Description: Lists of men$^{?}$.
CTH: 234 "*Listes d'hommes.*"$^{?}$
Dating and Script: MH/MS.
Remarks: One-sided small fragment with two columns. There are no striking features to ascribe this text to CTH 140 "*Fragments de traités ou protocoles passés avec les Gasgas*" as suggested by the *Konkordanz*.
Measurements: 2.4 × 2.8 × 1.3 cm.
Bibliography: N/A.

Bo 8766

Left column

§ 1' 1']-*ị*
(broken off)

Right column

§ 1' 1' (traces)
2' ^{m}*Šu-na-ị-*[*li*(-)[1)]
3' ^{URU}*Tạ-ḫ*[*a-na*$^{?}$-
4' ^{URU}*Tạ-ḫ*[*a-na*$^{?}$-

---

§ 2' 5' SAG.M[EŠ$^{?}$
6' VIII LÚ.M[EŠ
(broken off)

Text-critical note: [1)] For ^{m}Šunaili and ^{URU}Taḫ[ana$^{?}$ . . .] in lines 3'–4' see KBo 16.66 IV$^{?}$ 1-2 (CTH 234.2; likewise MH/MS).

81. Bo 8767

Description: Festival.
CTH: 670 "*Fragments divers.*"
Dating and Script: MS$^{?}$.
Remarks: One-sided small fragment with two columns. Whether right column lines 1'–4' could be an indirect join to KUB 25.3 IV 35'–38' (CTH 634.2.A) cannot be examined physically.
Measurements: 2.8 × 3.1 × 0.9 cm.
Bibliography: N/A.

Bo 8767

Left column

§ 1' 1'-3' (traces)
4']-*x̣-ŠU*
5']-*ŠU*
(broken off)

Right column[1)]

§ 1' 1' ^{LÚ}*pa[l-ṷa-tal-la-aš pal-ṷa-a-iz-zi* . . . $^{?}$]

---

§ 2' 2' GAL *ME-Š[E-TI*$_4$ . . . $^{?}$ ^{NINDA}*ta-pár-ṷa*$_a$*-šu-un*]
3' *tar-ku[m-mi*$^{?}$*-ịa*$^{?}$*-iz-zi*[2)]]

---

§ 3' 4' ⸤^{NINDA}⸥[*ta-pár-ṷa*$_a$*-šu-uš*
(broken off)

Text-critical notes: [1)] If the posited indirect join with Bo 8767 is correct, KUB 25.3 IV 34'–40' would then read as follows: 34' [. . . *UŠ-K*]*É-EN* (§) 35'(= 1') ^{LÚ}*pa[l-ṷa-tal-la-aš pal-ṷa-a-iz]-zi* 36'(= 2') GAL *ME-Š[E-TI*$_4$ ^{NINDA}*t]a-pár-ṷa*$_a$*-šu-un* 37'(= 3') *tar-ku[m-mi-ịa-iz]-zi* (§) 38'(= 4') ⸤^{NINDA}⸥[*ta-pár-ṷa*$_a$*-šu-u*]*š* 39' [*ṷa-aš-šu-u-ṷa-an*]*-zi* 40' [^{NINDA}*ṷa-ga-t*]*a-aš šar-ru-ma-an-zi* (similarly in KUB 25.9 IV 31–33 [CTH 634.2.B]). [2)] Alternatively restore with the form *tar-ku[m-ma-a-iz-zi]*; cf. KBo 45.5:3'.

82. Bo 8768

Description: Cult inventory or festival.
CTH: 530 or 670 “*Fragments divers.*”
Dating and Script: LNS.
Remarks: One-sided fragment from the left portion (with inscribed edge) of a very thick tablet.
Measurements: 2.8 × 3.2 × 1.1 cm.
Bibliography: N/A.

Bo 8768 (left column)

Bo 8768 (left edge)

Left column

§ 1’ . . .

——

§ 2’ 1’ ⌜^{d}U⌝ [$^{URU?}$
2’ ^{d}NISAB⌜A⌝(-)[
3’ ^{d}U ^{URU}*Ḫu̯r-š*[*a*$^{?}$-[1)]
4’ $^{LÚ.MEŠ}$GURUŠ(-)*x̣*(-)[
5’ $^{⌞LÚ.ME⌟Š}$SANG[A(-)
(broken off)

Left edge

§ 1 1]-*x̣-an-kán* [

——

§ 2 2](-)*x̣-u̯*[*a*$^{?}$(-)
(broken off)

Text-critical note: [1)] Cf. ^{d}U ^{URU}Ḫurša (KBo 2.7 obv. 18-20’), ^{d}U ^{URU}Ḫuršalašši (KBo 2.1 II 32), and ^{d}U ^{URU}Ḫuršanašši (KBo 10.20 III 45).

83. Bo 8769

Description: N/A.
CTH: 832 "*Fragments en langue hittite de nature inconnue.*"
Dating and Script: OH$^{?}$/NS.
Remarks: One-sided, slightly abraded fragment. The context could be of historical nature; cf. *Konkordanz*: "CTH 215.?"
Measurements: 3.8 × 2.4 × 0.9 cm.
Bibliography: N/A.

Bo 8769

§ 1' 1']-x̣ $^{m?}$x̣-[
2']-x̣-*in* ẹ$^{?}$-[
3' -*a*]*n*$^{?}$ *Ú-U*[*L*
4' (-)*š*]*u*$^{?}$-*ul-l*[*i*-
5']-x̣ *ta-an*[1)] *ḫar*[2)]-[
6']-x̣
7'](-)⸢*š*⸣*i*(-)[
(broken off)

Text-critical notes: [1)] Due to space between *ta-an* and the preceding sign no other word can be considered here. [2)] Alternatively read "*ḫur*".

84. Bo 8770

Description: N/A.
CTH: 832 "*Fragments en langue hittite de nature inconnue.*"
Dating and Script: NS.
Remarks: One-sided, slightly abraded fragment.
Measurements: 2.0 × 2.6 × 1.1 cm.
Bibliography: N/A.

Bo 8770

§ 1' 1'] ⸢*ma*$^{?}$-*a*⸣-*an* ⸢MUN⸣[US.LUGAL(?)

2'](-)*x̤*$^{?}$-*ạt*$^{?}$-*mạ* MỤNUS.⸢L⸣[UGAL$^{?}$

3']-*x̣* DUMU$^{?}$ [1)]-*la*-*x̤*-[

4'](-)*x̤*-*a*$^{?}$-*la*-*i*[*t*(-)

5'](-)*x̤*$^{?}$-*ạ*-*ir* *x̣*(-)[

(broken off)

Text-critical note: [1)] It is hard to decide if the sign is "DUMU" or "*i*". The entire word can also be read as PN ^{m}*I-la-l*[*i-ú-ma*(-) . . .] that can be related to the "Šukziya Affair" of the Telipinu Edict (O. Soysal, OrNS 59 [1990] 271–79); cf. also the possible mention of MUNUS.LUGAL "queen" in the preceding lines.

85. Bo 8771

Description: N/A.
CTH: 832 "*Fragments en langue hittite de nature inconnue.*"
Dating and Script: MS$^{?}$.
Remarks: One-sided fragment from the right column of a tablet that is too small to classify.
Measurements: 2.2 × 1.6 × 0.9 cm.
Bibliography: N/A.

Bo 8771

Right column

§ 1' . . .

———

§ 2' 1' *nạ-x̣*(-)[
2' *na-aš-t*[*a*
3' *na-a*[*t*(-)
4' *ḫu-i*[*š*$^{?}$-

———

§ 3' 5' *nam-m*[*a*(-)
6' ⌞*x-x*⌟(-)[
(broken off)

86. Bo 8772

Description: N/A.
CTH: 832 “*Fragments en langue hittite de nature inconnue.*”
Dating and Script: LNS.
Remarks: One-sided, slightly abraded fragment.
Measurements: 2.4 × 2.2 × 1.3 cm.
Bibliography: N/A.

Bo 8772

§ 1’ 1’ *ḫ*]*u-ẹl-p*[*í*(?)(-)
2’ . . .

---

§ 2’ 3’]-*tạ ša-ra-a* [
4’ I-E]N(?) *up-pa-an-za* [
5’] *da-*[
(broken off)

87. Bo 8773

Description: Ritual.
CTH: 449 "*Fragments de rituels nommant les dieux infernaux.*"
Dating and Script: (E)NS$^{?}$.
Remarks: One-sided fragment. Because of the mention of the Primeval / Underworld Deities [N]amšara and Mi[nki] this fragment should rather relate to CTH 446 or 449, but not CTH 448 as stated at the *Konkordanz*.
Measurements: 2.4 × 3.6 × 1.0 cm.
Bibliography: N/A.

Bo 8773

§ 1' 1' *]⸢ne$^{?}$-x-x⸣(-)[*

---

§ 2' 2' *^{d}Na]-⸢am⸣-ša-ra-aš ⸢^{d}Mi⸣-[in-ki-iš*
3' *pát-te]-eš-ni ták-na-a-az a-[*[1]
4' *](-)x̣(-)an-na-ạš ḫu-i-da-a-a[r*[2]
5' *-l]a-aš pạ$^{?}$-ạš-pa-na-a-aš*[3] *l[a-*
6' *]⸤x-x-x$^{?}$-x x-x-x$^{?}$-x⸥[*
(broken off)

Text-critical notes: [1] In this context we hardly expect the cult term *taknaz dā-* "to take from the earth." [2] To understand as [*ták-š*]*a-an-na-ạš ḫu-i-da-a-a*[*r*] "the animal[s] of the [plain f]ield" or DINGIR-*na-ạš ḫu-i-da-a-a*[*r*] "the god's animal[s]" ? For the latter see KBo 10.25 VI 4'–5' // KBo 30.14 V 8': DINGIR.MEŠ-*na-aš* / [(*ḫu-u*)]-*ị-tar*. [3] On *pašpana-* see CHD P/2 (1995) 209 "an insect pest". The noun seems to denote here the insect among others [. . . -*l*]*a-aš* and *l*[*a-* . . .] in a list of the animals (line 4'). The incomplete nouns could be restored as [*mušgall*]*aš* "[caterpil]lar$^{?}$" and *l*[*alawešaš*] "a[nt]" respectively, if one considers the list of insects in KUB 3.94 II 18–26.

88. Bo 8774

Description: Ritual or festival.
CTH: 470 "*Fragments de rituels*" or 670 "*Fragments divers.*"
Dating and Script: LNS.
Remarks: One-sided fragment.
Measurements: 3.6 × 3.7 × 1.0 cm.
Bibliography: N/A.

Bo 8774

§ 1' 1'](-)⌜*x-x-x-x-x*?⌝(-)[
2' EGI]R-*ŠU* GEŠTIN-*a*[*n*
3' *l*]*a-ḫu-u-u̯a-i* [

---

§ 2' 4' [. . . ? EGI]⌜R?⌝-*ŠU šu-up-pa*(-)[
5' D]UMU?-*aš IŠ-TU* ^{KU}[$^{Š?}$
6'] *na-aš-tạ* ^{GIŠ}[

---

§ 3' 7' [. . . ? EGI]⌞R?⌟-*ŠU* III NINDA.[
8'](-)⌞*e*?⌟-[
(broken off)

89. Bo 8776

Description: Festival.
CTH: 670 "*Fragments divers.*"
Dating and Script: OH$^{?}$/NS.
Remarks: One-sided fragment.
Measurements: 3.9 × 4.2 × 1.2 cm.
Bibliography: N/A.

Bo 8776

§ 1' 1' [L]UGAL-*uš-kán I*⌜*Š*⌝-*T*⌜*U*⌝ *x̤*(-)[
2' *ụ-iz-zi* ^{GIŠ}*ḫa-lụ*-[*ga-an-ni-i̯a*$^{?}$*-az kat-ta ti-i̯a-zi*(?)]
3' [II] DUMU.MEŠ.É.GAL I ^{L}[^{Ú}*ME-ŠE-TI*$_4$]
4' [L]UGAL-*i pí-ra-a*[*n ḫu-u*$^{?}$*-i*$^{?}$*-i̯a-an-te*$^{?}$*-eš*$^{?}$][1]

---

§ 2' 5' [L]UGAL-*uš* ^{d}UTU-*aš* [É-*ri*(?)[2]
6' [*pa-i*]*z-zi t*[*a-aš*$^{?}$(-)
7' [^{LÚ}A]LAN.Z[U$_9$ *me-ma-i*
8' [*ḫal-z*]*a-i* ^{L}[^{Ú}
9' [. . .]-⌞*x-x*$^{?}$⌟-[
(broken off)

Text-critical notes: [1] For restorations of lines 2'–4' see KUB 59.36 V 3'–6'. [2] Cf. KBo 30.13 rev. 11'. Alternatively restore *pár-na* (KBo 10.26 I 10).

90. Bo 8777

Description: N/A.
CTH: 831 "*Fragments en langue inconnue ou indéterminée.*"
Dating and Script: (L)NS.
Remarks: One-sided fragment. Whether a historical text is present here as suggested at the *Konkordanz* (CTH 215.?), depends on the interpretation of the words in lines 4' and 6'; see text-critical notes below.
Measurements: 3.3 × 2.8 × 2.9 cm.
Bibliography: N/A.

Bo 8777

§ 1' 1' (traces)
2']-⸢*x*⸣-*na x̣-x̣*$^{?}$(-)[

---

§ 2' 3'](-)*x̣*(-)*an-da-i̯a-a*⸢*z*$^{?}$⸣(-)[
4'](-)*x̤-ip-ri* ^{GIŠ}*ši*$^{?}$-[[1)]
5']-*x̣-li ạ-x̣*(-)[
6']-*x̤-ma a-aḫ-x̤*$^{?}$(-)[[2)]
7']-*x̣-zi x̤*$^{?}$(-)[

---

§ 3' 8'] ⸤*an*⸥-[
(broken off)

Text-critical notes: [1)] Or to be read [DUMU.MEŠ$^{?}$ *Š*]*I-IP-RI* ^{GIŠ}ŠUK[UR . . .] ? [2)] Alternatively, but less likely, read *zạ*$^{?}$-*aḫ-ḫ*[*i*$^{?}$- . . .].

91. Bo 8778

Description: Prayer.

CTH: 385 "*Fragments de prières à la déesse d'Arinna.*"

Dating and Script: NS.

Remarks: One-sided small fragment from the right portion (with inscribed edge) of a tablet. Lines 1'–6' of Bo 8778 duplicate KUB 57.60 II 11'–18' (CTH 385) and KUB 57.63 II 17–26 (CTH 385.10.A) from where the restorations are taken. Thus, the assignment to CTH 212.159 at the *Konkordanz* is to be revised.

Measurements: 4.6 × 2.5 × 3.5 cm.

Bibliography: A. Archi, in: FsOtten^{2} (1988) 18–21.

Bo 8778 obv. (II$^{?}$)

Bo 8778 obv. (II$^{?}$ right edge)

Obverse (II$^{?}$)

§ 1' 1' [(^{d}UTU-*u-i ma-iš-za-aš-ti-iš ku-e-el m*)]⌈*i-iš-ri*⌉-[*u*$^{1)}$-(*u̯*)]*a-a*⌈*n-z*⌉[(*a*)]

2' [(*ḫa-ap-pár-nu-u̯a-aš-ḫi-iš ku-e-el l*)]*a-lu-uk-ki-u*$^{!\ 2)}$-*u̯a*$^{3)}$-*an-t*[(*e-eš*)]

3' [(*la-ba-ar-na-an* ^{LÚ}SANGA-*KA* ^{f}*ta-u̯a-an-na-an-na-an-da-an*)]

4' [(*ši-u̯a-an-za*)-*an-n*(*a-an-da-an Q*)]*A-DU* DUMU.MEŠ-*ŠU*

5' [(DUMU.DUMU.MEŠ-*ŠU ap-pa-ši-u̯a*)-*a*(*t-ta*)-*z*]*a*$^{4)}$ *pa-aḫ-š*[(*i*)]

6' [(*nu-uš ma-i̯a-an-da-aḫ-ḫe-eš-ki uk-tu-ri-i̯a-a*)]*ḫ*$^{?}$-[(*ḫe-eš*)]-⌊*ki*⌋

(broken off)

Text-critical notes: $^{1)}$ Due to the length of the lacuna here is an extra -*u*- expected which is not present in KUB 57.60 II 12' and KUB 57.63 II 18. $^{2)}$ It seems that the sign is initially intented as "*nu*." $^{3)}$ KUB 57.60 II 13' omits -*u̯a*-. $^{4)}$ KUB 57.60 II 16': *a̭p-pa̭-ši-u̯a-an*$^{(!)}$-*ta-az*; KUB 57.63 II 24: *ap-pa-ši-u̯*[*a-a*]*t-ta̭-a̭z*.

92. Bo 8779

Description: Festival.
CTH: 685 "*Fragments de fêtes pour les dieux KAL.*"
Dating and Script: NS.
Remarks: The lines of Bo 8779 seem to be close to the left column divider or left edge.
Measurements: 2.9 × 3.6 × 0.8 cm.
Bibliography: N/A.

Bo 8779

§ 1' 1' [*na*]-⌈*at-ša-a*⌉[*n*

---

§ 2' 2' [. . .]-*x̣ ḫa-an-te-e*⌈*z-zi*⌉ [*pal-ši*(?)
3' [*Ú*]-*ỤL ku-in-ki ḫal-z*[*i-*
4' [^{LÚ}SA]NGẠ ^{d}LAMMA ^{URU}*Ḫa-at-t*[*i*[1)]
5' [^{LÚ}NA]R ^{d}LAMMA ^{URU}*Ḫa-at-t*[*i*
6' [. . . $^{?}$]⌊x$^{?}$.x⌋.GAL ^{URU}*Ḫa-at-t*[*i*

---

§ 3' 7' (traces)
(broken off)

Text-critical note: [1)] Lines 4'–6' are comparable with KUB 53.11 I 6'–8' (CTH 685).

93. Bo 8780

Description: Festival.

CTH: 613 "*AN.TAḪ.ŠUM*^{sar} *18*^{e}*/19*^{e} *jours: au dieu Pihassassi.*"

Dating and Script: LNS.

Remarks: One-sided fragment from the upper part (with edge) of a tablet of which lines 2–7 are duplicate of, or parallel to KUB 11.13 II 1–8 (CTH 613.1.A) from where the restorations are adopted.

Measurements: 3.5 × 3.0 × 1.0 cm.

Bibliography: N/A.

Bo 8780

§ 1 1 [LÚ ^{GIŠ}GIDRU *A-NA* ^{L}]$^{\text{Ú.MEŠ}}$NAR *x̣*-[

2 [. . . *nu*$^{?}$ ^{L}]^{Ú}SẠGI.A *u̯*⌜*a*⌝-[*aš-ša-an-za* . . . $^{?}$]

3 [*pí-ra-a*]*n*$^{?}$ *ḫu-u-u̯a-a-i* *x̤*$^{?}$-[

---

§ 2 4 [$^{\text{LÚ.MEŠ}}$NAR GI]Š ^{d}INANNA.ḪI.A *kar-ap-p*[*a-an-zi*[1]]

5 [*na-aš-kán an-d*]*a*[2] *ú-da*! [3]-*an-z*[*i*]

6 [$^{\text{LÚ.MEŠ}}$*ḫal-li-i̯a-r*]*ị-uš*[(!)]-*ma-aš*[4] [

7 [^{GIŠ}*za-ḫur-ti-uš* EGIR-*a*]⌞*n* *kar*⌟-*ap-p*[*a-a*$^{?}$-*an*[5] *ḫar-kán-zi*]

(broken off)

Text-critical notes: [1] KUB 11.13 II 4: *kar-pa-a-an-zi.* [2] KUB 11.13 II 5: *an-da-an.* [3] The sign is written incompletely. [4] KUB 11.13 II 6: $^{\text{LÚ.MEŠ}}$*ḫal-li-i̯a-re-e-eš-ma-aš.* [5] KUB 11.13 II 8: *kar-pa-a-an.*

94. Bo 8781

Description: Ritual$^{?}$.
CTH: 470 "*Fragments de rituels.*"
Dating and Script: LNS.
Remarks: One-sided fragment with two columns.
Measurements: 1.9 × 3.3 × 0.9 cm.
Bibliography: N/A.

Bo 8781

Left column

§ 1' 1']-*x̣*
2']-*x̣-ša*
3' -*z*]*i*$^{?}$
4'](-)⌞*x-x-x*⌟
(broken off)

Right column

§ 1' 1' ⌜*x-x*⌝(-)[
2' ZI-*ŠU n*⌜*a*⌝-*x̣*$^{?}$(-)[
3' *ma-a-an-ma-a*[*š*
4' *na-aš-ma* DUMU.MU[NUS(-)[1)]
5' ^{TÚG}*zi-iz-z*[*i*$^{?}$-[2)]
6' ⌞*x-x-x-x*$^{?}$⌟(-)[
(broken off)

Text-critical notes: [1)] Alternatively DUMU.MU[NUS.LUGAL]. For DUMU.MUNUS "girl" or DUMU.MUNUS.LUGAL "princess" preceded by the alternating conjunction *našma* "or" see e.g., KUB 39.6 rev. 14 (CTH 450.II.1); KUB 32.133 I 9 (CTH 482); KUB 39.73:14' // KUB 39.71+ IV 48 (CTH 718.1.E and A). [2)] This hapax cannot be related any lemma known from the Boğazköy documents; probably to be read ^{TÚG}*SÍ-IS-S*[*Í*- . . .] to Akkadian *sissiktu* "fringe, hem, edge (of a garment)" cf. CAD S (1984) 322. For occurrences in the Hittite texts see KUB 7.13 obv. 37, KUB 41.21 I 14', and KUB 58.75 rev. 6'.

95. Bo 8782

Description: Cult inventory.
CTH: 530 "*Fragments divers.*"
Dating and Script: LNS.
Remarks: One-sided fragment. The assignment to CTH 670.2916 at the *Konkordanz* is to be revised.
Measurements: 2.9 × 4.8 × 1.4 cm.
Bibliography: N/A.

Bo 8782

§ 1' 1' *-an]-zị* ⸢VI NINDA⸣.[

2' *BI-IB-RU-kán*(?)] *šụ-un-nạ-an-zi* [

3' I ^{DUG}*ḫu-u*$^{?}$*-up-p*]*ár* KAŠ ^{GIŠ}ZAG.GAR.RA-*ni* [

4' ^{DUG}*ḫ*]*ar-ši aš-ša-nu-ma-aš ḫal-z*[*i-i̯a-ri*

5' (-)*d*]*a*$^{?}$*-an-zi* [

---

§ 2' . . .

(broken off)

96. Bo 8783

Description: Festival.
CTH: 670 "*Fragments divers.*"
Dating and Script: LNS (unusual slanted script).
Remarks: One-sided fragment. Some signs are impressed into the clay very slightly.
Measurements: 2.4 × 4.6 × 1.1 cm.
Bibliography: N/A.

Bo 8783

§ 1' 1' (traces)

---

§ 2' 2'](-)*ti-i̯a-an-za* I UD⌜U.A$^{?}$.LU⌝[M$^{?}$

3' BA]L-*ti* II UDU.BABBAR$^{?}$ I UDU.GE$_{6}$$^{?}$[

4'] *A-NA* ^{d}NIN.URTA BAL-*t*[*i*

5']⌞ (-)*x*$^{?}$-*x*⌟-*z*[*i*

(broken off)

97. Bo 8784

Description: Ritual or festival.
CTH: 470 "*Fragments de rituels*" or 670 "*Fragments divers.*"
Dating and Script: NS.
Remarks: One-sided small fragment.
Measurements: 3.1 × 3.1 × 0.9 cm.
Bibliography: N/A.

Bo 8784

§ 1' 1']-⌜*x-x*?⌝ *N*⌜*A*⌝[*M-MA-AN-TU*$_4$(?)
2'] *na-aḫ-ši-i*[*š*[1)]
3' NI]NDA.SIG.MEŠ III NINDA.[
4']-*ni*? *ŠA* 1/2 ⌞*UP-N*⌟[*I*
5' D]UG*KU-KU-U*⌞*B*⌟[

---

§ 2' . . .
(broken off)

Text-critical note: [1)] This is the shorter spelling for *na-aḫ-ḫa-ši-iš*; see KBo 11.24 + 23 I 7, KUB 32.133 I 14.98.

98. Bo 8785

Description: Festival.
CTH: 670 "*Fragments divers.*"
Dating and Script: NS.
Remarks: One-sided fragment. It is remarkable that the verticals of some signs seem to be impressed into the clay more firmly than usual; e.g., "*i̯a*", "*e*" and "*Ù*".
Measurements: 4.3 × 4.9 × 0.7 cm.
Bibliography: N/A.

Bo 8785

§ 1'	1'	]⸢*x*⸣[
	2'	]-*x̣* *up-p*⸢*a-an*⸣-[*zi*?]
§ 2'	3'	] É.LUGAL(-)*ši*(-)*i*-[
	4'	] *ịš-ki-i̯ạ-az-z*[*i*[1)]
	5'	](-)*x̣*[2)]-*ši-i̯a-aš*?(-) *x̣*(-)[
§ 3'	6'	]-*x̣* *pí-ra-ạn pa-iz-z*[*i*
	7'	*A*?-*NA*] É̤ ^{d}U *pa-iz-zi ḫal-x̣*-[
	8'	*I-NA* É](-)*x̤*-*x̤*?-*x̣* Ù *I-NA* Ẹ́? [^{d} . . .

§ 4' 9' *I-NA* É] ^{d}U Ù *Ị-NA* É̩ [^{d} . . .

10'](-)⌞*x*$^{?}$ *x-x-x-x*⌟ *pé-ẹ-d*[*a*$^{?}$-

(broken off)

Text-critical notes: [1] If this is a pres. sg. 3 form of *iškiya-* "to smear, anoint" it would be a rare spelling beside the usual *iš-ki-iz-zi*, *iš-ki-i̭a-zi* and *iš-ki-i̭a-iz-zi*. [2] Is this sign "*gul*" ? The interpretation of the word still remains impossible.

99. Bo 8786

Description: Festival.

CTH: 594 "*Au printemps, à Tippuwa*" or 634 "*Grande fête d'Arinna.*"

Dating and Script: NS.

Remarks: One-sided small fragment from the left portion (with edge) of a tablet. The remaining context concerns the cultic scene where the king throws away the linen cloth, and the royal body-guards pick it up from where they are squatting. Thus, lines 1'–6' can be duplicate of, or parallel to KBo 13.224:6'–10' (CTH 594.G), KUB 25.3 III 25–29 (CTH 634.2.A) and KUB 59.8 V 10'–16' (CTH 594 or 634).

Measurements: 3.3 × 2.7 × 1.8 cm.

Bibliography: N/A.

Bo 8786

§ 1' 1' ⌜TU⌝$_7$.ḪI.⌜A *ta*⌝-[*ru-up-ta-ri*]

2' $^{\text{LÚ.MEŠ}}$MUḪALDIM ^{GI}[^{Š} . . . [1)] *da-an-zi*]

---

§ 2' 3' LUGAL-*uš* GADA-*a*[*n ar-ḫa*]

4' *pé-eš-ši-i̯a-z*[*i*?]

5' *nu ma-a-a*⸤*n* $^{\text{LÚ.}}$⸥[^{MEŠ}*ME-ŠE-TI*$_4$ *ku-e-ez*]

6' ⸤*pár-aš-na-a*⸥[*n ḫar-kán-zi*]

(broken off)

Text-critical note: [1)] To complete either with ^{GIŠ}*GA-AN-NU-UM* (KUB 25.3 III 26), ^{GIŠ}*ḫa-ap-ša-al-li* (KUB 59.8 V 12'), or ^{GIŠ}*ki-iš-te-mu-uš* (KBo 13.224:7').

100. Bo 8787

Description: Cult inventory.
CTH: 510 *“Idoles et fêtes de villes.”*
Dating and Script: LNS.
Remarks: One-sided fragment. Bo 8787 is from the same text genre of KUB 38.6 + Bo 6741 (CTH 510.A), KUB 38.10 (CTH 510.B), KUB 57.58, and KUB 57.106.
Measurements: 4.7 × 3.6 × 1.4 cm.
Bibliography: N/A.

Bo 8787

§ 1’ 1’ [. . . $^{?}$ *ku-e-da-ni-i̯a A-NA* DINGIR-*LIM*] Ị EZẸN$_{4}$.⌜MEŠ⌝[. . . $^{?}$]
2’ [I-*EN*$^{?}$ $^{\text{EZEN}_4}$*zé-e*$^{?}$*-na-aš* I-*EN*$^{?}$ EZEN$_{4}$ *D*]*I*$_{12}$-*ŠI* [

---

§ 2’ 3’ [^{URU} . . . (a number) DINGIR.MEŠ $^{\text{NA}_4}$ZI.KI]N(?) ^{d} x̣ ^{d} x̣ ^{d} x̣(.)[[1)]
4’](-)⌞*x-dạ*$^{?}$⌟*-ni*$^{?}$*-i̯a-ạš*[2)] [
5’ ^{d}L]AMMA$^{?}$ ^{KỤR}[*L*]*a-u̯a-ta-aš*[3)][
6’] ^{ḍ}U ^{d}U *ḫu-u-u̯a-ri-i̯a-u̯*[*a-*[4)]
7’ ^{d}U ^{URU}*N*]*e-ri-ik-ka*$_{4}$ ^{d}U ^{URU}*Kaš-da-*[*ma*
8’]⌞^{d}*Mil*⌟*-ku-ụš* ^{d}*Pí-ḫa-mị-ị*[*š*
9’](-)⌞*x̣*$^{?}$*-ša-x̣*⌟(-)[
(broken off)

Text-critical notes: [1)] Cf. KUB 38.6 I 9’, 13’, 17’, 21’, 33’: The deities are always listed in the sequence ^{d}U ^{d}UTU ^{d}LAMMA ^{d}U ^{URU}[. . .]. [2)] Cf. KUB 38.10 IV 14. If this is part of a geographical name, $^{\text{KUR/URU}}$Adaniyaš could be taken into consideration. [3)] Elsewhere mentioned as ^{KUR}*La-u̯a-ta* (KUB 38.6 I 24’, 30’, KUB 57.58:8’, KUB 57.106 II 16). [4)] This epithet of the Stormgod is sofar unattested. For the initial element cf. ^{d}Ḫuwariyanzipa.

101. Bo 8788

Description: N/A.
CTH: 832 "*Fragments en langue hittite de nature inconnue.*"
Dating and Script: (L)NS.
Remarks: Two-sided fragment from the upper and lower portions (with edges) of a tablet that is moderately abraded. The side with the upper part is almost illegible.
Measurements: 2.3 × 3.9 × 1.9 cm.
Bibliography: N/A.

Bo 8788 (side with upper part)

Bo 8788 (right edge)

Bo 8788 (side with lower part)

Side with upper part

§ 1 1](-)x̤-rụ-uk$^{?}$-x̣

2]-x̤-ịš$^{?}$

3–4 (illegible signs)

5] (-)x̤$^{?}$(-)⌞i-e(?)⌟-zị

6 . . .

(broken off)

Side with lower part

§ 1’ 1’ (traces$^{?}$)

2’] ⌜NINDA$^{?}$⌝.LẠ̀L Ì$^{?}$ ẸM-⌜ṢA⌝(?) x̣-x̣$^{?}$

3’]-x̣ DÙ-an-zị x̤$^{?}$

4’]-x̣- x̤$^{?}$

(bottom of the tablet)

102. Bo 8789

Description: Kizzuwatnan festival.

CTH: 720 "*Fragments divers.*"

Dating and Script: N/A.

Remarks: One-sided, moderately abraded fragment from the left portion (perhaps upper edge) of a tablet. Because of the keywords ^{LÚ}AZU and ^{d}*IŠTAR* Bo 8789 is most likely a fragment from an Ištar/Šauška cult, e.g., CTH 615, 712–16 and 720.

Measurements: 2.7 × 3.9 × 2.0 cm.

Bibliography: N/A.

Bo 8789

§ 1 1 *mạ-ạḫ-ḫa-ạn-ma*(-)*x̣*$^{?}$(-)[

2 *nu A-NẠ* ^{d}*IŠTẠR* [

3 *nu* ^{LÚ}AZU ^{GIŠ}*x̣-x̣*[1)](-)*x̣-x̣*(-)[

4 *A-NA* ^{GIŠ}*x̣-x̣*(-)*x̣-x̣*(-)[

5 *x̣-x̣-x̣-x̣*(-)*ạn*$^{?}$*-x̣*(-)*x̣*(-)[

6 (traces)

(broken off)

Text-critical note: [1)] Judging from the sign traces, the undeterminable designation of the wooden object in lines 3 and 4 appears to be the same word, probably ^{GIŠ}BANŠUR and not ^{GIŠ}ERIN.

105. Bo 8792

Description: Festival.
CTH: 670 "*Fragments divers.*"
Dating and Script: OH/NS.
Remarks: One-sided tiny fragment.
Measurements: 3.0 × 3.6 × 1.7 cm.
Bibliography: N/A.

Bo 8792

§ 1' 1'](-/.)x̣[1)] *p̣ár-šụ-ụl-lị* [
2' *pa-ra-a e-e*]*p-zi ta-a*[*š*(-)
3'] *pé-e-da-i* [

(broken off)

Text-critical note: [1)] According to the sign traces the word preceding *paršulli* is unlikely to be "NINDA". Thus, the word here is either without any determinative in the sense of "crumb" or to be interpreted as the bread designation [NINDA.GUR$_4$.R]A *paršulli*; cf. KBo 23.61:5'.

106. Bo 8794

Description: Festival.
CTH: 670 "*Fragments divers.*"
Dating and Script: (E)NS.
Remarks: One-sided fragment from the right column of a tablet.
Measurements: 3.5 × 4.5 × 1.9 cm.
Bibliography: N/A.

Bo 8794

Right column

§ 1' 1' MUNU⌜S.L⌝[UGAL(?)(-)[1]

---

§ 2' 2' *ma-a-a*[*n*(-)
3' *a-ri* ⌜MUNUS.LU⌝[GAL(?)[2]
4' *a-ru-u̯a-a-iz-* [*zi*]

---

§ 3' 5' ^{LÚ}ALAM.ZU$_9$ *me-ma-*[*i*]
6' [^{L}]⌞^{Ú}*pal*⌟-*u̯a-tal-la-* *a*[*š*]
7' [*pal-u̯a-a-i*]*z-* [*zi*]
(broken off)

Text-critical notes: [1] Or: N⌜I⌝[N.DINGIR] ? See the following note. [2] According to the sign traces to be read more likely this way; the possibility of ⌜NIN⌝.[DINGIR], however, cannot be ruled out.

107. Bo 8795

Description: N/A.
CTH: 832 "*Fragments en langue hittite de nature inconnue.*"
Dating and Script: NS.
Remarks: One-sided fragment. Despite the assignment to CTH 470 "*Fragments de rituels*" at the *Konkordanz* there is no clear evidence for a religious content of this fragment.
Measurements: 4.2 × 3.4 × 1.4 cm.
Bibliography: N/A.

Bo 8795

§ 1' 1'](-)*x̤*$^{?}$-*rị*(-)*x̤*$^{?}$(-)*x̣*(-)*x̤*$^{?}$(-)[
2' *k*]*a-ru-ú ḫa*-[1)
3' -*i̯*]*a-nu-un* [

---

§ 2' 4'](-)*ẹ-eš-ša-an-z*[*i*
5' -*a*]*n-zi-pát x̣*-[
6']-⌞*an*$^{?}$-*za*⌟ *x̤*-[
(broken off)

Text-critical note: 1) In combination with the preceding word *karū* 'formerly' one expects here *ḫatrai-* 'to write' or *ḫandai-* 'to prepare'.

108. Bo 8796 + VS 28.30

Description: Festival.

CTH: 591.I.b.A "*Fête du mois.*"

Dating and Script: OH/LNS.

Remarks: Bo 8796 is a one-sided fragment, and lines 1'–6' directly join VS 28.30 IV 8–13. Duplicate is KBo 45.3 obv. 5–8; parallel passages are KBo 10.39:9'–13'; KBo 17.88 + KBo 24.116 + KBo 20.67 III 7'–11', IV 21–24 (CTH 591.I.a.A) from where the restorations are taken.

Measurements: 2.8 × 2.6 × 0.8 cm.

Bibliography: J. Klinger, StBoT 37 (1996) 366–68 (text edition of VAT 7481 = VS 28.30 without Bo 8796); D. Groddek, DBH 6 (2002) 59 (transliteration of VS 28.30 without Bo 8796); H. A. Hoffner, SMEA 49/I (2007) 379–80 (on higher numbers in KBo 17.88+ III 10', IV 23).

Bo 8796

VS 28.30 + Bo 8796 rev. IV (composite image)

Reverse IV

(Line numbers of Bo 8796 are in parentheses)

§ 1 . . .

8 (= 1') ⌜DINGIR⌝-*mu̯-uš*[1] *ša-am-ni-i̯a-an-ta-ru*

9 (= 2') ^{LÚ}GUR[U]Š-*a̤n-ti* ^{d}UTU-*šum-mi*

10 (= 3') *ta-u̯a-an-*[(*n*)]*a̤-ni*[2] *e-u̯a-li*[3]

11 (= 4') *da-lu-ga-*[*u*]*š* MU.KAM.ḪI.A-*uš pé-eš-kán-d*[*u*]

12 (= 5') ⸤IX⸥-*an ta-lu̯-ri-i*![4] IX-*an*

13 (= 6') *x̤-an-ku-ut-ti*[5] MU̯-*an a-aš-šu-ša-aš*

14 (= 7') [*ḫa-lu-ga-aš*[6]] ⌜*ú*⌝-*e̤-mi̤-i̤š-ki̤-i̤d-du̯*

(Bo 8796 breaks here off; text continues in VS 28.30 IV 15 ff.)

Text-critical notes: [1] KBo 45.3 obv. 5: *ši-mu-uš* on which see E. Neu, HS 111 (1998) 55 60. [2] KBo 45.3 obv. 6: [(*t*)]*a-u̯a-an-na-a̤n-na*. [3] KBo 45.3 obv. 6: *i-u̯a-*[(*li*)]. [4] The first sign "*ta*" has here a unique form, similar to "*ša*" in VS 28.30 IV 28. Contrary to the handcopy in the edition volume, the last sign "*i*" is written over an erased "*in*"; for the tablet photo see hethiter.net/: PhotArch BoFN01347. Based on this reading, both hapax legomena *ta-lu-ri-i* and *x̤-an-ku-ut-ti* in the following line are in agreement in word ending or (nominal) case. [5] The first sign is broken and ends with a vertical, making many alternative readings possible; thus, it is indeterminable. Similarly, KBo 45.3 obv. 7 has [(*x-an-ku-u*)]*t-ti* MU-*an*. The phrase IX-*an ta-lu-ri-i* and IX-*an x̤-an-ku-ut-ti* here and partially in KBo 45.3 obv. 7 may indicate numbers or qualities of "year(s)" as the analogous passages in KBo 17.88 + KBo 24.116 + KBo 20.67 III 10', IV 23 and KBo 10.39:12' mention higher numbers of "years": IX-*an LI-IM* . . . IX-*an* SIG$_7$-*an* . . . IX-*an* "GAŠAN"-*ti* (or "GAŠAN+TI") MU(.KAM).ḪI.A-*uš*; on which see H. A. Hoffner, SMEA 49/I, 379f. [6] Restoration follows KBo 17.88 + KBo 24.116 + KBo 20.67 III 11' and IV 24.

109. Bo 8797

Description: N/A.
CTH: 832 "*Fragments en langue hittite de nature inconnue.*"
Dating and Script: OS.
Remarks: One-sided fragment. Tablet layout, features and script remind us of royal land-donation texts (CTH 222).
Measurements: 3.2 × 2.7 × 1.8 cm.
Bibliography: N/A.

Bo 8797

§ 1′ 1′ . . . [1]

---

§ 2′ 2′ ^{URU} . . .]-*ra̤-aš* ^{ỤRU}*Tu-u-m*[*a*$^{?}$-
3′ ^{URU} . . .]-⌞*x*⌟-*aš* ^{URU}*Ša-aḫ̮-mi*-[
4′ ^{URU} . . .]-*x̣-u̯a-aš-na-aš-ša*(-)[
5′ ^{GIŠ}T]ỊR(?) *I-N*[*A*
6′] I-⌞*ŠU*$^{?}$⌟[2][
7′]⌞*x̣-x̣*$^{?}$⌟[
(broken off)

Text-critical notes: [1] Lower part of the seal-field ? [2] Alternatively read proper name ^{m}*Š*⌞*u*⌟-[. . .] ?

110. Bo 8799

Description: Festival.
CTH: 670 “*Fragments divers.*”
Dating and Script: NS.
Remarks: One-sided fragment. An earlier suggestion that if Bo 8799 lines 1’–4’ directly join KBo 10.29 IV 1–4 (CTH 669.26) has been not confirmed since Bo 8799 obviously does not belong to the top portion of a tablet.
Measurements: 3.3 × 2.9 × 0.4 cm.
Bibliography: N/A.

Bo 8799

§ 1’ . . .

——

§ 2’ 1’ [^{LÚ}ALA]N.ZU$_9$ *me-m*[*a-i*]
2’ [^{LÚ}*pal-u̯*]*a-a-tal-la-aš*
3’ [*pal-u̯a-a*$^{?}$*-i*]*z-zi*
4’ [^{LÚ}*ki-i-ta-š*]*a*[1)] *ḫal-za-a̯-*⌞*i*⌟

————————

§ 3’ 5’ (traces)
(broken off)

Text-critical note: [1)] Alternatively read [^{LÚ}*ki-i-t*]*a*‹*-aš*›.

111. Bo 8800

Description: Festival.
CTH: 627 "*Fête du KI.LAM.*"
Dating and Script: (L)NS.
Remarks: Bo 8800 is one-sided fragment, and lines 2'–7' duplicate KBo 10.24 IV 11–17 (CTH 627.1.b.A) and IBoT 2.100 rt. col. 4'–7' (CTH 627.1.b.F) from where the restorations are adopted.
Measurements: 3.8 × 2.6 × 0.6 cm.
Bibliography: N/A.

Bo 8800

§ 1' 1' (traces$^{?}$)
2' [(^{GIŠ})]*ḫ̮ụ-ṳ-lụ-g̣ạ-a*⌜*n*⌝-[(*ni-i̯a e-ša*)]
3' [(*t*)]*a* LUGAL-*i* ⌞EGIR⌟-[(*an i-i̯a-at-ta*)]

---

§ 2' 4' [(^{L})]$^{\text{⌜Ú⌝.MEŠ}}$ GALA [($^{\text{MUNUS.MEŠ}}$*ar-kam-mi-i̯a-le-eš*)]
5' [(L)]UGAL-*i pí-r*[(*a-an* EGIR-*an-na*)]
6' *ḫ̮ụ-ṳ*$^{?}$*-i-i̯*⌞*a*⌟-[(*an-te-eš* ^{GIŠ}*ar-kam-mi*)]
7' [(*gal*)]-*ga*[(*l-tu-u-ri u̯a-al-ḫ̮a-an-ni-iš-kán-zi*)]
(broken off)

112. Bo 8801

Description: Hurrian.
CTH: 791 "*Fragments en langue hourrite de nature inconnue.*"
Dating and Script: N/A.
Remarks: One-sided small fragment.
Measurements: 3.4 × 2.3 × 1.1 cm.
Bibliography: H.-S. Schuster, HHB I (1974) 14 n. 32.

Bo 8801

§ 1'	1'	-*ḫ*]*u*$^?$
	2'	]-*tap*
§ 2'	3'	]-*x̣-ma t*[*u-*
	4'	-*n*]*i*$^?$-*eš* ⌜*x*⌟(eras.$^?$)(-)*ša-x̣*(-)[
§ 3'	5'	](-)*x̣-un-ni-da-x̣*(-)[
	6'	-*u*]*š*$^?$ *ti-k*[*i-*
§ 4'	7'	]⌞*x-x-x*⌟[

(broken off)

113. Bo 8802

Description: Ritual or festival.
CTH: 470 "*Fragments de rituels*" or 670 "*Fragments divers.*"
Dating and Script: NS.
Remarks: One-sided fragment.
Measurements: 1.9 × 3.4 × 0.6 cm.
Bibliography: N/A.

Bo 8802

§ 1' 1' ^{LÚ}SA]⌜NG⌝[A(?)
2'] *ẹ-e*⌜*p-z*⌝[*i*
3' *a*]*n*$^{?}$-*dạ ú-u̯a-t*⌜*e-e*⌝[*z-zi*
4' -*p*]*a*$^{?}$ ^{KUŠ}*kur-ši kat-ta-x̣*[1)](-)[
5']-⌞*x̣ ap-pa-an-z*⌟[*i*$^{?}$
(broken off)

Text-critical note: [1)] Unlikely *kat-ta-a*[*n*].

114. Bo 8803

Description: Cult inventory or list of materials for a festival$^{?}$.
CTH: 530 "*Fragments divers.*" At the *Konkordanz*: CTH 460 "*Aufzählen magischer Substanzen.*"
Dating and Script: LNS.
Remarks: One-sided fragment.
Measurements: 3.6 × 3.3 × 0.6 cm.
Bibliography: N/A.

Bo 8803

§ 1' 1']⸢*x*$^{?}$⸣[
2' -*š*]*a*$^{?}$-*aš*(-)⌞*x*⌟(eras.)-⸢*x*⸣(-)[
3'] ⸢*š*⸣*i-it-tar* *š*⸢*u*$^{?}$⸣-[
4'] I U$_{4}$.SAKAR KÙ.BABB[AR
5'] I GU$_{4}$.NIGA VIII U[DU$^{?}$(.)][1)]

---

§ 2' 6'] I̩ GU$_{4}$.LÍL[2)] VIII UDU+x̣(.)[3)][
7'](-)⌞*x-x*⌟-*kạn*$^{?}$ *x̣*(-)[
8']⌞*x-x*$^{?}$*-x*⌟[
(broken off)

Text-critical notes: [1)] For these animals and their quantities cf. KBo 38.80 obv. 7. [2)] GU$_{4}$.LÍL "ox of the steppe = wild ox" is otherwise attested only in KBo 12.44:11'; cf. also GU$_{4}$.MAḪ.LÍL known from KBo 5.5 IV 4'. [3)] The kind of animals listed here does not permit a reading PÉ[Š] "mou[se]". I would tentatively suggest ^{UDU}GUK[KAL$^{?}$+KUN] "fa[t-tailed] sheep" with a ligature writing. For the Middle Hittite sign combination of this rare logogram see Chr. Rüster – E. Neu, HZL no. 252.

115. Bo 9441 + KBo 3.18 + 19 + 17 + Bo 7303

Description: Literary.

CTH: 311.2.B "*Naram-Sin en Asie Mineure.*"

Dating and Script: OH/NS. At the *Konkordanz* labeled as "LNS."

Remarks: Bo 9441 is one-sided fragment, and lines 1'–7' directly join KBo 3.18 + 19 + 17 + Bo 7303 III 11–17. Duplicate is KBo 3.16 + III 7–13 (CTH 311.2.A) from where the restorations are adopted. Bo 7303 is not included here.

Measurements: 2.6 × 2.8 × 1.3 cm.

Bibliography: H. G. Güterbock, ZA 44 (1938) 54–57 (textual treatment of KBo 3.18+ and KBo 3.16 without joins); O. Soysal, NABU 2015/3, 116 (transliteration and remarks); S. Košak, hethiter.net/: hetkonk (v. 1.91). http://www.hethport.uni-wuerzburg.de/hetskiz/sk.php?f=Bo%203060

Bo 9441

KBo 3.18 + 19 + 17 + Bo 9441 + Bo 7303 rev. III
(composite image; Bo 7303 is not included)

Reverse III

(Line numbers of Bo 9441 are in parentheses)

. . .

§ 3 11 (= 1') [(*ki*)]-*iš-šị-ri-ịt-tạ*[1] *te-eḫ-ḫi* ^{d}*IŠTAR-ša-aš- ši*[2]

12 (= 2') [*a-a*]*p-pa tar-aš-k*⸤*i-iz*⸥*-zi i-it šu-up-pí-i̯a-aḫ-ḫ*⸤*u*⸥-[(*ut*)]

13 (= 3') [*šu*]-*up-pa-i̯a-aš*[3] ^{GIŠ}Ṇ[(Á-*aš*)] ⸤*še*⸥*-eš-ki-aḫ-ḫu-ti*[4] DINGIR.MEŠ-*K*[(*A*)]

14 (= 4') [*d*]*ạ-a-ri-*[5]*nu-ut nu* [(DINGIR.MEŠ-*KA m*)]⸤*u-g*⸥*a-a*[6]*-i* ^{m}*NA-RA-A*[(*M-*^{d}*SÎN-na-aš*)]

15 (= 5') [(*šu*)]-*up-pí-i̯a-aḫ-ḫ*[(*a-ti šu-up-pa-i̯*)]⸤*a*⸥*-aš* ^{GIŠ}NÁ-[(*aš*)]

16 (= 6') [*še*]-*iš-kị-iš-kị*-[(*u-u̯a-an d*)]⸢*a-a-iš*⸣ DINGIR.M[EŠ-*Š*]⸤*U*⸥

17 (= 7') [(*d*)]*ạ-ạ-rị-*[7]*nu-ut* [(*n*)]*u* DINGIR.MEŠ-*ŠU*[8] *mu-ki-iš-ki-u-an*[9] *d*[(*a-a-i*)]*š*

(Bo 9441 breaks here off; text continues in Bo 7303 + KBo 3.18 + III 18ff.)

Text-critical notes: [1] KBo 3.16 + III 7: *ke-eš-šar-ta.* [2] KBo 3.16 + III 7: ^{d}*IŠTAR*$^{!}$*-iš-ša-aš-ši.* [3] KBo 3.16 + III 9: [*šu-up*]*-pí-i̯a-aš.* [4] KBo 3.16 + III 9: *še-eš-ki-i̯a-aḫ-ḫu-ut.* [5] KBo 3.16 + III 10 adds *-i̯a-*. [6] KBo 3.16 + III 10 omits *-a-*. [7] KBo 3.16 + III 13: *da-ri-i̯a-nu-ut.* [8] KBo 3.16 + III 13 omits *-ŠU.* [9] KBo 3.16 + III 13: *mu-ki-iš«-eš»-ki-u-u̯a-an.*

116. Bo 9442

Description: Festival?.
CTH: 670 "*Fragments divers.*"
Dating and Script: NS.
Remarks: One-sided fragment from the upper-right portion (with edges) of a tablet.
Measurements: 3.5 × 3.3 × 2.1 cm.
Bibliography: N/A.

Bo 9442

§ 1 1]-*x̣*
2]-*x̣ ši-pa-an-dạ-x̣*-[
3 *tá*]*k*?-*ši-iš-šar*[1)]
4]-*x̣ e-ša-ri*
5 *ša*?-*r*]*a-a*[2)]
6 -*š*]*a*
7]-*ịt*
8]-⌞*un*?⌟
(broken off)

Text-critical notes: [1)] For this spelling see [*tá*]*k-ši-iš-šar* in VS 28.14 obv. 10. For an alternative reading *ạ-ši-iš-šar* (= *aševšar*) there is no supporting occurrence known to me. [2)] Or to be restored as [*pa-r*]*a-a*.

117. Bo 9443

Description: Ritual or festival.
CTH: 470 "*Fragments de rituels*" or 670 "*Fragments divers.*"
Dating and Script: NS.
Remarks: One-sided fragment.
Measurements: 4.5 × 2.8 × 1.6 cm.
Bibliography: N/A.

Bo 9443

§ 1' . . .

———

§ 2' 1' $^{\mathrm{UZU?}}$]EME.Ḫ̮[I.A(-)
2'](-)*x̣-ku-it*(-)[
3'] LUGAL *I-NA* [
4']-*ạr*(-)*pa-an*-[
5' *A-NA*(?)] ^{d}U[1)] *ši-i*[*p-pa-an*-

———

§ 3' 6'] *Ạ-NA* LỤGAL(./-)*x̣*?[
7'] *Ụ́-ỤL*(-)[
8' (traces)
(broken off)

Text-critical note: [1)] Or: [. . . LÚ] ^{d}U.

118. Bo 9444

Description: Hurrian.
CTH: 791 "*Fragments en langue hourrite de nature inconnue.*"
Dating and Script: NS.
Remarks: One-sided fragment from the lower portion (with bottom part) of a tablet.
Measurements: 4.1 × 3.2 × 2.1 cm.
Bibliography: N/A.

Bo 9444

§ 1' 1'] ⌜*ta*⌝-[
2'](-)*x̣-šạ-a*-[
3'](-)⌜*x*⌝-*a*(-)*u̯a*$_a$-*a-ni*-[
4'] *pé-e-tu-ụ́*-[[1)]
5' -*t*]*i-ni-še-ni x̣*-[

(bottom of the tablet)

Text-critical note: [1)] This word may belong to *pé-(e)-tu-ú-ḫa* known from the Hurrian "Kešši Story" KUB 47.1+ I 9, IV 5' (CTH 361.II.1). Cf. E. Laroche, GLH (1978-79) 199 and Th. Richter, BGH (2012) 319.

119. Bo 9445

Description: N/A.
CTH: 832 "*Fragments en langue hittite de nature inconnue.*"
Dating and Script: N/A.
Remarks: One-sided fragment from the right portion (with edge) of a tablet.
Measurements: 5.1 × 2.8 × 2.5 cm.
Bibliography: N/A.

Bo 9445

Bo 9445 (right edge)

§ 1' . . .

———

§ 2' 1' *-t*]*i-iš-šạ*$^{?}$

2'–3' . . .

4']*-x̣*$^{?}$ *ẹ-ẹš-tạ*

5']˻*x-x*˼ [

(broken off)

120. Bo 9446

Description: Ritual.
CTH: 470 "*Fragments de rituels.*"
Dating and Script: NS.
Remarks: Bo 9446 is one-sided fragment, and lines 3'–6' are similar to KBo 55.94 II 2–8 (CTH 470.1779).
Measurements: 2.9 × 3.4 × 2.2 cm.
Bibliography: N/A.

Bo 9446

§ 1' 1']⌈^{DUG}*KU-KU-UB* KAŠ$^{?}$⌉[
2'] TUR-*TÌ* ^{GIŠ}*ỊN*-[*BI*
3' ^{GIŠ}*SE*$_{20}$]-*Ẹ*$^{?}$-*ER-DU*$_4$ GIŠ.KÍN *kar-š*[*i*$^{?}$[1]-
4' ^{GIŠ}NU.Ú]R.MA.ḪI.A[2] ^{GIŠ}*x*(.)[
5' ^{GIŠ}*IN-B*]*I* *ḫu-el-p*[*í* ^{GIŠ}ḪAŠḪUR(?)[3]
6' ^{GIŠ}ŠENNU]R ^{GIŠ}U$_4$.Ḫ[I.IN ^{GIŠ}GEŠTIN(?)[4]
7']⌊*x-x*⌋[
(broken off)

Text-critical notes: [1] In Bo 9446 line 3' and in KBo 55.94 II 2 the same incomplete word appears to be *kar-š*[*i-* . . .] rather than *kar-šu*$^{?}$-[. . .] as read by H. Ertem, Flora (1974) 136. It can be interpreted with the preceding logogram as GIŠ.KÍN *karš*[*iyan*(*t*)-] 'cu[t$^{?}$] tree fruit(s)' and compared with GIŠ.KÍN.ḪI.A *duwarnanda* 'cracked/shelled tree fruits' in KBo 10.34 I 24. [2] The broken first sign which ends with double vertical does not permit a reading [^{GI}]^{Š}PÈŠ.ḪI.A. [3] For restoration cf. KBo 55.94 II 7. [4] Cf. KBo 55.94 II 8.

121. Bo 9447

Description: Ritual.

CTH: 470 "*Fragments de rituels.*"

Dating and Script: LNS.

Remarks: Two-sided small fragment from the top and bottom portion (with both edges) of a tablet of which content (lines 1–4) is similar to KUB 58.110 III 1'–5' (CTH 448.4.1.b.H), Bo 3367 + Bo 7039 obv.$^{?}$ 4'–9' (CTH 448.4.1.b.C) and KBo 55.94 II 14–18 (CTH 470.1779).

Measurements: 1.7 × 4.8 × 1.7 cm.

Bibliography: N/A.

Bo 9447 side with upper part (left); side with lower part (right)

§ 1 1 [. . . $^{?}$ III ^{KUŠ}DÙG.GAN] ZÌ.DA.DUR$_5$ IỊI ^{KUŠ}DỤG.G[AN[1)]

2 ZÌ.DA ŠE$^{?}$ *z]é-e-ṇa-an-da-aš*[2)] IỊI ^{KUŠ}D[ÙG.GAN

3](-)*x̣-x̣-mi-iš*[3)] IỊI ^{KUŠ}DỤG.GẠN [

4]-*x̣-ạš*$^{?}$ III ^{KUŠ}DỤG.G⌊AN⌋[

(broken off)

Other side

§ 1' 1'] *a*⌈*n-da*⌉ [

(bottom of the tablet)

Text-critical notes: [1)] One expects here leather bags with following ZÌ.DA.ḪÁD.DU.A 'dry flour' as an alternative to ZÌ.DA.DUR$_5$ 'moist flour'; cf. KBo 55.94 II 14. [2)] For restoration see KBo 13.248 I 18'. [3)] Possibly designation of a grain, or alternatively to read [. . .](-)*x̣-x̣* GE$_6$-*iš* 'black . . .'.

122. Bo 9448

Description: Festival.
CTH: 670 "*Fragments divers.*"
Dating and Script: NS.
Remarks: One-sided small fragment with two columns from the lower portion (with bottom part) of a tablet.
Measurements: 4.3 × 3.6 × 1.9 cm.
Bibliography: N/A.

Bo 9448

Bo 9448 right column

Right column

§ 1' 1' *x̤*(-)[
2' *n*[*u*(-)
3' *an-x̤*(-)[1)][
4' *QA-TA*⸢*M*⸣(-)[[2)]
5' *ku-e-x̤*[?](-)[
6' DUMU.MỤNUS.LUGA[L(-)
(bottom of the tablet)

Text-critical notes: [1)] Alternatively read as divine name ^{d}*x̤*(-)[. . .]. [2)] Or: *QA-TA*⸢*M*⸣-[*MA*].

123. Bo 9449 + Bo 4422 + KUB 39.104

Description: Ritual.

CTH: 400.A *"Rituel d'Iriya, pour la purification d'une ville."*

Dating and Script: MH/LNS.

Remarks: Bo 9449 is one-sided, pre-ruled fragment, and lines 1'–5' directly join Bo 4422 + KUB 39.104 IV 8'–12' (CTH 400.A). Duplicates are KUB 30.34+ IV 23–28 (CTH 400.C) and ABoT 2.24 obv. 6'–11' (CTH 400.J) from where the restorations are adopted.

Measurements: 2.8 × 2.5 × 1.8 cm.

Bibliography: http://www.hethport.uni-wuerzburg.de/hetskiz/sk.php?f=691/z (a sketch of joins KUB 39.104 + Bo 4422 + Bo 8334. However, the latter piece hardly belongs here).

Bo 9449

Bo 4422 + KUB 39.104 + Bo 9449 rev. IV

Bo 4422 + KUB 39.104 + Bo 9449 rev. IV (detail)

Reverse IV

(Line numbers of Bo 9449 are in parentheses)

§ 1' 8' (= 1') ⌜*a-ki*⌝*-ir nu-uš a-pé-e-*<*da-*>*ni*[1] *pí-d*[(*i pé-e-da-at-ti*)]

---

§ 2' 9' (= 2') *nu* MÁŠ.GAL*-an u̯a-ar-nu-u̯a-an-zi* [(*šu-u-ra-šu-u-ra-an-na*)]

10' (= 3') <*ḫa-*>*a-ri-i̯a-an-zi̯*[2] *nu te-ez-zi ki-i̯*[(*a-aš-ta ma-aḫ-ḫa-an*)]

11' (= 4') MÁŠ.GAL *šu-u-ra-šu-u-ra-aš-ša kat-t*[(*a-an ták-na-za pa-a-ir*)]

12' (= 5') *k*⌞*i-i-kán*⌟ *ŠA* ^{URU}*Ḫa-at-ti i-na-a*[(*n e-eš-ḫar NI-IŠ* DINGIR-*LIM*)]

(Bo 9449 breaks here off; text continues in KUB 39.104+ IV 13' ff.)

Text-critical notes: [1] KUB 30.34+ IV 24: Likewise with faulty spelling *a-pé-e-*<*da-*>*ni*. [2] KUB 30.34+ IV 26 and ABoT 2.24 obv. 9': *ḫa-ri-i̯a-an-zi*.

124. Bo 9450

Description: N/A.

CTH: 39 "*Fragments en vieux-hittite, de nature inconnue*" or 832 "*Fragments en langue hittite de nature inconnue.*"

Dating and Script: NS.

Remarks: One-sided fragment. The predicate *dāir* in line 5' is in favor of a mythical or historical story rather than a religious description (ritual, festival etc.). The rare word *annaššar* and ^{d}Inar (lines 2'–3') remind us of the narrative in KUB 43.75 (CTH 39), which uses, however, ^{d}LAMA instead of ^{d}Inar in a historical context. Thus, the present piece could belong to another example of KUB 43.75.

Measurements: 4.5 × 3.3 × 1.5 cm.

Bibliography: N/A.

§ 1' . . .

______

______

§ 2' 1']-*an ḫar-kán-z*[*i*

2']-*zi* ^{d}*I-na-a*[*r*(-)

3' *a*]*n-na-aš-šar*[1)] *š*[*a*$^{?}$-

4'] *ta-mạ-i*(-)*x̣*(-)[

5'](-)⌞*x-i*⌟ *da-a-ir* [

6'](-)*x̣-x̣*(-)[

7' (traces$^{?}$)

(broken off)

Bo 9450

Text-critical note: [1)] According to J. Puhvel, HED 1 (1984) 64, *an-na-aš-šar* may relate formal to *annašnant-* 'pillar$^{?}$', which meaning is unproven. The same word occurs in its complete form also in KUB 43.75 obv. 12' and 20'. However, the context there is obscure, and an alternative reading *an-na-aš*^{SAR} as a possible plant designation does not help any further. I tend now to retract my earlier interpretation NAGGA-*aš-šar* "tin" for the passages in KUB 43.75 (O. Soysal, Murš. I [1989] 72, 73, 107) since the phonetic reading of NAGGA has been recently determined as *arzili-* by O. Soysal, HS 119 (2006) 109 ff.

125. Bo 9457

Description: N/A.
CTH: 832 "*Fragments en langue hittite de nature inconnue.*"
Dating and Script: (L)NS.
Remarks: One-sided small fragment from the right portion (with edge) of a tablet. The right edge is partially inscribed with signs overrun from the other side.
Measurements: 4.0 × 2.5 × 2.6 cm.
Bibliography: N/A.

Bo 9457

Bo 9457 right edge

Bo 9457 other side

Bo 9457 right edge

§ 1’ 1’ *](-)ḫụ-i⸢z-du?-za?⸣(-)[. . .]-⸢x̣ pí?-d⸣a-ụ́*[1]

---

§ 2’ 2’ *]-ạ*[2] *tar-uḫ-zi*

3’ . . .

4’ *]-eš-zi*

---

§ 3’ 5’ *-a]n?*

6’ *-a]n? šu-up-pí*

7’ *](-)x̣-an-kán ne-eḫ-ḫị*

8’ *-ká]n? ta-me-ek-⸤ta⸥*

9’ *]⸤x̣⸥[*

(broken off)

Other side

§ 1’ 1’ *-u]š?-zi*

2’ *Ú-U]L(?)-an te-ez-zi*

---

§ 2’ 3’ *]-x̣-ta*

(broken off)

Text-critical notes: [1] The last signs ⸢x̣ *pí?-d⸣a-ú* are seen on the right edge of the other side of the fragment after line 3’. [2] Or: [. . . .ḪI].Ạ.

126. Bo 9459

Description: Ritual.
CTH: 470 "*Fragments de rituels.*"
Dating and Script: NS.
Remarks: One-sided fragment from the left portion (with edge) of a tablet.
Measurements: 4.3 × 1.5 × 1.4 cm.
Bibliography: N/A.

§ 1′ 1′ ⸢Ù$^{?}$⸣[

---

§ 2′ 2′ *u̯a-ạ*$^{?}$-[
3′ *A-NA* [
4′ *na-aš-t*[*a*

---

§ 3′ 5′ *iš-tar-r*[*a-*[1)]
6′ *ḫur-ta-x̣*(-)[2)][

---

§ 4′ 7′ EGIR-*an-d*[*a-ma*$^{?}$(-)
8′ *A-NA* ⸢x⸣ E[N.SÍSKUR(?)
9′ *an-da-m*[*a*(-)

---

§ 5′ 10′ ⸤*x-a*$^{?}$*-li*$^{?}$⸥(-)[
(broken off)

Bo 9459

Text-critical notes: [1)] If this word is Hittite, despite the spelling with geminated *-rr-*, it may belong to *ištar*(*a*)*k*(*iya*)- "to become sick" and hardly to the Hattian *ištarrazil* "(dark) earth". Cf. also *iš-da-ra-u-u̯a-a*⸢*n-za*⸣ and ⸤*iš*⸥*-ta-ra-a-u-u̯a-an-za* of unknown meaning which occurs in KBo 40.372:3′, 11′. [2)] If a Hittite word, this is to be related to *ḫurt-* 'to curse' or *ḫurtai-* 'curse'.

127. Bo 9460

Description: Ritual$^?$.
CTH: 470 "*Fragments de rituels.*"
Dating and Script: NS.
Remarks: One-sided fragment with two columns.
Measurements: 4.2 × 2.3 × 0.6 cm.
Bibliography: N/A.

Left column

§ 1' 1']-*ạ*$^?$
2'–5' . . .
6' -*z*]*i*$^?$
7'–8' . . .
9']-⌞*x*$^?$-*a*$^?$-*x*⌟
(broken off)

Right column

§ 1' 1' *x̣*(./-)[
2' *š*[*a*-
3' SU[D$^?$-

---

§ 2' 4' *ku-ị*[*t-ma*$^?$*-an*$^?$(-)
5' *kị-ị*(-)[
6' *nu-kạ́*[*n*
7' I ŠẠḪ(.)[
8' ^{UZU}NÍG.[GIG(.)
9' *nu kiš-*[*an*
10' ⌞*pu-uḫ-x̣*⌟(-)[1)][
(bottom of the tablet)

Bo 9460

Text-critical note: [1)] Or Akkadian ⌞*PU-UḪ-ŠÚ*⌟ 'his substitute'?

128. Bo 9461

Description: Ritual or festival.
CTH: 470 "*Fragments de rituels*" or 670 "*Fragments divers.*"
Dating and Script: NS.
Remarks: One-sided fragment.
Measurements: 4.8 × 1.2 × 1.8 cm.
Bibliography: N/A.

§ 1' 1']-*x̣ x̣*-[
2']-*x̣* ^{GIŠ}[
3']-*x̣* GUŠK[IN
4' -*š*]*a*$^{?}$-*an*(-) [

---

§ 2' 5']-*x̣*-*ma*-*ká*[*n*
6' *P*]*A*-*NI* [

---

§ 3' 7'](-)*x̣*-*la*-*a*-[
8']-*aš* *ạn*-[
9'](-)*x̣*-*ša*-*an*(-)[

---

§ 4' 10'] *PA*-*NI* [
11' NINDA].SIG.ME[Š
12']-⌞*x*⌟ *x̣*-[
(broken off)

Bo 9461

129. Bo 9462

Description: Festival.

CTH: 670 "*Fragments divers.*"

Dating and Script: NS.

Remarks: One-sided fragment. The left portion is very close to the edge, so that nothing is missing at the beginning of the lines. The textual features, including repetitive *lu-kat-ti-ma*, are more similar to the *nuntarriyašḫaš*–festival, e.g., KUB 51.15 rev. 2'–13' (CTH 626.Ü 6) than to the AN.TAḪ.ŠUM^{SAR}–festival, e.g., KBo 10.20 I 19 ff., II 5 ff., III 4 ff., IV 3 ff. (CTH 604.A).

Measurements: 3.3 × 2.5 × 1.3 cm.

Bibliography: N/A.

Bo 9462

§ 1' 1' *lu-kat-ti-*⸢*ma*⸣(-)[

2' $^{\text{EZEN}_4}$*zé-e-na-ạn-*[*ta*$^?$*-aš*$^?$

3' I DUG.KA.GAG.A [

---

§ 2' 4' *lu-kat-ti-ma* ṾI$^?$ [1)][

5' III UDU.ḪI.A I$^?$ [

---

§ 3' 6' ⸤*lu*⸥*-kat-ti-ma*(-)[

7']⸤*x* É$^?$(./-)*x*⸥[

(broken off)

Text-critical note: [1)] For reasons of space after the sign *-ma* unlikely to read *lu-kat-ti-ma-z*[*a*].

130. Bo 9463

Description: N/A.
CTH: 832 "*Fragments en langue hittite de nature inconnue.*"
Dating and Script: (L)NS.
Remarks: One-sided fragment with two or three columns that is too small to classify.
Measurements: 3.9 × 4.2 × 1.2 cm.
Bibliography: N/A.

Bo 9463

Left (or middle?) column

(Only remnants of a broken sign are seen)

Right (or middle?) column

§ 1' 1'–3' (traces)
4']-*x̣-kạ́n* [
5' *na-at da-*[
6' *nu-ut-ta a-x̣-*[

---

§ 2' 7']-⌞*x x̣*⌟-[
(broken off)

131. Bo 9464

Description: Festival.
CTH: 670 "*Fragments divers.*"
Dating and Script: LNS.
Remarks: One-sided fragment from the top right portion (with edges) of a tablet.
Measurements: 3.8 × 3.0 × 1.7 cm.
Bibliography: N/A.

Bo 9464

§ 1 1 *A-N*]*A*(?) *PA-NI* DINGIR-*LIM*
2 GIŠBANŠ]ỤR(?) *šẹ-er da-a-i*

---

§ 2 3 DUM]⌞U.É⌟.GAL
4 NINDA].⌞GU⌟R$_4$.RA
(broken off)

132. Bo 9465 (+$^{?}$) KUB 28.104

Description: Festival.

CTH: 744.11 *"Fragments de fêtes contenant des chants et récitations en hatti."*

Dating and Script: NS.

Remarks: Bo 9465 is one-sided fragment. For lines 2'–5' see KUB 28.104 IV 4'–10' and V 10'–14' from where the restorations here are adopted. I suspect that Bo 9465 belongs rather to the same tablet as KUB 28.104 than is its duplicate. Compare the "LUGAL" signs in "MUNUS.LUGAL" with additional petite verticals here in line 5' and in KUB 28.104 IV 14'. Further analogous passages are KBo 30.140 obv. 4'– rev. 2 and KBo 43.221:5'–9'.

Measurements: 2.8 × 4.0 × 2.1 cm.

Bibliography: N/A.

Bo 9465

§ 1' 1' (traces)

2' [$^{\text{LÚ.MEŠ}}$SAG]I GAL.ḪI.A ⌜*ú*⌝-[*da-an-z*]*i* [

3' [^{LÚ}SAGI I] NINDA.GUR$_4$.RA *EM-ṢA* TUR

4' [*a-ra-aḫ-za*] *ú-da-i* [1)]

---

§ 2' 5' [$^{\text{LÚ.MEŠ}}$SAGI L]UGAL-*i* MUNUS.LUGAL-*i̯a* [

6' [GAL.ḪI.A *pí-an-zi*] ⸤^{LÚ}SAGI DINGIR⸥-[*LIM*

(broken off)

Text-critical note: [1)] Here is an unidentified sign curving up from a lower line, or reaching from the other side of the tablet.

133. Bo 9466

Description: Historical or prayer?.

CTH: 3.2 "*Fragments nommant la ville de Zalpa.*"

Dating and Script: OH/(L)NS.

Remarks: Bo 9466 is a one-sided fragment, and lines 4'–6' duplicate KBo 12.18 I 1'–4' and KBo 50.3:6'–9' from where the restorations are adopted. The left portion is very close to the edge, so that nothing is missing at the beginning of the lines.

Measurements: 3.1 × 1.6 × 1.1 cm.

Bibliography: O. Soysal, Murš. I (1989) 75–78, 108–110; C. Corti, Eothen 11 (= GsImparati; 2002) 172–175; O. Soysal, ZA 95 (2005) 129–130 (on the fragment KBo 50.3 which is cited as unpublished Bo 69/580).

Bo 9466

§ 1' 1' *šu-m[e-eš(-)*[1]

2' *ú-ẹ-[*

3' *nu-uš(-)[*

---

§ 2' 4' *ki-nu-n[(a-aš-ta šu-me-e)š*

5' *šu-me-eš(-)x̣(-)[*[1]

6' *[ḫ]˻u˼-ur-[(ta-al-li-i̯a-at-t)e-ni*?

7' *]˻x˼[*

(broken off)

Text-critical note: [1] Thus, the reading *[la-l]a-me-eš* ? at the *Konkordanz* (S. Košak, hethiter.net/: hetkonk (v. 1.91)) should now be corrected.

134. Bo 9470

Description: Festival.
CTH: 670 "*Fragments divers.*"
Dating and Script: NS.
Remarks: Two-sided fragment from the right portion (with partially inscribed edge) of a tablet. Reverse$^{?}$ lines 1'–4' appear to be duplicate of, or parallel to KUB 58.4 V 14'–17' (CTH 651).
Measurements: 4.4 × 1.8 × 1.8 cm.
Bibliography: N/A.

Bo 9470 obv.$^{?}$

Bo 9470 obv.$^{?}$ (right edge)

Bo 9470 rev.$^{?}$

Bo 9470 rev.$^{?}$ (right edge)

Obverse$^{?}$

§ 1' 1' *-e]n*$^{?}$[1)]

---

§ 2' 2']-*x̣-me-lị*[2)] *da-a-i*
3']-*x̣*$^{?}$

---

§ 3' 4']-*ịa-zi*
5' IZI$^{?}$-*i*]*t*[3)] *za-nu-an-zi*

---

§ 4' 6' ^{URU}*N*]*e-ri-ịk*
7' EGI]R-*pạ tị-an-zi*

(broken off)

Reverse?

§ 1' 1'] SỊR-*RU*

---

§ 2' 2' A]D.KID

3' NINDA.GU]R_4.RA

4' *ki-i*]*t-ta*

5'–6' (traces)

(broken off)

Text-critical notes: 1) Perhaps [*UŠ-KE-E*]*N*. 2) [*A-NA* ^d*Ḫa-š*]*a-me-lị* ? 3) Alternatively restore as [*ḫa-ap-pí-ni-i*]*t*.

135. Bo 9471

Description: N/A.
CTH: 832 "*Fragments en langue hittite de nature inconnue.*"
Dating and Script: NS.
Remarks: One-sided tiny fragment that cannot be classified.
Measurements: 3.2 × 2.8 × 1.1 cm.
Bibliography: N/A.

Bo 9471

§ 1' 1' ANŠE.K]UR.RA.⌜MEŠ⌝ [
2' A]NŠE.KUR.RA.MEŠ *x̣*-[
3'] *na-aš a-u*[*t*? 1)-

---

§ 2' 4']-*x̣-zi-pí-i̯*[*a*(-) 2)
5'](-)⌞*x*?-*x-x*⌟ *x̣*-[
(broken off)

Text-critical notes: 1) Or less probably *a-ś*[*i*(-) . . .]. 2) It appears to be a proper name.

136. Bo 9472

Description: Festival.
CTH: 670 "*Fragments divers.*"
Dating and Script: NS.
Remarks: One-sided fragment from the right portion (with partially inscribed edge) of a tablet.
Measurements: 3.3 × 3.5 × 0.8 cm.
Bibliography: N/A.

Bo 9472

§ 1' 1'](-)⌜*ú*$^{?}$-*ša*⌝(-)*x̣*(-)[
2'] *ti-an-zi* [
3' ^{KU}]^{Š}NÍG.BÀR *x̣*[1)][
4' -*z*]*a*$^{?}$ *ku-it-ma-an* DUMU-*a*[*š*$^{?}$]
5']-*ị*$^{?}$ *nu-uš-ša-an* DUMU-*a*[*š*$^{?}$]
6' *E*]*M*$^{?}$-*ṢÚ*
7' -*z*]⌞*i*⌟ [
(broken off)

Text-critical note: [1)] A sign overrun from the other side of the tablet.

137. Bo 9474

Description: Instruction$^{?}$.
CTH: 275 "*Fragments de protocoles (ou de traités ?).*"
Dating and Script: (L)MS$^{?}$.
Remarks: One-sided fragment.
Measurements: 3.9 × 3.6 × 1.8 cm.
Bibliography: N/A.

Bo 9474

§ 1’	1’	]-*x̤-iš-nạ*$^{?}$(-)[
	2’	*ta*$^{?}$]-*ma-a-iš* [
	3’	-*a*]*n*$^{?}$ *MA-ḪAR* [$^{1)}$
	4’	*ku*$^{?}$]-*ẹ-da-ni-mạ* [
	5’	*ma-ni*]-*i̯ạ-aḫ-ḫi-i̯*[*a*(-)
	6’	]-*na* *a*[*r*-

(broken off)

Text-critical note: **1)** To restore [^{d}UTU-*ŠI*] ? Cf. KUB 13.2+ I 19’–22’, II 43’–45’ (CTH 261.I.B) where the context also contains the lexemes *ma-ni-i̯a-aḫ-ḫi-i̯a* (I 22’) and *ku-e-da-ni-ma* (II 45’) as here.

138. Bo 9476

Description: Festival.
CTH: 670 “*Fragments divers.*”
Dating and Script: OH$^{?}$/NS.
Remarks: One-sided small fragment.
Measurements: 4.1 × 3.0 × 2.5 cm.
Bibliography: N/A.

Bo 9476

§ 1’ 1’ *](-)⸢pa$^{?}$⸣(-)[*
2’ *](-)x̤$^{?}$-šị-ú x̣-[*
3’ *UŠ-K]Ẹ́-EN-NU tẹ$^{?}$(-)[*
4’ *-u]š-x̤ ú-u̯[a-*
5’ L]$^{Ú.ME.EŠ}$*ME-ŠE-[TI$_4$(-)*
6’ *(-)t]a$^{?}$-aš(-)pa$^{?}$-an-x̣(-)[*
7’ *-n]i$^{?}$ x̣-x̣-x̣-x̣$^{?}$(-)[*
(broken off)

139. Bo 9477

Description: Festival.
CTH: 670 "*Fragments divers.*"
Dating and Script: NS.
Remarks: One-sided small fragment.
Measurements: 3.0 × 3.7 × 1.9 cm.
Bibliography: N/A.

Bo 9477

§ 1' 1' (traces)

2']-x̣ *ḫu-⌜u-x?⌝-*[

---

§ 2' 3' LÚ.MEŠ*ḫé-eš*]-*tu-um-né-eš*[1] *pí-*[

4' É]*ḫẹ-eš-ta-a pẹ-⌞e?⌟-*[[2]

5']-x̣-*kán-zi* [

6']-x̣ *ḫu-x̣-x?-*[

(broken off)

Text critical-notes: [1] Cf. the rare attested plural form LÚ.MEŠ*ḫé-eš-tu-u-um-né-eš* in KBo 25.171 II? 7' (CTH 675). [2] *pẹ-⌞e?⌟-*[*da-an-zi*] ?

140. Bo 9478

Description: Conjuration and mythology$^{?}$.
CTH: 457 "*Conjurations et mythes.*"
Dating and Script: MH$^{?}$/MS.
Remarks: One-sided fragment. Archaic lexical features like *ú-el-lu-u̯a*, *ták-ku* and the whole context remind us of the narrative in KUB 43.60 I (CTH 457.7.1).
Measurements: 2.9 × 5.2 × 0.7 cm.
Bibliography: N/A.

Bo 9478

§ 1' 1']⸢*x* *x*⸣[
2']⸢*x*- *x*-*e*⸣- *da*(-) [

---

§ 2' 3'] *a-i̥š-šir*[1] *nu-u̯a ku-it-ta*(-)*x̣*(-)[
4' UDU.Ḫ]I.A[2] *ú-el-lu-u̯a*[3] *tar-na-aš gi-im-r*[*a*-
5']-*i̥ ku-it-ta* SIG$_5$-*ta-ti ták-ku ú-ẹ*$^{?}$-[
6' *d*]*a*$^{?}$-*a-na*[4] *ša-li-ga-ri nu-za-an tu-ik-k*[*i*-
7']-*x̣-ša-aš da-a-i* IV-*na ša-li-ga-*⸤*r*⸥[*i*
8' *n*]*u* ⸤DUMU.L⸥Ú.U$_{19}$.LU GU$_4$.ḪI.A UDU.ḪI.A ⸤*ú-e*⸥[*l-lu-u̯a*(?)[5]
9' . . .

---

§ 3' 10']-⸤*x̣-mi*$^{?}$⸥(-)[
(broken off)

Text critical-notes: [1)] So far, the verb *aiš*(*š*)- is known only from the hippological texts and describes an animal (horse) action or condition ('to become hot[?]'); J. Friedrich – A. Kammenhuber, HW[2] I (1975) 50; J. Puhvel, HED I (1984) 11 f. [2)] Compare and restore mutually with line 8'. [3)] For the allative form *ú-el-lu-u̯a* see KUB 43.60 I 36. [4)] Ordinal number *dān=a* "and second" follows IV-*na* in the next line. The sign remnants would less likely support the reading [*t*]*a-a-na* as attested in KBo 20.40 V 6' in this spelling. [5)] Compare and restore mutually with line 4'.

141. Bo 9479

Description: Mythological.
CTH: 323.1.C "*Disparition et retour du Soleil (mugawar).*"
Dating and Script: OH/MS.
Remarks: Bo 9479 is a one-sided fragment, and lines 2'–8' duplicate VBoT 58 IV 12–18 (CTH 323.1.A) from where the restorations are taken. According to the sign forms and ductus Bo 9479 may belong to the same tablet as KUB 36.44 + KUB 53.20 (CTH 323.1.B).
Measurements: 3.0 × 2.8 × 0.6 cm.
Bibliography: *Konkordanz der hethitischen Keilschrifttafeln* (http://www.hethport.uni-wuerzburg.de/hetkonk/).

Bo 9479

§ 1' 1' (traces)
2' [(*pa-a-ú ku-iš* ^{LÚ}MÁŠDA *nu-ut-ta* I UDU *p*)]*a-a-u̯*

§ 2' 3' [^{d}UT(U-*u-u̯a-aš* ^{d}*Te-li-pí-nu-u̯a-aš-ša mu-g*)]*a-a-u-u̯a-aš QA-TI* [

§ 3' 5' [*nu tar-n*(*a-az ki-i* I ^{DUG}ḪAB.ḪAB ZABAR *Ù NA-A*)]*K-TÁM-ŠU*$^{\text{(!)1)}}$ ZA[(BAR)]
6' [. . . (ZABAR *A-NA NA-AK-TÁM-MI zi-i*)]*k-kán-te-eš* I ^{GI}[(^{Š}IG ZABA)R]
7' [^{GIŠ}*a-ri-i*(*m-pa-aš* ZABAR II ^{GIŠ}AB ZABAR I ^{GI})]^{Š}GAG ZABA[(R I ^{GIŠ}MAR ZABA)R]
8' [I ^{GIŠ}NÍG.GUL (ZABAR I ^{GIŠ}*al-ki-iš-ta-aš ip-p*)]*í-aš* I ^{GIŠ}*al-*[(*ki-iš-ta-aš*)]
9' [. . . (I ^{GIŠ}*šu-ú-ni-la-aš* ^{GIŠ}*la-aḫ-ḫu-ra-aš* TUR)] ⌞DUḪ⌟.LÀL *t*[(*úḫ-ḫu-x*)- . . .]
10']⌞*x x*⌟[
(broken off)

Text-critical note: $^{\text{1)}}$ Scribal error for "*MA*" as it occurs in VBoT 58 IV14 as well.

142. Bo 9480

Description: (Cult$^{?}$) inventory.
CTH: 242 "*Inventaires de métaux, d'outils et d'armes*" or 530 "*Fragments divers.*"
Dating and Script: NH/LNS.
Remarks: One-sided fragment.
Measurements: 3.5 × 2.6 × 0.9 cm.
Bibliography: N/A.

Bo 9480

§ 1' 1' (traces$^{?}$)
2' *u̯a-a*]*k-šur* VI ^{GIŠ}*x̣*[1](./-)[
3' -*š*]*a-a-an an-d*[*a*
4'] Ị$^{?}$ ^{DUG}*ḫu-up-pár* [
5']-*ša da-x̣-x̣*$^{?}$(-)[
6'](.)*x̣*.ḪI.A *pí-x̣*-[
7' x$^{?}$]+⌞I⌟ GÍN.GÍN [
8']⌞*x-x-x*⌟[
(broken off)

Text-critical note: [1] To read [. . . ^{URUDU}*u̯a-a*]*k-šur* VI ^{GIŠ}PẠN [. . .] ? Cf. KUB 60.1+ rev. III$^{?}$ 19': [^{UR}]^{UDU}*u̯a-ak-šur* IV ^{GIŠ}P[AN].

143. Bo 9482

Description: Festival.
CTH: 660 "*Offrandes à des images royales*," 669 "*Grands fragments de fêtes*" or 670 "*Fragments divers.*"
Dating and Script: NS.
Remarks: One-sided fragment.
Measurements: 2.9 × 2.8 × 0.8 cm.
Bibliography: N/A.

Bo 9482

§ 1'   . . .

———

§ 2'   1'   [. . .$^{?}$ [1)]] ^{LÚ}MUḪ̮ALDIM-*aš* $^{UZU̯}$[[2)]
2'   [. . .$^{?}$]-x̣$^{?}$ II-*ŠU dạ-a-i* [2)] x̣$^{?}$-[
3'   [. . .$^{?}$] ^{d}*Šu-u̯a-lị-i̯[a-at-ti*$^{?}$
4'   ] ALA[N$^{?}$(.)[3)]

———

§ 3'   5'   (traces$^{?}$)
(broken off)

Text-critical notes: [1)] Perhaps nothing is missing here. [2)] For lines 1'–2' see KBo 21.49 + KBo 39.87 II 14'–15' (CTH 660): ^{LÚ}MUḪ̮ALDIM ^{UZU}NÍG.GIG *iš-ta-na-na-aš* / ⸤II-*ŠU*⸥ *da-a-i*; similarly KBo 38.120 + KBo 30.92 rev. 1–2 (CTH 660.4). [3)] Can be completed as [^{LÚ}]ALA[N.ZU$_{9}$] ? Cf. the context of KUB 30.41(+) I 21'-24' (CTH 669.19) where $^{LÚ.MEŠ}$MUḪ̮ALDIM, ^{d}*Šu-u̯a-li-i̯a-at-ti* and ^{LÚ}ALAN.ZU$_{9}$ are co-attested.

144. Bo 9483

Description: Festival.
CTH: 670 *“Fragments divers.”*
Dating and Script: NS.
Remarks: One-sided fragment.
Measurements: 2.7 × 2.4 × 1.0 cm.
Bibliography: N/A.

Bo 9483

§ 1’	1’	]⌈x̣⌉[
§ 2’	2’	$^{\text{LÚ.MEŠ?}}$]SAG[I(.)
	3’	](-)x̣(-)*pí-an*-x̣(-)[
	4’	^{LÚ}SAN]GA-*i* GAL [
	5’	]-x̣? *ka-a-r*[*i-i̯a-*
	6’	]-⌊*x-eš*⌋-*ša*(-)[
	7’	]⌊*x*-x̣?⌋[
		(broken off)

145. Bo 9484

Description: Festival.
CTH: 670 "*Fragments divers.*"
Dating and Script: NS.
Remarks: One-sided small fragment that is heavily burnt and abraded.
Measurements: 2.5 × 2.4 × 1.4 cm.
Bibliography: N/A.

Bo 9484

§ 1' 1' *A-NA*(?) ^{d}*Pa*]-⌜*ap-pa-i̯a*⌝[
2' *A-NA*(?) ^{d}*I*]*š-du-uš-t*[*a-i̯a*
3'] *A̤-NA* DỊNGIR-*LIM*[1)][
4'](-)*x̤-pa*(-)*an-dạ*?-[

---

§ 2' 5']-*x̤-mạ* ⌞*x*⌟-[
(broken off)

Text-critical note: [1)] Or to be read as divine name ^{d}*Ši*-[. . .] ?

146. Bo 9485

Description: Festival.
CTH: 670 “*Fragments divers.*”
Dating and Script: NS.
Remarks: One-sided small fragment from the right column of a tablet. The co-attestation of ᵈUTU ᵁᴿᵁ[Arinna] (line 2’) and the bread designation ᴺᴵᴺᴰᴬ*mī*[*umīu-*] (line 4’) in a near context suggest that Bo 9485 is a fragment to the 5th day of the *nuntarriyašḫaš*-festival (CTH 626; KBo 2.15 IV 5’–9’ // KUB 25.14 IV 2’–5’).
Measurements: 3.3 × 3.1 × 0.8 cm.
Bibliography: N/A.

Bo 9485

Right column

§ 1’ 1’ (traces?)
2’ ᵈUTU ᵁᴿ⌜ᵁ⌝[*A-ri-in-na*1)
3’ *tal-la-* *ị*? 2)[

---

§ 2’ 4’ ⌞IX? ᴺᴵᴺᴰᴬ⌟*mi-*⌞*i*⌟*-*[*ú-mi-i*?*-ú*(-)
(broken off)

Text-critical notes: 1) Or written as semi-logographically ᵁᴿᵁPÚ-*na*. If this piece belongs to CTH 626 the restoration can be extended as ᵈUTU ᵁᴿ⌜ᵁ⌝[*A-ri-in-na ŠA* ᶠ . . . (name of a Hittite queen)]. 2) This word is perhaps not related to ⁽ᴰᵁᴳ⁾*tallai-*, but rather a verb *tallai- =? *talliya-* “to evoke (a deity).”

147. Bo 9486

Description: Festival.
CTH: 670 "*Fragments divers.*"
Dating and Script: NS.
Remarks: One-sided small fragment.
Measurements: 2.7 × 3.1 × 0.8 cm.
Bibliography: N/A.

Bo 9486

§ 1' 1' -*z*]⌜*i-iš*⌝(?)(-)[
2' *pár-š*]*ụ-ụl-lị* GA.KIN.A[G[1)]
3' ^{U}]⌞^{ZU}ḪA⌟.LA KU$_6$.ḪI.A *x̤*(./-)[
4']⌞Ì⌟.GIŠ(?) I *x̤*? [
5']-*x̣* *x̤*-[
(broken off)

Text-critical note: [1)] For lines 2'-3' cf. KBo 30.37 I 5'-6' (CTH 674.?) and KBo 38.36:2'-6' (CTH 652).

148. Bo 9487

Description: Cult inventory.
CTH: 530 *"Fragments divers."*
Dating and Script: NH/LNS.
Remarks: One-sided fragment. Bo 9487 and KUB 12.4 (CTH 530) show similar script and text structure, so they could belong to the same tablet.
Measurements: 3.6 × 2.6 × 1.5 cm.
Bibliography: N/A.

Bo 9487

§ 1' 1']⌜*x*⌝[
2' *A*$^{?}$-*N*]*A* É-*Š*[*U*[1)]
3'] ZỊ̀.DA.DỤR$_5$ [
4' *me*]-*ma-al* [
5' *u̯a-a*]*k-šur* II *x̣*[2)]-[

---

§ 2' 6' [EZEN$_4$] Ụ́.BAR$_8$-*i̯a-k*[*án ke-e-da-ni*
ḫa-an-da-an-za[3)]]

---

§ 3' 7' ^{L}]^{Ú}SANGA ⌞$^{d?}$⌟[
8']⌞*x*⌟[
(broken off)

Text-critical notes: [1)] Cf. KUB 12.4 IV 12. [2)] [I *u̯a-a*]*k-šur* II *N*[*AM-MA-AN-TU$_4$*] ? See KUB 12.4 IV 1. [3)] Restoration follows KUB 12.4 IV 6. Cf. similarly, but with slight spelling variations KBo 26.190 II 5': [EZ]EN$_4$ Ú.BAR$_8$-*i̯a-kán ke-e-da-ni-pát ḫa-an-da-za*.

149. Bo 9488

Description: (Purification) ritual?.
CTH: 470 "*Fragments de rituels.*"
Dating and Script: N/A. The script is clearly older than NS (cf. the signs "*it*", "*mu*", "*tar*" etc.)
Remarks: One-sided fragment.
Measurements: 3.6 × 2.5 × 1.5 cm.
Bibliography: N/A.

Bo 9488

§ 1'	1'	](-)⸢*x-ši*?-*x*⸣(-)[
§ 2'	2'	] *nu* DINGIR-*LIM*(-)*x̣*?(-)[
	3'	*IŠ*]-*TỤ* ^{ỤRU}*Ḫ̮a*-[
	4'	] *Ạ-NA* Ẹ́-*Š*[*U*?
§ 3'	5'	] *ụ́-e-ed-dụ* [
	6'	(-)*m*]*i-nụ-ma-aš mu*-⸢*ú*?⸣-[[1)]
	7'	*pa-a*]*p-rạ-a-tar*[2)] *u̯a-aš-tú*[*l*
§ 4'	8'	]-⸤*x̣ mu-x-x*⸥(-)[
		(broken off)

Text-critical notes: [1)] To the word (⸗)*mulatar* (an evil quality) ? [2)] According to the sign traces the reading [*ḫ̮*]*a-rạ-a-tar* is less probable.

150. Bo 9489

Description: Treaty or (military) protocol?.
CTH: 212 "*Traités (ou protocoles): fragments.*"
Dating and Script: MS?.
Remarks: One-sided fragment from the left portion (with edge) of a tablet.
Measurements: 2.9 × 2.7 × 1.7 cm.
Bibliography: N/A.

Bo 9489

§ 1' 1' ⸢x-x?⸣(-)[
2' *e-eš-t*[*u*
3' *tu-uz*[1)]*-z*[*i*?-
4' *pí-ra-an i-i̯*[*a-*

---

§ 2' 5' *na-aš-ta tu-u*[*z-zi*?-
6' (traces)
(broken off)

Text-critical notes: **1)** This is the rare form with an additional horizontal, Chr. Rüster – E. Neu, HZL (1989) no. 340.3.

151. Bo 9490 + KBo 28.108

Description: Treaty.
CTH: 29.A "*Traité de Tahurwaili avec Eheya du Kizzuwatna.*"
Dating and Script: Taḫurwaili/MS.
Remarks: Bo 9490 is a one-sided fragment, and lines 7'–13' directly join KBo 28.108 obv. 1'–7' (see *Konkordanz*).
Measurements: 4.2 × 2.5 × 1.6 cm.
Bibliography: G. F. del Monte, OrAnt 20 (1981) 211 and 212 n. 21 (without the joined piece Bo 9490); *Konkordanz der hethitischen Keilschrifttafeln*, http://www.hethport.uni-wuerzburg.de/hetskiz/sk.php?f=170/u.

Bo 9490

Bo 9490 + KBo 28.108 obv. (left) and detail (right)

Obverse

(Line numbers of KBo 28.108 are in parentheses)

§ 1' 1' [. . .]⌜x̣ x⌝[
2' [. . .]-x̣-*bi*-⌜x⌝(-)[

---

§ 2' 3' [. . .] ^m^*E-ḫé-i̯a* ⌜URU x⌝[
4' [. . .]-x̣ *pa-ni-iš* URU^KI^ [
5' [. . .]-x̣-*bi* KUR-*šu* URU.DIDLI^?^.[ḪI^?^.A^?^-*šu*^?^

---

§ 3'	6'		[. . .] URU^{KI} ÌR *ša* $^{m⌜}$*E*⌝-[*ḫé-i̯a*
	7'	(= 1')	⌜*i-n*⌝[*a pa*$^{?}$]-*ni-šu la-a i-qá*[*b-bi*
	8'	(= 2')	*i-na p*[*a*$^{?}$-*ni*$^{?}$]-*šu la-a i-ip-*[*pu*$^{?}$-*uš*$^{?}$ [1]

---

§ 4'	9'	(= 3')	^{LÚ}*mu-un-na-ab-tu*$_{4}$ *i-n*[*a*(-)[2]
	10'	(= 4')	*ul-lu-ú ạ-na ul-l*[*i-i*

---

§ 5'	11'	(= 5')	URU^{KI} *ša* LỤGAL.GAL *ša ạ-*[*na* ^{m}*E-ḫé-i̯a*
	12'	(= 6')	*a-na qa-ti* LỤGAL.GAL *ú-*[*ta-ar-ru*[3]
	13'	(= 7')	*ša a-na* LUGAL.GAL *i-x̣-*[[4]

(Bo 9490 breaks here off; text continues in KBo 28.108:8'ff.)

Text-critical notes: [1] Cf. the Išputaḫšu-Treaty KUB 31.82:3' (CTH 21.I.2). [2] Rather preposition *i-na* than verbal form *i-na-ak-kir* (cf. KBo 28.108:17'). [3] Due to the initial sign "*ú*" as it appears in Bo 9490 line 12' the restoration here with *ut-ta-na-a-ar* (following a similar clause in KUB 31.82:7') is no longer tenable (pace G. F. del Monte, OrAnt 20, 211). [4] Due to the initial sign "*i*" as it appears in Bo 9490 line 13' the restoration for here with *ut-ta-na-a-ar* is impossible (pace G. F. del Monte, OrAnt 20, 211).

152. Bo 9491

Description: Festival.
CTH: 670 "*Fragments divers.*"
Dating and Script: LNS.
Remarks: One-sided fragment with two columns.
Measurements: 3.2 × 4.1 × 1.1 cm.
Bibliography: N/A.

Bo 9491

Left column

§ 1' 1' -*z*]*i*
2' -*z*]*i*
(broken off)

Right column

§ 1' 1'](.)⸢*x̣*.MEŠ⸣ *x̣*-[
2' *nạ-aš-kán* [
3' EGIR-*pa š*[*a*$^{?}$-

---

§ 2' 4' ^{LÚ}SANGA-*kán Ạ*-[*NA* ^{d} . . .
5' ^{d}U ^{URU}*Ḫa-a*[*t*$^{?}$-*ti*$^{?}$ 1)
6' *Ù A*-⌞*NA* ^{d}⌟[

---

§ 3' 7' ⌞^{LÚ}SAN⌟[GA$^{?}$(-)
(broken off)

Text-critical note: 1) Or: ^{d}U ^{URU}*Ḫa-l*[*a-ap*].

153. Bo 9492

Description: N/A.
CTH: 832 "*Fragments en langue hittite de nature inconnue.*"
Dating and Script: NS.
Remarks: One-sided, moderately abraded fragment. Most of the signs are hard to recognize.
Measurements: 3.8 × 2.4 × 1.1 cm.
Bibliography: N/A.

Bo 9492

§ 1' 1']-x̣ DINGIR.MẸŠ-*eš* *nẹ*-[
2']-*x̣*-*zị* $^{LÚ.MEŠ}$*x̣*(.)[
3' -*a*]*n*$^{?}$-*dụ* DINGIR.MẸŠ(-)[
4'](-)*an*$^{?}$-*dạ* *š*[*u*$^{?}$-

§ 2' 5']-*ịạ*-*zị*(?) *x̣*-[
6']-*x̣* *dạ*-*r*[*a*(?)-
7'](.)*x̣*.MẸŠ$^{?}$ *ạn*-[

§ 3' 8']-*x̣* [
(broken off)

154. Bo 9493

Description: Ritual.
CTH: 460 "*Listes d'ingrédients pour des rituels.*"
Dating and Script: NS.
Remarks: One-sided fragment of which each line is seemingly written across two columns.
Measurements: 2.7 × 3.2 × 0.8 cm.
Bibliography: N/A.

Bo 9493

Column I$^?$ and II$^?$

§ 1' 1' ^{TÚG}NÍG].⸢LÁM⸣.ḪI.⸢A[1] Š⸣[A
2']-x̣ ⸢x⸥ (eras.) [

---

§ 2' 3' ^{TÚG}*ka-ri-ú-u*]*l-li*[2] I ^{TÚG}BAR.S[I
4']-⸤x *e*$^?$⸣-*pa-an-du*[3] [
5' -*i*]*š*$^?$ VI SÍG *pa-a-*[*i*$^?$]

---

§ 3' 6'] ⸤*x-x-x*$^?$*-x*⸥ [
(broken off)

Text-critical notes: [1] Cf. KBo 18.194 (obv.) 3' (listings of articles of attire). This rare plural usage is instead of regular ^{TÚG}NÍG.LÁM.MEŠ. [2] For co-attestation of ^{TÚG}*kariulli* and ^{TÚG}BAR.SI see KBo 13.160 I 10' and KUB 17.18 II 21'-22'. [3] If the reading is correct, this is an alternate spelling for *i-pa-an-du/tu*, which denotes a valuable object of attire$^?$ (most recently O. Soysal, JAOS 136 [2016] 424). Cf. also the attestation *e-pa-an-d*[*u*$^?$] in KBo 22.147 obv. II$^?$ 14'.

155. Bo 9494

Description: Ritual?.
CTH: 470 "*Fragments de rituels.*"
Dating and Script: NS.
Remarks: One-sided small fragment.
Measurements: 2.4 × 2.8 × 1.1 cm.
Bibliography: N/A.

Bo 9494

§ 1' 1'](-)⌜*x-x*⌝(-)[
2']-*x̣-az ạr-*[*ḫa*?
3' *t*]*ar-na-an ḫar-tén*1)[
4']-*a-an gi-i*[*m-*
5']-*x̣ na-an* [
(broken off)

Text-critical note: 1) For *tarnan ḫarten* see KUB 14.13 + KUB 23.124 I 23 (CTH 378.IV.A), KUB 12.55 + 57 IV 10-11 (CTH 453.4.A) and KUB 60.161 II 7 (CTH 448.2.1.4.A). The usage *tarna-* with preceding noun(s) in ablative case (here lines 2'-3') recalls rather the context in KUB 12.55 + 57 IV 8-11.

156. Bo 9495

Description: Festival$^{?}$.
CTH: 670 “*Fragments divers.*”
Dating and Script: NS.
Remarks: One-sided fragment.
Measurements: 2.9 × 3.8 × 1.6 cm.
Bibliography: N/A.

Bo 9495

§ 1’ 1’]⸢*x*(-)*x̣*⸣[
2’ $^{LÚ.ME}$]^{Š}MUḪ̮ALDIM(?) *e*⸢*l-u̯*⸣[*a*$^{?}$-
3’]-*x̣-at*[1)] *a-rụ-u̯ạ-*⸢*ạ*$^{?}$*-x̣*⸣-[
4’]-*me*$^{?}$*-iš-mi nu-kán* DINGIR.MEŠ *ḫ̮ụ-u-*[*ma-an-te-eš*(?)
5’]-*x̤-zi nu* ^{GIŠ}IG *x̣*$^{?}$ [
6’ -*z*]*i nu-kán* $^{LÚ.ME}$[^{Š}
7’](-)⸤*x-at*$^{?}$*-x*⸥(-)[
(broken off)

Text-critical note: [1)] Alternatively to read [. . . -*z*]*i-la* ?

157. Bo 9497

Description: Ritual.
CTH: 409 "*Rituel de Tunnawiya, contre l'impureté*" or 448 "*Rituels à la déesse solaire de la terre*" ?
Dating and Script: MH$^{?}$/MS$^{?}$.
Remarks: One-sided fragment with two columns from the lower portion (with bottom part) of a tablet.
Measurements: 3.3 × 4.0 × 1.7 cm.
Bibliography: N/A.

Bo 9497

Left column

(Nothing preserved)

Right column

§ 2' 1' [. . .$^{?}$ *i*]*m-m*[*a*(-)

2' [*n*]*a-at-ká*⌈*n*⌉ [

3' *n̩am-ma* ÉSAG.ḪI.A̩ x̩$^{?}$-[

---

§ 2' 4' ^{MUNUS}ŠU.GI[1)]-*ma-*⌊*kán*⌋[2)] [

5' *nu k*⌊*u-iš-ki*$^{?}$⌋[

(bottom of the tablet)

Text-critical notes: [1)] This "*gi*" sign is resembles with the older forms. [2)] For co-attestation ÉSAG "grain-storage pit" and ^{MUNUS}ŠU.GI "Old Woman" in a near context see e.g., KBo 21.1+ III 8'-13' (CTH 409.II.Tf01.A), KUB 20.1 III 15-16 (CTH 719.1), KUB 35.34:2'-7' (CTH 762.5), KUB 55.45+ II 1-13 (CTH 409.II.Tf01.D), KUB 60.161 II 13-15 (CTH 448.2.1.4.A).

158. Bo 9498

Description: N/A.
CTH: 832 "*Fragments en langue hittite de nature inconnue.*"
Dating and Script: NS.
Remarks: One-sided fragment.
Measurements: 4.3 × 2.9 × 1.0 cm.
Bibliography: N/A.

Bo 9498

§ 1' 1' *-i]⌜š? da-me?-ẋ?⌝-[*
2' *]-ẋ[1]-e* EGIR-*pa [*
3' *-k]án? an-da [*
4' *]-ẋ-u̯a-aš-ši-ká[n*
5' *]-ẋ nu-u̯a-za i[š-*
6' *ša?-r]a-a[2] ti-i-i̯[a-*
7' *]-ni[3] me-mi-an [*
8' *-z]⸤i⸥ ᵈZạ?-[*
9' *](-)ẋ-x(-)[*
(broken off)

Text-critical notes: [1] The sign is probably "*me*". Thus, [*M*]*E-E* or [*ŠA-M*]*E-E* ? [2] Or: [*pa-r*]*a-a*. [3] To be restored as [*u*]-*ni me-mi-an* ? Cf. KBo 16.6 lower edge 4, KBo 50.30 + KUB 14.17 II 8', 13', KUB 6.41 I 34, 36 and KUB 14.24:19' (all Murš. II).

159. Bo 9500

Description: N/A.
CTH: 832 "*Fragments en langue hittite de nature inconnue.*"
Dating and Script: NS.
Remarks: One-sided fragment from the left portion (with edge) of a tablet that is too small to classify.
Measurements: 2.5 × 2.3 × 3.0 cm.
Bibliography: N/A.

Bo 9500

§ 1' 1' ⌜*x*⌝-[
2' *ŠA* [
3' *na-aš*(-)[
4' *nu-uš-š*[*a*?-*an*?
5' *nam-ma̤*(-)[
6' ⌞*nu*(-)*x-x̣*?⌟(-)[
(broken off)

160. Bo 9501

Description: N/A.
CTH: 832 "*Fragments en langue hittite de nature inconnue.*"
Dating and Script: NS.
Remarks: One-sided small fragment from the right? column of a tablet.
Measurements: 2.3 × 1.7 × 2.0 cm.
Bibliography: N/A.

Bo 9501

Right? column[1)]

§ 1' 1' ⌜*nam*⌝-*ma e*-[
2' *na-aš-ta a*[*n*?-
3' *ḫu̯-u̯a-ap-p*[*a*? [2)]-
4' *na-aš-ta a*[*n*-
5' [*Š*]⌞*A*? *x-x*⌟(-)[
(broken off)

Text-critical notes: **1)** The signs appear to be close to the edge or column-divider, so that nothing is missing at the beginning of the lines. **2)** Alternatively read *ḫu̯-u̯a-ap-p*[*í*(-) . . .].

161. Bo 9502

Description: Cult inventory or festival$^{?}$.
CTH: 530 or 670 “*Fragments divers.*”
Dating and Script: LNS$^{?}$.
Remarks: Fragment with the inscribed right edge of a tablet.
Measurements: 5.3 × 2.4 × 2.5 cm.
Bibliography: N/A.

Bo 9502

§ 1’ 1’]-*x̣-e*
2’]-*x̣* DÙ-*an-za* [1)]
3’ ^{URU}*G*]*a-aš-du-ḫa*[2)]
4’ . . .
5’]-*x̣-ši*
6’-7’ (traces)
8’]-*uš ša-ḫu-i̯a-an-ti*[3)]
9’]-*x̣-ta-ri* [4)]
10’-11’ . . .

---

§ 2’ 12’]-*x̤*
(broken off)

Text-critical notes: 1) There is an illegible sign as runover from the other side of the tablet. 2) The geographical name ^{URU}*Ka-aš-du-ḫa* is known only from KUB 53.16 V 15' and 17' (CTH 652). 3) This hapax is either a Hittite part. sg. d.-l. or a Luwian predicate in pres. pl. 3 of unknown meaning. Whether *šaḫuyanti* may be considered as a cognate of Luwian lemmas listed under **šaḫui-* (*šaḫuidala-*, *šaḫuidara-* etc.) by E. Laroche, DLL (1959) 84 and H. C. Melchert, CLL (1993) 184 cannot be assured yet. 4) There are some illegible signs as runover from the other side of the tablet.

162. Bo 9503

Description: Historical?.
CTH: 215 *"Fragments non caractérisés."*
Dating and Script: NS.
Remarks: Two-sided small fragment from the top (rev.?) and bottom (obv.?) part of a tablet.
Measurements: 3.0 × 3.5 × 2.5 cm.
Bibliography: N/A.

Bo 9503 obv.?

Bo 9503 rev.?

Obverse?

§ 1' 1' . . .

______

§ 2' 2' Š]*A* KUR LÚKÚR [

______

(bottom of the tablet)

Reverse?

§ 1 1 -*i*]*š*?

2 *ku*]-*ẹ-da-ni-i*[*k-ki*]

3]-*x̣-u-i-ẹ*?-[

4]-⌞*x̣-pí*?⌟(-)[

(broken off)

163. Bo 9504

Description: Historical.

CTH: 215 "*Fragments non caractérisés.*"

Dating and Script: (E)NH.

Remarks: One-sided fragment of which each paragraph is written as single line. In this respect Bo 9504 shows similarities to KUB 31.8 (CTH 40.VI.b.6). Furthermore, both fragments have identical (archaic) "URU" signs (here line 3' and KUB 31.8 line 4') and narrative in pret. sg. 1 (here line 2' and KUB 31.8 line 10'). Thus, they may possibly belong to the same tablet.

Measurements: 3.7 × 3.6 × 1.1 cm.

Bibliography: N/A.

Bo 9504

§ 1' 1'](-)⌜*x*⌝-*u̯*⌜*a*⌝-[

---

§ 2' 2'] *ụ́-tạḫ-ḫ̮ụ-ụn*[1)] [

---

§ 3' 3']-*x̣* URU-*an ša-x̣*-[

---

§ 4' 4'](-)⸤*az-zi-i̯*⸥[*a*(?)(-)

(broken off)

Text-critical note: [1)] This spelling is attested, however incomplete, also in KBo 3.22 rev. 58 (OS): *ú-taḫ-ḫ*[*u-un*].

164. Bo 9505

Description: Oracle$^{?}$.
CTH: 582 "*Fragments d'oracles.*"
Dating and Script: NS.
Remarks: One-sided fragment from the lower portion (with bottom part) of a tablet that is slightly abraded. The script is a bit careless and sometimes difficult to read.
Measurements: 3.4 × 4.6 × 0.8 cm.
Bibliography: N/A.

Bo 9505

§ 1' 1']-*p̣í-ịz*(?) *Ụ́-Ụ*[*L*(?) $^{1)}$

____

____

§ 2' 2'] *ạ-pé-e-da-ni-ma-k*[*án*$^{?}$
3' *a-p*]*é-e-ez* KAŠ$^{?2)}$-*ni-i*[*t*$^{?}$(-)
4'] DINGIR-*LIM-mạ ku-ịt*$^{?}$(-)[
5'] *na-at-za I-N*[*A*$^{?}$

____

(bottom of the tablet)

Text-critical notes: $^{1)}$ To be restored as [*a*]-*p̣í-ịz Ụ́-Ụ*[*L* SI×SÁ-*at*] ? Cf. KUB 16.32+ II 18': *a-pí-iz UL* SI×SÁ-*at* (likewise followed by a paragraph stroke). $^{2)}$ The sign is a clear "*pí*".

165. Bo 9506

Description: Cult inventory$^{?}$.
CTH: 530 "*Fragments divers.*"
Dating and Script: LNS.
Remarks: One-sided fragment from the right portion (with edge) of a tablet.
Measurements: 5.1 × 2.6 × 1.1 cm.
Bibliography: N/A.

Bo 9506

§ 1' 1'](-)x̣-*še-e*[*š*(-)
2' . . .

---

§ 2' 3'](.)x̣(.)ŠẸ$^{?}$ *ḫar-z*[*i*]

---

§ 3' 4' Z]Ì.DA.DUR$_5$ KÙ$^{?}$ [1)].GẠ
5' -*t*]*a*
6'-7' . . .
8']-x̣-*ša-ma-kán*
9']-x̣ ^{d}U
10' *UP*$^{?}$]-*NỊ* 1/2 *ši-iš-x̣*$^{?}$(-)[
11']⌞*A-N*⌟*A* ^{d}Ụ$^{?}$
(broken off)

Text-critical note: [1)] The shape of this sign is obscure. For ZÌ.DA.DUR$_5$ "moist flour" and KÙ.GA "pure" in near context see KUB 51.31 I 4-5 (CTH 530).

166. Bo 9507

Description: Festival.

CTH: 626 *"Fête de la "hâte" (nuntarriyashas)."*

Dating and Script: OH/NS.

Remarks: Bo 9507 is a one-sided fragment, and lines 1'–7' are duplicate of KUB 10.14 I 3–9 (CTH 626.Tg06.III.1.D) and parallel to KUB 11.34+ IV 22'–30' (CTH 626.Tg06.III.1.A) and KUB 44.9 obv. III 3–11 (CTH 626.Tg06.III.1.I) from where the restorations are taken. Although Bo 9507 lines 1'–4' and KUB 10.14 I 3–6 would perfecly fit for a direct join, the different line numbers and paragraph strokes after § 2 of both fragments do not permit this.

Measurements: 3.8 × 3.8 × 1.4 cm.

Bibliography: N/A.

Bo 9507

§ 1' 1' [*me-ma-i* (^{LÚ}*pal-u̯a-tal-la-aš*[1] *p*)]*ạl-u̯ạ-ạ*-⸢*iz*⸣-[*zi* . . . $^{?}$]

---

§ 2' 2' [(^{LÚ}SAGI.A I ^{NINDA}*u̯a-ge-eš-š*)*a*]*r a-aš-ka-a*[*z ú-da-a*$^{?}$*-i*]

3' [(LUGAL-*i pa-a-i* LUGAL-*uš pár-ši-i̯*)]*a ták-kán u̯*[*a-a-ki* ^{LÚ}SAGI.A-*aš*$^{?}$*-kán*]

4' [(LUGAL-*i* NINDA.GUR$_{4}$.RA *e-ep-zi n*)]*ạ-an-kán p*[*a-ra-a pé-e-da-i*]

---

§ 3' 5'$^{?}$ [($^{\text{LÚ.MEŠ}}$ḪUB.BÍ *tar-ku-u̯a-an*)*-zi*(?)][2] [

---

§ 4' 6" [(*pár-aš-na-u-aš-kán* ^{LÚ}SAG)I.A-*aš*] *ụ-ị*[*z-zi*]

7" [(LUGAL MUNUS.LUGAL TUŠ-*aš* ^{d}*Wa*$_{a}$*-a*)*-ḫi-ši-i*]*n a-k*[*u-u̯a*$^{?}$*-an-zi*]

(broken off)

Text-critical notes: 1) KUB 10.14 I 3 reads erroneously ^{LÚ}*pal-u̯a-tal-la-«tal-la-»aš*. 2) The reconstruction of this paragraph is highly problematic, and the field here could be vacat as well: it looks a bit narrow for writing, and the phrase $^{LÚ.MEŠ}$ḪUB.BÍ *tarkuwanzi* "the dancers dance" never occurs in a separate paragraph as supposed here, which is rather customary for *parašnauaš=kan* ^{LÚ}SAGI.A-*aš uizzi* "the cupbearer of squtting comes" in the following line.

167. Bo 9508

Description: Festival.
CTH: 670 "*Fragments divers.*"
Dating and Script: NS.
Remarks: Bo 9508 is a one-sided fragment, and lines 1'–6' duplicate KBo 47.84 V$^{?}$ 2'–6' (CTH 592), KBo 52.113 V$^{?}$ 1'–7' (CTH 606.?) and KUB 10.54 IV 12'–16' (CTH 669.3.A) from where the restorations are adopted.
Measurements: 3.2 × 4.5 × 1.1 cm.
Bibliography: N/A.

Bo 9508

§ 1' 1'] ⌜*na-a*⌝[(*n-kán* ^{GIŠ}BANŠUR-*i*)]

2' [(*da-a-i nu*)] *ḫu-u-m*[(*a-an-du-uš*)]

3' [(^{NINDA}*ḫar-šu*)]-*uš*[1] *pár*-[(*ši-i̯a*)]

4' [(*na-aš*)]-*kán*[2] LÚ ^{GI}[(^{Š}BANŠUR-*aš*[3]))]

5' [(^{GIŠ}BANŠ)]UR-<*i*>[4] *ḫar-ap*-[(*zi*)]

---

§ 2' 6' [(I NINDA.GUR$_4$.R)]⌞A-*ma*⌟-*ká*[(*n* LÚ ^{GIŠ}BANŠUR)]

(broken off)

Text-critical notes: [1] KBo 52.113 V$^{?}$ 4': ^{NINDA}*ḫar-ša-uš*; KUB 10.54 IV 14': NINDA.GUR$_4$.RA.ḪI.A. [2] KBo 52.113 V$^{?}$ 5': *na-an-kán*. [3] KUB 10.54 IV 15' omits -*aš*. [4] Or: [*A-NA* ^{GIŠ}BANŠ]UR which is less probably due to space reasons.

168. Bo 9509

Description: Ritual.

CTH: 470 "*Fragments de rituels.*"

Dating and Script: NS.

Remarks: Bo 9509 is a one-sided fragment. My early suggestion that Bo 9509 lines 1'–7' might directly join KUB 8.39 lines 4'–10' (CTH 470.235) has been not fully confirmed due to syntactical problems. The context of Bo 9509 is very similar to KUB 8.39: 4'–10' from where the restorations are adopted.

Measurements: 3.4 × 2.9 × 1.8 cm.

Bibliography: N/A.

Bo 9509

Bo 9509 (right edge)

§ 1' . . .

---

§ 2'
1' *ḫu-u-i]t-tị-[i̯a*$^{?}$*-at*$^{?}$*-ti*$^{?}$]
2' *ḫu-u-i]*⌜*t*⌝*-ti-i̯ạ-ạ[t*$^{?}$*-ti*$^{?}$]
3'] *nụ-ụš-ši-iš-tạ* ⌜*kar-a*⌝[*p-zi*]
4' *kar-a]p-dụ nu a-pa-a-at-t[a]*
5' *-a]*⌞*n*$^{?}$⌟*-za*
6' *-š]i-kán kar-ap-du-*⌜*ma*$^{?}$⌝
7' *ir-ḫ]a-a-iz-zi*

---

§ 3' 8'](-)⌞*x-x-an*$^{?}$*-x*⌟(-)[. . .]⌞*x x*⌟

(broken off)

169. Bo 9511 + KBo 3.38

Description: Historical.

CTH: 3.1.B "*Fragments nommant la ville de Zalpa.*"

Dating and Script: OH/NS.

Remarks: Bo 9511 is one-sided fragment, and its lines 1'–5' directly join KUB 3.38 rev. 28'–32' (see *Konkordanz*). Duplicate is KBo 22.2 rev. 10'–15' (OS; CTH 3.1.A) from where the restorations are adopted.

Measurements: 4.7 × 2.0 × 2.1 cm.

Bibliography: S. Košak, hethiter.net/: hetkonk (v.1.91).

Bo 9511

Bo 9511 + KBo 3.38 rev. (composite image)

Reverse

(Line numbers of Bo 9511 are in parentheses)

§ 4' 27' [(*I-N*)]*A* MU.III.KAM LUGAL-*uš I-NA* ^{URU}*Za-ạl-pa pa-it* LU[GAL-*u*]*š* ^{URU}*Za-al-pa* MU.III.KAM *kat-ta*

28' (= 1') ⸢*e-eš-t*⸣*a ta-ba-ar-na-aš* ^{m}*Ḫa-ạp-pí-in* URU-*ạz kạt-ta ú-e-ek-ta*

29' (= 2') *Ù* L[(Ú.M)]EŠ URU-*LIM Ú-UL pí-ạn-zị nu-uš dam-m*[*i-i*]*š-šir*$_9$[1)] *še-a e-ki-ir*

30' (= 3') LUGAL-*uš* ^{U}[(^{R})]^{U}*Ḫa-at-tu-ši* DỊNGIR.MEŠ-*na-aš ạ-ru-u̯a-u-u̯a-an-z*[(*i*)] *ụ̯-it Ù* $^{\text{LÚ.MEŠ}}$GAL

31' (= 4') *a-pí-i̯a da-a-li-iš ša-aš Ạ-NA* LÚ.MEŠ URU-*LIM te-e*[*t*] *ú-uk-u̯a* LUGAL-*uš-me-e*[*t*]

32' (= 5') *ki-iš-ḫ̮*[(*a*)]-*ạt Ù* ÉRIN.MEŠ *kạt-te-eš-ši nu* URU-*LAM Ẹ̣L*-[*Q*]*É QA-TI*

---

§ 5' 33' (= 6') . . .

(broken off)

Text-critical note: [1)] Written with the sign "*šar* = *šir*$_9$"; for this value see Chr. Rüster - E. Neu, HZL (1989) under no. 353.

170. Bo 9512

Description: Ritual or festival.
CTH: 470 "*Fragments de rituels*" or 670 "*Fragments divers*."
Dating and Script: NS.
Remarks: Two-sided fragment from the top (obv.$^{?}$) and bottom (rev.$^{?}$) right portion (with edges) of a tablet.
Measurements: 2.9 × 2.0 × 1.8 cm.
Bibliography: N/A.

Bo 9512 obv.$^{?}$

Bo 9512 rev.$^{?}$

Obverse$^{?}$

§ 1	1	-*z*]*i*$^{?}$
	2	]-*x̣*
	3	. . .
	4	]-*x̣*-*ti*-*i̯ạ*(-)[. . . $^{?}$]
	5	(-)*u̯*]*a*-*ạr*-[. . . $^{?}$]
	6	](-)*ụ́*$^{?}$-*u̯a*-*a*[*n*-

(broken off)

Reverse$^{?}$

§ 1'	1'	.Ḫ]⌜I.A⌝-*i̯ạ*
	2'	G]UNNI.MEŠ

(bottom of the tablet)

171. Bo 9513

Description: N/A.
CTH: 832 "*Fragments en langue hittite de nature inconnue.*"
Dating and Script: MS.
Remarks: One-sided fragment from the upper portion (with edge) of a tablet.
Measurements: 2.5 × 3.0 × 1.1 cm.
Bibliography: N/A.

Bo 9513

§ 1 1 *ge*$^{?\,1)}$-*e*]*n-zu-aš te-x̣*-[
2] ^{LÚ}SIPA.UDU x̣-[

---

§ 2 3 *ge*$^{?\,2)}$-*en*]-*zu-aš* [
4]-*e-e*[*l*(-)

(broken off)

Text-critical notes: [1)] Or alternatively read [. . . ^{d}E]N.ZU-*aš* ? [2)] Or alternatively read [. . . ^{d}EN].ZU-*aš* ? A restoration with *ták-ku* (*I-NA* ITU.x.KAM) ^{d}EN.ZU-*aš* "if the moon . . . (in the . . . th month)" as protasis of a lunar omen seems to be less probable due to mention of ^{LÚ}SIPA.UDU "shepherd" in line 2.

172. Bo 9514 + Bo 3251

Description: Festival.

CTH: 674 *"Fragments nommant la fête du wuruli."*

Dating and Script: LNS.

Remarks: Bo 9514 is a one-sided fragment, and lines 5'–9' directly join other unpublished piece Bo 3251 II 14'–18' (CTH 674).

Measurements: 3.4 × 3.0 × 0.3 cm.

Bibliography: V. Haas, KN (1970) 254; F. Fuscagni, HPMM 6 (2007) 18–19 (both without Bo 9514).

Bo 9514

Bo 9514 + Bo 3251 obv. II

Bo 9514 + Bo 3251 obv. II (detail of the "patch-join")

Obverse II

(Line numbers of Bo 9514 in parantheses)

§ 1’	10’ (= 1’)	*(-)i]š$^{?}$-ḫ̮a-aš-x̣(-)[*
	11’ (= 2’)	*]-x̣$^{?}$-a$^{?}$-aš*[1] *i-i̯[a-*
	12’ (= 3’)	*]-x̣$^{?}$ zị*[2]*-nu-pí(-)[*
	13’ (= 4’)	^{URU}*N]e-ri-i[k(-)*

---

§ 2’	14’ (= 5’)	*]-⸢a$^{?}$-a⸣n pa-ra-a* U$_4$.KAM-*ạt u̯a-ar-[*
	15’ (= 6’)	*-e]š* DINGIR.MEŠ *u̯a-ar-ap-p[a]-an-zi* ÙKU.Ḫ[I.A(-)
	16’ (= 7’)	*u̯a-a]r-ap-zi ne-ku-uz me-e-ḫu-ni [*
	17’ (= 8’)	*-k]án$^{?}$* ^{É}*k⸤a⸥-rị-im-ma-na-aš a[n-da(-)*
	18’ (= 9’)	*]⸤ x x$^{?}$ ḫal⸥-za-a-i* ^{GIŠ}*mu-kar [*

(Bo 9514 breaks here off; text continues in Bo 3251 II 19’ ff.)

Text-critical notes: [1)] Or read [. . .]-*i̯ạ-aš.* [2)] Although this sign slightly differs from “*zi*” in line 7’, it is unlikely “*gi*”. However, a word *zinupi-* is hitherto unknown. Considering a scribal error “*zi*” for “*gi*” one might suggest *kinupi-*, which designates a kind of vessel.

173. Bo 9515

Description: Oracle.
CTH: 568 "*Sur la célébration de plusieurs fêtes.*"
Dating and Script: NH/NS.
Remarks: One-sided fragment.
Measurements: 3.6 × 3.0 × 0.9 cm.
Bibliography: N/A.

Bo 9515

§ 1' 1' *ša]-kṳ-⸢u̯a-aš-šar(?)-x̣(-)x̤*$^?$⸣ [1)][
2'](-)x̤ Ị$^?$-ŠỤ *ḫa-pu-ša-an-z[i* [2)]

---

§ 2' 3' EZEN$_4$] ⸤NÍG⸥.MỤNUS.ÚS.SÁ[3)] EZEN$_4$ MU.[KAM$^?$ [4)]
4'](-)x̤$^?$ DÙ-*an-zi* GAM-*a[n-na*[5)]

---

§ 3' 5' EZEN$_4$ NÍG.M]UNUS.ÚS.SÁ EZẸN$_4$ [MU.KAM$^?$
6' D]Ù-*an-zi* GAM-[*an-na*

---

§ 4' 7' E]ZEN$_4$ M[U.KAM$^?$
8' DÙ-*an-z]i* [
(broken off)

Text-critical notes: [1)] To read and restore as [EZEN$_4$ *ša]-kṳ-⸢u̯a-aš-šar-an*⸣ or [EZEN$_4$.ḪI.A *ša]-kṳ-⸢u̯a-aš-šar-uš*⸣ ?; cf. KBo 14.21 II 14' (CTH 565), KUB 50.34 II 2 (CTH 568.F). [2)] For the cult expression EZEN$_4$ x-*ŠU ḫapušanzi* "they will make up the uncelebrated festival x-time(s)" see e.g., KBo 2.6 + KUB 18.51 II 16-18 (CTH 569.3.I), KBo 14.21 I 9', 13'-14'. [3)] For NÍG.MUNUS.ÚS(.SÁ) "bride price" see Chr. Rüster - E. Neu, HZL (1989) under no. 369. Only a few attestations of EZEN$_4$ NÍG.MUNUS.ÚS(.SÁ) (Hitt. = EZEN$_4$ *kušata-*) "dowry-festival" are known to me: ẸZEN$_4$ NÍG.MUNUS.ÚS.SÁ$^!$-*aš* (KBo 16.63 obv. between lines 15'-16') and incomplete EZEN$_4$ NÍG.MUNUS.[ÚS.SÁ$^?$] (KUB 46.29 obv. 11'). [4)] Perhaps to be reconstructed as EZEN$_4$ MU.[KAM (*ŠA*) MU.x.KAM]; cf. KBo 14.21 I 55, II 13'. [5)] Cf. KBo 14.21 I 56: DÙ-*an-zi kat-ta-an-na*.

174. Bo 9516 + KUB 17.24

Description: Festival.
CTH: 691.2 "*Fête witass(iy)as.*"
Dating and Script: MH/(E)NS.
Remarks: Bo 9516 is a one-sided fragment, and line 5' directly joins KUB 17.24 III 1' (CTH 691.2). All restorations are taken from KUB 17.24 III 2'–7' and partially from parallel KBo 29.72 + KBo 14.96 II 7'–12' (CTH 692.5.D).
Measurements: 1.7 × 3.0 × 1.4 cm.
Bibliography: N/A.

Bo 9516

Bo 9516 + KUB 17.24 rev. III (composite image)

Bo 9516 + KUB 17.24 rev. III (composite image, detail)

Reverse III

(Line numbers of KUB 17.24 are in parentheses)

§ 1' 1' ⸢EN.SIS⸣[KUR-*kán* 1 UDU *A-NA* ^{d}*Ḫu-u̯a-aš-ša-an-na*[1] *ši-pa-an-ti*]

2' *nu* ^{LÚ}MUḪALDIM U[DU *ḫu-u-e-ek-zi* ^{UZU}*a-ú-li-iš*]

3' *ši-i-e-ez-zi* ^{LÚ}SA[GI-*aš-ma*[2] *A-NA* EN.SISKUR *a-ku-u̯a-an-na*]

4' *pa-a-i nu* EN.SISKUR ^{d}[*Ḫu-u̯a-aš-ša-an-na-an e-ku-zi*[3]]

5' (= 1') ^{LÚ}NA̤R S̤ÌR-*RU̥* ⸢I NINDA.GUR$_{4}$.RA⸣ [*pár-ši-i̯a*]

(Bo 9516 breaks off here; text continues in KUB 17.24 III 2'ff.)

Text-critical notes: [1] The restorations with the name of ^{d}Ḫuwaššanna here and in line 4' are certain since in the following paragraph (KUB 17.24 III 2', 6') the receiver of the offerings is mentioned as *ŠA* ^{d}*Ḫuwaššanna attaš* ^{d}[UTU]; further occurrences are compiled by B. H. L. van Gessel, Onomasticon I (1998) 172. For the sequence of ^{d}Ḫuwaššanna → ^{d}UTU see KBo 29.72 + KBo 14.96 II 7' and 13'. [2] Cf. KBo 29.72 + KBo 14.96 II 9'. [3] Cf. KBo 29.72 + KBo 14.96 II 11'.

175. Bo 9517

Description: Festival.
CTH: 500 "*Fragments de rituels (ou de fêtes) du Kizzuwatna*" or 670 "*Fragments divers.*"
Dating and Script: NS.
Remarks: One-sided fragment from the right column of a tablet.
Measurements: 3.3 × 1.9 × 1.0 cm.
Bibliography: N/A.

Bo 9517

Right column

§ 1' 1' (traces)
2' *na-ạt x̣-[*
3' *ti-it-t[a-nu-*
4' ^{DUG}*ḫu-u-up-[ru*$^?$*-uš*$^?$*-ḫi*$^?$(-)[1)]

---

§ 2' 5' *nu-kán* ^{L}[^{Ú}
6' $^{\text{LÚ.MEŠ}}$BA[LAG.DI(-)
7' *na-aš m[a*$^?$*-*
8' *ụš*$^?$*-⌞x-x*$^?$⌟(-)[

(broken off)

Text-critical note: [1)] Alternatively restore as ^{DUG}*ḫu-u-up-[pár*$^?$(-) . . .].

176. Bo 9518 + Bo 4744 + KUB 26.1a

Description: Instruction.

CTH: 255.2.E "*Instructions de Tudhaliya IV aux majordomes* (LÚ.SAG)."

Dating and Script: Tudḫ. IV / (L)NS.

Remarks: Bo 9518 is a one-sided fragment, and lines 1'–8' directly join Bo 4744 I 3'–10' + KUB 26.1a obv. I 1'–2' (CTH 255.2.E). Duplicate is KUB 26.8 I 25'–36' (CTH 255.2.B) from where the restorations are taken.

Bo 4744 was recently published by R. Akdoğan, AoF 40 (2013) 2–4 (with text copy), however, treated there as a duplicate of KUB 26.1a. For the join Bo 4744 (+) KUB 26.1a see *Konkordanz* (http://www.hethport.uni-wuerzburg.de). The first four lines of Bo 4744 are now lost.

Measurements: 3.5 × 2.5 × 1.1 cm.

Bibliography: E. von Schuler, HDA (1957) 10 (text edition of CTH 255); J. L. Miller, Royal Hittite Instructions (2013) 298–99 (latest text edition of CTH 255); R. Akdoğan, AoF 40, 2–4; O. Soysal, NABU 2015/3, 113–14 (transliteration, translation and remarks).

Bo 9518

Bo 4744 + Bo 9518

Bo 4744 + Bo 9518 + KUB 26.1a obv. I
(composite image)

Obverse I

(Line numbers of Bo 9518 in parentheses)

§ 1' 1' *ag-g*[(*a*$^{?}$)-

2' *IŠ-T*[(*U* ZI LUGAL *x*)-

3' (= 1') *le-ẹ k*⌜*u*⌝-[(*iš-ki a-uš-z*)*i*

4' (= 2') *ku-e-dạ-n*[(*i-ik-ki*) . . . (*nu-za A-NA* ^{d}UTU-*ŠI*) . . . $^{?}$]

5’ (= 3’) *ar-lụ-u̯a-x̤*(-)$^{1)}$[. . . $^{?}$ (*ḫa-at-te*$_9$*-eš-šar*)(-) . . . $^{?}$ *le-e*(?)]

6’ (= 4’) *i-i̯a-zi* [(*na-aš-kán ta-me*)*-e-da-ni an-da-an*]

7’ (= 5’) *le-e ku-ẹ-*[(*da*)*-ni-ik-ki pa-iz-zi*]

---

§ 2’ 8’ (= 6’) *na-aš-ma* ^{LÚ}*a-r*⌞*a-a*⌟[*š̌*$^{?}$(-) . . . (*a-aš-šu-uš*)]

9’ (= 7’) ^{d}UTU-*ŠI-ma-aš-š*⌞*i*⌟ *mẹ-*⸢*m*⸣[*a-aḫ*$^{?}$*-ḫi*$^{?}$ (EGIR GAM-*u̯a-ra-a*)*n-kán kar-aš*(?)]

10’ (= 8’) *nạ-ạn-za-an-kán* EGIR GAM [(*Ú-UL*) *kar-aš-zi* . . . $^{?}$]

(Bo 9518 breaks here off; text continues in Bo 4744 I 11’ ff. + KUB 26.1a :3’ ff.)

Text-critical note: $^{1)}$ The sign “*lu*” has an initial vertical, and the incomplete word is a hapax of unknown meaning (something unfavorable ?). There are slight traces that begin with a *winkelhaken*, thus the sign may be “*ši*” or “*ar*”. G. Beckman suggests the reading *ar-ku-u̯a-a*[*r*] (personal communication).

177. Bo 9519

Description: Ritual$^?$.
CTH: 470 "*Fragments de rituels.*"
Dating and Script: NH/LNS.
Remarks: One-sided fragment.
Measurements: 3.5 × 2.3 × 0.5 cm.
Bibliography: N/A.

Bo 9519

§ 1'	1'	-]⸢*iz-zi*⸣ [
	2'	-*k*]*án* DỊNGIR-*LUM k*[*u-iš*$^?$
	3'	-*e*]*š-kán-zi n*[*u*$^?$ [1)](-)
	4'	DI]NGIR.MEŠ-*aš pí-ra-a*[*n*
	5'	-*r*]⌞*a-a*⌟(?)[2)] *ú-u̯a-an- z*[*i*
	6'	]-*x̣* DUMU.LÚ.U_{19}.LU-*UṬ*$^?$-[*TI*$^?$
	7'	*ku-u*]-*uš tar-pa-li*-[*uš*(-)[3)]
	8'	*ti*]-⌞*i*⌟*t-ta-nu-mi*[4)] [
	9'	]-⌞*x̣*$^?$-*u*$^?$⌟-*en* ⌞*na-a*⌟[*t*$^?$(-)
	(broken off)	

Text-critical notes: [1)] Or read *n*[*a*-. . .]. [2)] Restore [*pa-r*]⌞*a-a*⌟ or [*ša-r*]⌞*a-a*⌟ ? [3)] This unique spelling is against the customary form *tar-pa-al-li*-°. [4)] For the phrase *kūš tarpalliuš titta*- "to install these substitutes" see KUB 60.161 II 8 (CTH 448.2.1.4.A).

178. Bo 9520

Description: Sumerian.
CTH: 819 “Fragments.”
Dating and Script: NS.
Remarks: One-sided fragment.
Measurements: 2.5 × 3.7 × 2.1 cm.
Bibliography: N/A.

Bo 9520

§ 1' 1']-⌜*x*(-)*ir*$^{?}$⌝ [
2']-*x̣*$^{?}$-*x̣* [

---

§ 2' 3' [1]]-*x̣* *nạm-tar*$^{?}$ *nu-gạ́l*$^{?}$ *á-gál* *š*⌜*ub-x*⌝-[

---

§ 3' 4' ^{d}*E*]*n-ki lugal-ab-zu* [2] -*ke*$_4$ [3][
5'](-)*x̣*$^{?}$-*x̣-ra ḫé-éb-ba*$^{?}$ [4]-*an-sụm*(-)*x̣*-[
6' [. . . $^{?}$]

---

§ 4' 7'']-⌞*x*⌟ *la*-[
(broken off)

Text-critical notes: [1] This single-line paragraph is written with a small and careless script. [2] “[E]nki, the king of the *abzu*”; for further occurrences see A. W. Sjöberg, The Sumerian Dictionary, Part II (1994) 188 f. [3] With this reading I follow P. Michalowski (Ann Arbor, MI). [4] With this reading I follow J. Crisostomo (Ann Arbor, MI).

179. Bo 9522

Description: N/A.
CTH: 831 “*Fragments en langue inconnue ou indéterminée.*”
Dating and Script: N/A.
Remarks: One-sided fragment that is too small to classify.
Measurements: 4.1 × 2.9 × 1.5 cm.
Bibliography: N/A.

Bo 9522

§ 1’	1’	]-*x̣ a-x̣*(-)[
	2’	](-)*tu-x̣*(-)[
§ 2’	3’	](-)*at-x̣*(-)[
	4’	](-)*x̣*[1)]-*ḫ̮a-x̣*(-)[
	5’	](-)*x̣-kạ́n*?(-)[
	(broken off)	

Text-critical note: [1)] Sign is “*ri*” or “*ar*”.

180. Bo 9523

Description: N/A.
CTH: 832 "*Fragments en langue hittite de nature inconnue.*"
Dating and Script: N/A.
Remarks: One-sided fragment from the right portion (with edge) of a tablet that is too small to classify.
Measurements: 3.4 × 2.3 × 2.7 cm.
Bibliography: N/A.

Bo 9523

§ 1'	1'	]-*x̣*
§ 2'	2'	]-*it*
	3'-4' ...	
	5'	]-*x̣-zi*
	6'	]-*x̣*
	(broken off)	

181. Bo 9524

Description: Ritual or festival.
CTH: 470 "*Fragments de rituels*" or 670 "*Fragments divers.*"
Dating and Script: NS.
Remarks: Two-sided fragment from the top and bottom part (with edges) of a tablet.
Measurements: 2.1 × 4.4 × 1.6 cm.
Bibliography: N/A.

Bo 9524 obv.$^{?}$

Bo 9524 rev.$^{?}$

Obverse$^{?}$

§ 1' 1' *kụ-rạ-a*[*n-zi*$^{?}$
2' *nu* ÉRIN.MEŠ-*a*⸢*z*⸣ [
(bottom of the tablet)

Reverse$^{?}$

§ 1 1]⸤NINDA⸥.GỤR$_4$.RA.Ḫ̮I.A *ŠA* ZÌ.D[A(.)
2 (traces)
(broken off)

182. Bo 9525

Description: Ritual or festival.
CTH: 470 "*Fragments de rituels*" or 670 "*Fragments divers*."
Dating and Script: ENS$^{?}$.
Remarks: One-sided small fragment.
Measurements: 2.3 × 3.6 × 1.6 cm.
Bibliography: N/A.

Bo 9525

§ 1’ 1’]⸢MUNUS.LUGAL[1)](?)⸣(-)[ ](-)ẋ$^{?}$(-)[
2’] *ma-ạ-ạn an-tu-uḫ-š*[*i*$^{?}$(-)
3’] *ạ-ra-aḫ-za gị-i*⸤*m-r*⸥[*i*$^{?}$
4’](-)ẋ̤$^{?}$ *A-NA* ^{d}⸤*x-x*$^{?}$⸥(-)[

---

§ 2’ 5’](-)⸤*x-x*⸥(-)[
(broken off)

Text-critical note: [1)] If the reading ⸢MUNUS.LUGAL⸣ is correct, the mention of the queen (alongside with the king ?) here and *araḫza gimri* "outside to the countryside" (line 3’) recall the context of KBo 29.203 rev. 4’, KUB 35.136 + I 4’, 7’ and also KBo 23.57 lt. e. 1, which are all religious texts from the Luwian milieu (Ištanuwan and Lallupiyan; CTH 771-773).

183. Bo 9526 + KBo 6.10 + KBo 6.20

Description: Laws.

CTH: 292.II.b.A *"Deuxième série: 'si une vigne'."*

Dating and Script: OH/NS.

Remarks: Bo 9526 is a missing piece from the right edge of KBo 6.10 + KBo 6.20 obverse II and reverse III. Its lines II 1'–9' directly join KBo 6.10 + KBo 6.20 II 21–29', and III 1'–9' directly join KBo 6.10 + III 9'–17'. Duplicates are KUB 29.28 + I 10'–13' (OS; CTH 292.I.A) and KUB 29.29 + II 2'–8' (OS; CTH 292.I.A) from where the restorations are taken. For technical reasons, a composite image of Bo 9526 + KBo 6.10 + KBo 6.20 could not be generated.

Measurements: 4.1 × 1.7 × 2.5 cm.

Bibliography: J. Friedrich, HG (1959) 68 f., 70 f.; H. A. Hoffner, LH (1997) 116 f., 119–21 (both without Bo 9526); O. Soysal, NABU 2015/3, 114–16 (transliteration and remarks).

Bo 9526 obv. II (edge)

Bo 9526 rev. III (edge)

KBo 6.10 + KBo 6.20 + Bo 9526

Obverse II

(Line numbers of Bo 9526 in parentheses)

LH § 128/*25

§ 6' . . .

21' (= 1') *ta-i-e-ez-zi an-da-aš-še<<-aš-še>> a-pé-e-ni-šu-u-u̯a-an pạ-ạ-ị*

22' (= 2') *ták-ku ša*$^!$*-ma-na-az* NA[$_4$.ḪI.A-*u*]⌞*š*$^?$ *ku-iš-ki*[1)] *ta*⌟*-i-e-*[*e*]*z-zi*

23' (= 3') *A-NA* II NA$_4$ X NA$_4$.ḪI.A *pa-*[(*a*)]-⌜*i ták-ku*⌝ [. . . *-az*$^?$] ⌞^{NA4}*ḫu-u*⌟*-ḫạ-an*[2)]

24' (= 4') *na-aš-ma* ^{NA4}*ḫar-mi-i̯a-al-li ku-ịš-ki*

25' (= 5') *ta-i-e-ez-zi* II GÍN.GÍN KÙ.BABBAR *pa-a-i*

LH § 129/*26

§ 7' 26' (= 6') *ták-ku* <ŠA> ANŠE.KUR.RA *na-aš-ma* ˌ ANŠE.GÌR.NUN.NA ˌ ^{KUŠ}*an-na-nu-u*⌜*z*⌝-[*z*]*i*

27' (= 7') ^{KUŠ}*ga-az-zi-mu-el* [*ša-ku-u̯a*(?)-*a*]*l-li*[3)] *kat-ra-al* ZẠBAR

28' (= 8') *ku-iš-ki ta-a-i-e-e*[*z-zi ka-r*]*u-ú* I MA.NA KÙ.BABBAR *pẹ́-eš-kir*

29' (= 9') *ki-nu-na* ⌞XII⌟ GÍN.GÍN KÙ.BABB⌜AR⌝ [*pa-a-i*] *pár-na-aš-še-i̯a šu-u̯a-a-iz-zi*

(Bo 9526 breaks here off; text continues in KBo 6.10 + KBo 6.20 II 30' ff.)

KBo 6.10 + Bo 9526

Reverse III

(Line numbers of Bo 9526 in parantheses)

LH § 144/*33

§ 3' 9' (= 1') *ták-ku* ^{LÚ}ŠU.I ^{URUDU}*zi-na-*[*al-li a-ri-i*(*š-ši pa*)]-⌜*a*?-*i*?⌝

10' (= 2') *tu-uš ḫar-ni-ik-zi* [. . . *š*(*a-a-k*)*u-u̯a-*(*aš-ša-r*)]*u-uš* ⌜*pa-a*⌝-*i*

11'–13' (= 3'–5') . . .

LH § 145/*34

§ 4' 14' (= 6') *ták-ku* É.GU$_4$ *ku-iš-ki* [(*ú-e-te-ez-zi*)] *x̣*?

15' (= 7') VI GÍN.GÍN KÙ.BABBAR *pa-a-i t*[*ák-ku* . . . -(*uš*) *d*]*a-a-la-i*[4)]

16' (= 8') . . .

LH § 146a/*35a

§ 5' 17' (= 9') *ták-ku* É-*ir na-aš-ma* URU-*an n*[*a-aš-ma* (^{GIŠ}KI)]⌜RI$_5$ *na-aš*⌝-⌞*ma ú*⌟-*e*-⌞*ši-in*⌟

(Bo 9526 breaks here off; text continues in KBo 6.10 + III 18' ff.)

Text-critical notes: [1)] Contra J. Friedrich, HG 68 and H. A. Hoffner, LH 117, the handcopy in KBo 6.10 shows here some sign remnants. [2)] $^{\text{NA4}}$*ḫūḫa-* is known otherwise only from the oracular text KUB 5.9 obv. 33 and 34; see O. Soysal, NABU 2015/3, 115. [3)] Restoration with *šakuwal-* "eye-cover (of horse)" is a guess. Alternatively, [*pu-ri-i̯a-a*]*l-li* "lip-cover (of horse)" would be considerable as well. [4)] KUB 29.29 + II 7' has *ta-a-la-i*.

184. Bo 9527

Description: Ritual or festival.
CTH: 470 "*Fragments de rituels*" or 670 "*Fragments divers.*"
Dating and Script: NS.
Remarks: One-sided small fragment.
Measurements: 1.8 × 3.2 × 1.7 cm.
Bibliography: N/A.

Bo 9527

§ 1' 1' ^{GIŠ}BANŠ]⌜UR AD.KID NINDA[1)] *EM*⌝-[*ṢA*(?)
2' -*z*]*i na-at-kán* *x̤*$^{?}$-[
3'](-)⌞*x̣-kán*$^{?}$⌟(-) *x̤*$^{?}$(-)[

---

§ 2' 4']-⌞*an-zi*⌟(?)[
(broken off)

Text-critical note: [1)] Or to be read as number "IV" ?

185. Bo 9528

Description: N/A.
CTH: 832 "*Fragments en langue hittite de nature inconnue.*"
Dating and Script: NS.
Remarks: One-sided, lightly abraded fragment.
Measurements: 2.6 × 2.9 × 1.1 cm.
Bibliography: N/A.

Bo 9528

§ 1' 1'](-)⌜*x-x x̣-x̣*?⌝(-)[
2']-*LỊ-LỤ*[1)] *A-N*[*A*
3'](-)*x̣*(-)*x̣*?-*x̣-u-e-ni*? [2)][
4' *i-d*]*a-a-lụ*!? *x̣-x̣ x̣*-[
5'] IZI? *š*⌞*a*[3)]-*x*⌟-[
6' (traces?)
(broken off)

Text-critical notes: [1)] This word appears not to be Hittite. Thus, to be read Akkadian [*KI*]-*LỊ-LU* ? [2)] [. . .]-*x̣* ḪỤŠ-*u-e-ni* ? If this reading is correct, the text genre may be classified as oracle. [3)] Or alternatively read Š⌞*A x*⌟(./-)[. . .].

186. Bo 9529

Description: N/A.
CTH: 832 *"Fragments en langue hittite de nature inconnue."*
Dating and Script: NS.
Remarks: One-sided fragment.
Measurements: 4.1 × 3.7 × 0.8 cm.
Bibliography: N/A.

Bo 9529

§ 1' 1' (traces)
2' . . .

---

§ 2' 3' *gul*$^{?}$]-*lạ-ak-ku-an*[1] *a*[*n*$^{?}$-
4' *g*]*a-rị-ra-pí*[2] *ki-ị*(-)[
5'] *p̣í-i-e-et* [

---

§ 3' 6' -*t*]*e-en na-a*⸢*n*(-)*x*⸣(-)[
7']-*x̣-ni ga*-⸢*x̣*⸣-[
8']-*x̣ an*$^{?}$[3]-*x̣* (-)[
9'](-)⸢*x-x*$^{?}$⸣(-)[
(broken off)

Text-critical notes: [1] The signs -*ak-ku*- are written over erasure. The word *gullakkuwa*- "defiled, corrupt" usually exhibits the spelling *gul-la*-°; the only exception is *ku-ul-la-ak-ku-ụa-an* in KBo 13.98 rev.$^{?}$ 6'. [2] So far, the verb *karira*- "to eat (up), devour" is always paired with the preverb *arḫa*: KUB 7.1+ IV 11' (and dupls.), KUB 30.49+ IV$^{?}$ 24'. [3] Or: DINGIR/^{d}*x̣*(-)[. . .].

187. Bo 9530

Description: N/A.
CTH: 832 "*Fragments en langue hittite de nature inconnue.*"
Dating and Script: N/A.
Remarks: One-sided fragment from the left portion (with edge) of a tablet that is too small to classify.
Measurements: 3.3 × 2.7 × 1.6 cm.
Bibliography: N/A.

Bo 9530

§ 1' 1' *ma*$^{?}$-*x̣*$^{?}$-[
2' I ŠẠ$^{?}$.[
3' *na-ạn*(-)[
4' *x̣-x̣*(-)[

---

§ 2' 5'-6' (illegible signs)
(broken off)

188. Bo 9531

Description: N/A.
CTH: 832 "*Fragments en langue hittite de nature inconnue.*"
Dating and Script: NS.
Remarks: One-sided fragment that is too small to classify.
Measurements: 3.5 × 2.8 × 1.3 cm.
Bibliography: N/A.

Bo 9531

§ 1' 1' (traces)
2' *-a]n*$^{?}$*-zi*

---

§ 2' 3' *]-x̣-ta-an*
4' *-l]i*$^{?}$
5' *-š]ạ*$^{?}$*-an*
6' (traces)
(broken off)

189. Bo 9532

Description: N/A.
CTH: 832 "*Fragments en langue hittite de nature inconnue.*"
Dating and Script: LNS$^?$.
Remarks: One-sided fragment that is too small to classify.
Measurements: 4.0 × 2.7 × 1.4 cm.
Bibliography: N/A.

Bo 9532

§ 1' 1'](-)*x̣*-*x̣*(-)[
2']-*x̣* *x̣*-[
3']-*TỤ̀*$^?$ EGI⸢R⸣-[
4']-*ịt-tén* *Ụ̀*$^?$ [
5' -*a*]*n*$^?$ *ne*-*i̯*[*a*$^?$-[1)]

---

§ 2' 6' (traces$^?$)
(broken off)

Text-critical note: [1)] Or to be read IZI-*i*[*t*] ?

190. Bo 9534

Description: N/A.
CTH: 832 "*Fragments en langue hittite de nature inconnue.*"
Dating and Script: LNS.
Remarks: One-sided fragment.
Measurements: 2.9 × 2.8 × 2.5 cm.
Bibliography: N/A.

Bo 9534

§ 1' 1' (traces)

---

§ 2' 2' *-a]n$^{?}$-ni-eš ḫ[u-*[1)]
3' *-e]l-la-pa i-x̣-[*
4' *l]e-e ú-iz-zi [*
5' *](-)an-da e-ep-m[i*
6' *-i̭]a-aš-ša-an x̣-[*
7' *-a]ḫ$^{?}$-ḫa-an* ⌞IX-*x̣*⌟(-)[
(broken off)

Text-critical notes: [1)] To restore *[ḫa-a]n-né-eš ḫ[u-uḫ-ḫe-eš]* ?

191. Bo 9535

Description: Historical or instruction.

CTH: 215 "*Fragments non caractérisés*" or 275 "*Fragments de protocoles (ou de traités ?).*"

Dating and Script: NS.

Remarks: One-sided fragment. Extremely long shape of "*ni*" in line 2' reminds one of those used in KUB 26.81 I 6', 7' etc., KBo 55.60 lt. col. and rt. col. Both texts are (dynastic) protocol of a Tutḫaliya (CTH 275; on the latter see O. Soysal, JAOS 136 [2016] 422 f.), and I furthermore suspect that Bo 9535, KBo 55.60 and KUB 26.81 all not only belong to the same composition, but they may even be pieces of the same tablet.

Measurements: 3.0 × 2.9 × 1.3 cm.

Bibliography: N/A.

Bo 9535

§ 1' . . .

———

§ 2' 1']-x̤ x̣-[

2'](-)x̤-*ni*[1)](-)*ạ*[?]-[

3'] ÌR.MEŠ GA[L[? 2)]

4' -*e*]*š*[? 3)] *at-tạ*-[4)][

5'].⌞M⌟EŠ IGI-*z*⌜*i*⌝-[*uš*[?](-)[5)]

6' [LÚ.MEŠ(?)]S]AG [

(broken off)

Text-critical notes: [1)] [ŠE]Š-*ni* ? [2)] Cf. KBo 12.8 IV 24'. [3)] Or: [… .ME]Š. [4)] Most likely to *atta*- "father"; cf. *at-ti me-na-aḫ-ḫa-[an-da]* in KUB 26.81 IV 7. [5)] KUB 26.81 IV 2: [I]GI-*zi-uš-ša*.

APPENDIX 1: ADDENDA AND CORRIGENDA TO CHDS 2

Only a short time after the publication of CHDS 2 a number of additional direct joins and duplicates to the text group Bo 9536–Bo 9736 was announced at the *Konkordanz*. They were dicovered by colleagues from Germany. The following list of those fragments was checked and confirmed by us after physical examinations in the Ankara Museum. In December 2015 we were able to glue them together and take the new pictures of the joined pieces. For the inaccessible pieces deposited in other locations we gratefully utilized the composite images generated in Mainz. This section includes improved transliteraratons of the pertinent texts and the photos of the fragments Bo 9536 + KBo 48.254, Bo 9537 + KBo 19.74 and Bo 9598 which suffered in CHDS 2 from low visual quality due to technical difficulties. It is obvious that the rapid growth of the number of new joins and duplicates necessiates the constant update of this project on the unpublished texts as it is being first undertaken in this appendix.

Additional direct joins (all by D. Groddek and most recently posted as "Bemerkungen anläßlich der Edition eines Ensembles hethitischer Texte (CHDS 2)" are available at https://www.academia.edu and officially published in AoF 42 (2015) 127-141):

Bo 9542 + KUB 45.71 + KUB 45.48
Bo 9560 + 342/u (+) KUB 40.16
Bo 9582 + KUB 33.112 (+) KUB 36.2d
Bo 9583 + KUB 38.1
Bo 9594 + KUB 54.5
Bo 9605 + KBo 55.199 + Bo 3396 +
Bo 9614 + KUB 33.38
Bo 9630 (+) KUB 9.32 +
Bo 9650 + KUB 8.51
Bo 9705 + Bo 8282 + KUB 15.1

Additional duplicates (by D. Groddek and *J. L. Miller):

Bo 9538 (// KUB 59.13)
Bo 9562 (// KUB 13.2)*
Bo 9731 (// Bo 9083)

Bo 9536 + KBo 48.254

Due to a technical error the photo of these joined pieces appeared in CHDS 2 in black and white. Here are given the same pictures in correct color.

KBo 48.254 + Bo 9536

KBo 48.254 + Bo 9536 (detail)

Bo 9537 + KBo 19.74 + KUB 21.5

Due to a technical error the photo of these joined pieces appeared in CHDS 2 in black and white and a bit blury. Here are given new pictures taken in the Ankara Museum in June 2015. Since the tablets are moderately abraded the visual quality may be still not fully satisfactory.

KBo 19.74 + Bo 9537 (KUB 21.5 is not included)

KBo 19.74 + Bo 9537 (detail)

Bo 9538

Description: Festival.
CTH: 635 "*Fragments de fêtes de Zippalanda et du mont Daha*" or 685 "*Fragments de fêtes pour les dieux* KAL."
Remarks: Bo 9538 is a one-sided fragment, and lines 1'6' duplicate KUB 59.13 III! 7'-11' (CTH 685) from where the restorations are adopted.
Bibliography: S. Košak, hethiter.net/: hetkonk (v. 1.91).

§ 1' 1' ⌜III DUG.KA.GAG⌝.[(A) . . . ?]
2' *nu-kán* I UDU *A̤*-[(*N*)*A* Ḫ(UR.SAG*Da-a-ḫa*) *ši-pa-an-ti*]
3' I̤ ṲDU-*ma-kán* [(*A-NA* dLAMMA) *ŠA* ḪUR.SA(G*Da-a-ḫa*)]
4' [(*š*)]*i-pa̤-an-ti* I̤ [UDU-*ma-ká*(*n*[1]) *A-NA* dIMIN.IMIN.BI)]
5' [(*Š*)]*A* ḪUR.SA̤G[(*Da-a-ḫa-pát*) *ši-pa-an-ti*]
6' [GA(L.Ḫ)]⌞I.A-*ma*⌟-[(*kán ŠA* EZEN$_4$.ITU-*pát*! [2]))]
(broken off)

Text-critical notes: [1] M. Popko, THeth 21 (1994) 288 and D. Groddek, DBH 14 (2004) 24 read without -*kán*. [2] D. Groddek's (ibid.) reading EZEN$_4$.ITU MU seems to be less probable.

Bo 9542 + KUB 45.71 + KUB 45.48

Description: Lists of Hurrian deities in festivals.
CTH: 705 "*Fragments de listes divines analogues.*"
Dating and Script: MH/MS?.
Remarks: Bo 9542 is a one-sided fragment whose lines 1'–5' directly join KUB 45.71:1'–5' + KUB 45.48 III 1'.
Bibliography: S. Košak, hethiter.net/: hetkonk (v. 1.91).
http://www.hethport.uni-wuerzburg.de/hetskiz/sk.php?f=Bo%202951

Bo 9542 + KUB 45.71 + KUB 45.48

Bo 9542 + KUB 45.71 + KUB 45.48 (detail)

Reverse III

(Line number of KUB 45.48 III is in parenthesis)

§ 1' . . .

——

§ 2' 1' EGIR-*p*⌜*a-m*⌝[*a* 1 NINDA.SIG *A-NA* ᵈ*Ša-l*]⌜*u-uš* ᵈ⌝[*Pé-e*?-*te-en-ḫi*]

2' *pár-ši-i̯*⌜*a*⌝ [*še-ra-aš-ša-a*]*n* ⌜ᵁᶻᵁT⌝I *da-a-i* K[I.MIN]

---

§ 3' 3' Ẹ̣GIR-*pa-m*[*a* 1 NINDA.SIG] *A̧-NA* ᵈ*A-dam-ma* ᵈ*Ku-pa̧-p*[*a*]

4' ᵈ*Ḫa-šu-u*[*n-tar-ḫi pár-š*]*i-i̯a še-ra-aš-ša-an* ᵁᶻᵁT[I *da-a-i* KI.MIN]

---

§ 4' 5' (= 1') EGIR-*pa-ma* ⌜I NINDA.SIG⌝ *A̧-NA* ᵈ*Ur-šu-u-e I*[*š-kal-li*]

(Bo 9542 breaks off here; text continues in KUB 45.71:6' ff. + KUB 45.48 III 2' ff.)

Bo 9560 + 342/u (+) KUB 40.16

Description: Soldier's oath.
CTH: 427.B "*Le 'serment' militaire.*"
Dating and Script: MH/pre[?]-NS.
Remarks: Bo 9560 is a one-sided fragment, and its lines 2'-5' directly join 342/u:1'-4' (with its continuation in KUB 40.16 II 1' ff.). Duplicate is KBo 6.34 + II 27-31 (CTH 427.A) from where the restorations are taken.
Bibliography: S. Košak, hethiter.net/: hetkonk (v. 1.91).

http://www.hethport.uni-wuerzburg.de/hetskiz/sk.php?f=342/u

342/u + Bo 9560

Obverse II

(Line numbers of 342/u[1)] are in parentheses)

§ 1' 1' [. . . [?] (*QA-TAM-MA ma-al-la-an-d*)]⸢*u na-an*⸣ [(*QA-TAM-MA i-nu-uš-ki-du*)]

2' (= 1') [(*na-an*)] ⸢*QA-TAM-MA ḫar-ra*‹*-nu*›*-u*⸣*š-kán*[! 2)]*-du* ⸢x⸥ (eras.) [(*nu* ḪUL-*lu* ÚŠ-*kán*)]

3' (= 2') [(*pé-e*)]*-dạ-ú* *a-pé-e-ma* *da-ra-a*[(*n-zi*)]

4' (= 3') [(*a-pa-a*)]*-ạt* *e-eš-* *du* [

---

§ 2' 5' (= 4') [(*ke-e*)]-⸤*da-ni-ma A-NA* DIM_4⸥ [*m*]*a-aḫ-ḫa-an*[3)] [(*ḫa-aš-ša-tar-še-et* NU.GÁL)]

(Bo 9560 breaks off here; text continues in KUB 40.16 II 1' ff.)

Text-critical notes: [1)] The handcopy of this fragment is available in N. Oettinger, StBoT 22 (1976) 138 (Textbeilage). [2)] The corrupt sign in Bo 9560 exhibits a strange shape between "*it*" and "*kán*". Dupl. KBo 6.34 + II 28 has likewise erroneous *ḫar-ra*<*-nu*>*-uš-ki-it-ta* on which see N. Oettinger, StBoT 22, 34. Thus, the verb *ḫarranušk-* suffers here and in KBo 6.34 + from critical scribal errors and erasures in its writing. [3)] KBo 6.34 + II 31: GIM-*an*.

Bo 9561

Description: Treaty.

CTH: 68.N "*Traité avec Kupanta-dKAL du pays de Mira et Kuwaliya.*"

Remarks: Bo 9561 is a one-sided fragment, and lines 4'-6' duplicate KUB 19.52 + KBo 50.38 + III? 1'-3' (G. Beckman, ZA 87 [1997] 99), from where the restorations are taken.

Bibliography: O. Soysal, Anatolica 38 (2012) 174 (transliteration and remarks); S. Košak, hethiter.net/: hetkonk (v. 1.91).

§ 1' 1' *p*]⌈*í*?-*i̯a-an-du*?⌉1) [

2' -*š*]*i*? [

3' . . .

---

§ 2' 4' [*nam-ma ki-i ku-it ṬUP-PU tu-uk A-NA* mKu-pa-an-ta-dLAMMA (*i-i̯*)]*a-nu-un* [

5' [*ne-et-ták-kán* MU.KAM-*ti* MU.KAM-*ti pí-ra-an* III-Š(*U ḫal-z*)]*e-eš-kán-d*[(*u*)2)]

6' [*nu zi-ik* mKu-pa-an-ta-dLAMMA-*aš ke-e* (*A-WA-TE*MEŠ *p*))]*a-a̯ḫ-ši* [

7' (traces)

(broken off)

Text-critical notes: 1) Or less probably ⌈*u-i̯a-an-du*?⌉ 2) KUB 19.52 + III? 2': *ḫal-zi-iš-kán-d*⌈*u*⌉.

Bo 9562

Description: Instruction.

CTH: 261 "*Instructions aux chefs de postes (bêl madgalti).*"

Dating and Script: Arn. I / NS.

Remarks: Bo 9562 is a one-sided fragment, and lines 1'-4' duplicate KUB 13.2 I 16'-19' (CTH 261.I.B; Arn. I / NS) and KUB 31.86 + I 27'-29' (CTH 261.I.D; Arn. I / NS) from where the restorations are taken.

Bibliography: E. von Schuler, HDA (1957) 42; F. P. Daddi, StMed 14 (2003) 96-99; J. L. Miller, Royal Hittite Instructions (2013) 220-221; S. Košak, hethiter.net/: hetkonk (v. 1.91).

Obverse I

§ 1' 1' [(*u̯a-al-aḫ-zi nu* ÉRIN.MEŠ ^{LÚ}KÚR *u-ur-ki-in I-N*)]*A* Ụ$_4$.⸢III⸣.[(KAM *na-an-na-ú*)]

2' [(KASKAL.ḪI.A-*TÌ* U$_4$.II.KAM *ḫar-kán-du ku-i-ša-k*)]*án* ^{LÚ}KỤ́R-*mạ* Ụ̈-[(*UL ku-en-zi*)]

3' [(*nu* ^{LÚ}*BE-EL MA-AD-GAL*$_9$*-TI* ^{LÚ}DUGUD II *pé-e-da-an* III *p*)]*é-e-dạ-ạn*

4' [(IV *pé-e-da-an e-ep-du na-aš MA-ḪA*)]R ^{d}ỤTU-*ŠI up-pa-ụ́*[1)]

---

§ 2' 5' (traces$^{?}$)

(broken off)

Text-critical notes: [1)] KUB 13.2 I 19' and KUB 31.86 + I 29' have *ú-up-pa-ú*.

Bo 9582 + KUB 33.112 (+) KUB 36.2d

Description: Mythological.
CTH: 343.1.A *"La royauté du dieu KAL."*
Dating and Script: NS.
Remarks: Bo 9582 is a one-sided fragment, and lines 1'-8' directly join KUB 33.112 + III 23'-30'.
Bibliography: S. Košak, hethiter.net/: hetkonk (v. 1.91).
http://www.hethport.uni-wuerzburg.de/hetskiz/sk.php?f=443/u

KUB 36.2d (+) Bo 9582 + KUB 33.112 rev. III (composite image)

Reverse III

(Line numbers of Bo 9582 are in parentheses)

§ 2' 23' (= 1') *na-an A-NA* ^{d}LAMMA *ḫa-at-r[i-iš-k]⸢i-u-u̯⸣[a-a]⸤n⸥ da-a-iš*

24' (= 2') *i-ịt ki-i ud-da-a-ar Ạ-[NA* ^{d}L]AMMA *mẹ-[mi k]u-it-pát-u̯a-at-ta*

25' (= 3') *ne-pí-ši* LUGAL-*un i-i̯ạ-u-e[n nu-u̯]a-za* Ẹ̣ZE⸢N$_{4}$-*an*⸣ *Ú-UL*

26' (= 4') *kụ-u̯a-pí-ik-ki i-i̯a-at* [. . .]-*x̣*$^{?}$-*za Ú-UL ku-u̯ạ-pí-ik-ki ḫal-za-a-iš*

27' (= 5') ⸤*x x x*⸥ [$^{\text{ḪUR.S}}$]^{AG}*Na-ša-al-mạ* ỤGU *da-a-i*

28' (= 6') ^{UR}]^{U}*Ạp-zụ-u-i pa-ra-a na-ạ-i*

29' (= 7')]-*x̣*$^{?}$ *ụt-tar* Ẹ̣GIR-*an t[i-i]ḫ-ḫi*[1)] *nu* ^{LÚ}*Ṭ̣E*$_{4}$-*MỤ pạ-it*

30' (= 8')] *Ạ-NA* ^{d}LAMM⸤A⸥ [EGI]R-*pa QA-TAM-MA*
kạp-pụ-u-u̯a-it

---

§ 3' 31' (= 9')]⸤*x x x*⸥[ ] *iš-ta-ma-aš-tạ*

(Bo 9582 breaks off here; text continues in KUB 36.2d III 32' ff.)

Text-critical note: [1)] *ti-iḫ-ḫi* is a rare pres. sg. 1 form to *dai-* / *tiya-* "to place, put"; cf. KUB 17.28 I 28 (MH/NS), KUB 19.55 + rev. 42' (LNS).

Bo 9583 + KUB 38.1

Description: Cult inventory.
CTH: 501 "*Inventaire de Tarammeka, Kunkuniya, Wiyanawanta.*"
Dating and Script: NH/LNS.
Remarks: Bo 9583 is a one-sided fragment, and lines 4'-5' (also including a portion of the left edge) directly join KUB 38.1 IV 26'-27'/28'-29'[1].
Bibliography: S. Košak, hethiter.net/: hetkonk (v. 1.91).
http://www.hethport.uni-wuerzburg.de/hetskiz/sk.php?f=Bo%202496

Reverse IV

(Line numbers of Bo 9583 are in parentheses)

§ 5' 23' (= 1') ŠU.NÍGIN XXXVIII [
24' (= 2') ŠÀ VI *BI-IB-*[*RU*
25' (= 3') X *BI-IB-RU-m*[*a*
26' (= 4') VII ZA.ḪUM[2] II x̣(./-)[
27' (= 5') IV GAL ŠÀ II BABBA[R II? GE$_6^?$
(Bo 9583 breaks off here; text continues in KUB 38.1 IV 28'/30' ff.)

Left edge

. . . [*A-N*]⌞*A*⌟ ^{d}*A-la* EZEN$_4$ *x̣-x̣*?-[...?-*z*]*a*? [3]-*ni-iš* DỤ̀-*at* . . .

Text-critical notes: [1] The line numbers in the edition volume KUB 38.1 IV 28'-29' should be lowered based on the present join. [2] Thus, correct the transliteration ZA."LUM" in CHDS 2, 50. [3] Or: [. . . -*u*]*n-ni-iš*. This word designates a hitherto unknown festival which is dedicated to ^{d}Ala. L. Jakob-Rost's suggestion "Fr[ühjahrs-]Fest" in MIO 8 (1961) 182 with n. 88, is no longer tenable.

KUB 38.1 + Bo 9583 rev. IV

KUB 38.1 + Bo 9583 left edge

Bo 9583 + KUB 38.1 left edge (detail)

Bo 9594 + KUB 54.5

Description: Festival.
CTH: 694 "*Fragments de diverses fêtes*" (Culte de Huwassanna, déesse de Hubesna).
Dating and Script: MH/NS.
Remarks: Bo 9594 is a one-sided fragment, and lines 1'-6' directly join KUB 54.5 I 10'-15'.
Bibliography: S. Košak, hethiter.net/: hetkonk (v. 1.91).

KUB 54.5 + Bo 9594 obv. I

KUB 54.5 + Bo 9594 obv. I (detail)

Obverse I

(Line numbers of Bo 9594 are in parentheses)

§ 3' 10' (= 1') *na-aš-ta* MUNUS*ḫu-u-u̯a-*⌞*aš*⌟*-*⌜*š*⌝*a-a*[*n-na-al-*[1)]
11' (= 2') TÚG*ḫu-u-u̯a-al-tạ-az*[2)] [
12' (= 3') Ì!.DÙG.GA-*i̯a-aš-ša-an ku-x̣*(-)[
13' (= 4') *I-NA* GIŠBANŠUR *ki-it-t*[*a*(-)
14' (= 5') ⌞MUNUS*ḫu-u-u̯*⌟*a-aš-ša-an-na-al-l*[*i*(-)

---

§ 4' 15' (= 6') MUNUS]⌞*ḫu-u-u̯*⌟*a-aš*! [3)]*-ša-a*[*n-na-al-*[4)]
16' (= 7') (traces)
(broken off)

Text-critical notes: [1)] To complete with sg. nom. °-*la-aš* or °-*li-iš*. [2)] For TÚG*ḫu*(*wa*)*lta-* of unknown meaning see J. Friedrich - A. Kammenhuber et alii, HW² III/2 (Lfg. 19) (2010) 703 where the occurrence in KUB 54.5 I 11' is quoted in its incomplete form. The new join gives now a full sg. abl. TÚG*ḫūwaltaz*. This form may be detected also in KBo 17.105 + KBo 34.47 III 43' (TÚG?[*ḫ*]*u-u̯a-al-tạ-ạz*). [3)] This sign shows an unusual shape, possibly first intented to be written "*ša*" although no erasure is seen here. [4)] To complete with sg. nom. °-*la-aš* or sg. dat. °-*li*(-).

Bo 9598

Due to a technical error the photo of this fragment appeared in CHDS 2 cut off on its left side. Here is the original picture taken in the Ankara Museum in 2011.

Bo 9598

Bo 9605 + KBo 55.199 + Bo 3396 +

Description: Oracle.
CTH: 574.21 "*Oracles par l'oiseau Ḫurri.*"
Dating and Script: NS.
Remarks: Bo 3396 + Bo 9605 I? line 1' directly join KBo 55.199 line 7'. The permission to include Bo 3396 is by courtesy of Ms. Gül Demirayak who has the publication rights of this fragment.
Bibliography: S. Košak, hethiter.net/: hetkonk (v. 1.91).
http://www.hethport.uni-wuerzburg.de/hetskiz/sk.php?f=1096/u

KBo 55.199 + Bo 3396 + Bo 9605 + obv. I?

KBo 55.199 + Bo 3396 + Bo 9605 + obv. I$^?$ (detail)

Obverse I$^?$

(Line number of Bo 3396 + Bo 9605 + obv. I$^?$ is in parenthesis)

§ 1' 1'-4' . . .

---

§ 2' 5' [u̯a]-*aš-ku-uš ŠA* É.NA$_4$ DINGIR-*LIM*(-)x̣(-)[

6' [UDU$^?$] H̯Ạ.LA *ŠA* MU.II.KAM *kar-aš-*[*ša-an-za*[1)]

7' (= 1') NỊNDA.GỤR$_4$.RA U$_4$.KAM-*i̯ a-u̯a Ú-UL* [DÙ-*ir*(?)[2)]

(KBo 55.199 breaks here off; text continues in Bo 3396 + Bo 9605 + obv. I$^?$ 2' ff.; for a fuller text see CHDS 2 p. 73)

Text-critical notes: [1)] For restorations cf. Bo 3396 I$^?$ 10': UDU H̯A.LA-*i̯a k*[*ar-aš-ša-an-za*] (CHDS 2 p. 73 with n. 5) and KBo 55.199:3': [. . . H̯]A.LA *kar-aš-ša-an-za.* [2)] Cf. KUB 18.32:5': NINDA.GUR$_4$.RA *U$_4$-MI* DÙ-*ir*.

Bo 9614 + KUB 33.38

Description: Mythological.

CTH: 334.6.A “^{d}MAḪ, *déesse perdue et retrouvée (mugawar).*”

Dating and Script: OH/MS.

Remarks: Bo 9614 is a one-sided fragment from the top portion (with upper edge) of a tablet, and lines 1-4 directly join KUB 33.38 IV 1-4.

Bibliography: A. N. Asan, DBH 41 (2014) 290 (text edition without the join Bo 9614); S. Košak, hethiter.net/: hetkonk (v. 1.91). http://www.hethport.uni-wuerzburg.de/hetskiz/sk.php?f=Bo%202914

KUB 33.38 + Bo 9614 rev. IV (composite image)

Reverse IV

§ 1 1 [*nu*]-*zạ* ⸢AM⸣[A-*aš* DUMU-*ŠU*[? 1)] *ga-ni-eš-ta*] GU$_4$-*u*[*š*] AMẠR-*ŠỤ*

2 [*g*]*a-ni-eš-t*⸢*a* ỤDU-*ụš* S⸣[ILA$_4$-*SÚ*[? 1)] *g*]*a-ni-i*[*š*]- *ta* ⸢*x*⸣

3 [DI]NGIR-*LUM-ma* LUGAL MUNUS.LU⸢GAL *ga-ni-e*⸣*š-ta* Ụ̀ KUR ^{URU}*Ḫ̮a-at-ti*

4 [*g*]*a-ni-iš-ta nu-uš-za ḫ̮u-iš-ụ̯a-an-ni* [*i*]*n-na-ra-u-a*⸤*n*⸥-[*ni*]

5 ẸGIR.U$_4$-*MI* *kap-pu-u-* *i*[*t*]

(Bo 9614 breaks off here; text continues in KUB 33.38 IV 6 ff.)

Text-critical note: [1)] Restoration with the Akkadian possessive suffix -*ŠU*/-*SÚ* follows the usage AMAR-*ŠU* in line 1.

Bo 9630 (+?) KUB 9.32 +

Description: Ritual.

CTH: 394.C *"Rituel d'Ashella, contre une épidémie dans l'armée."*

Dating and Script: MH/NS.

Remarks: Bo 9630 is a one-sided fragment, and according to the *Konkordanz*, lines 1'-5' could indirectly join KUB 9.32 obv. 37-41. Duplicates are KUB 9.31 III 61-63 (CTH 394.A), KUB 41.17 III 10'-15' (CTH 394.E) and KBo 13.212:7'-10' (CTH 394.B) (all NS) from where the restorations are taken. However, the suggested join of Bo 9630 with KUB 9.32 seems, in agreement with F. Fuscagni (personal communication), highly problematic, since the ductus of Bo 9630 differs from KUB 9.32 as far as the text is preserved.

Bibliography: S. Košak, hethiter.net/: hetkonk (v. 1.91).

http://www.hethport.uni-wuerzburg.de/hetskiz/sk.php?f=Bo%202038

KUB 9.32 + Bo 9712 (+?) Bo 9630 obv. (composite image)

Obverse

(Line numbers of Bo 9630 are in parentheses)

§ 5 37 (= 1') *na-aš da-ga-an*[1)] *ḫa-at-ta-an-zi*[2)] *na-aš pít-tal-u̯a*[3)]*-ạn-t*[(*e-eš za-nu-u̯a*[4)])]*-ạn-*⸢*z*⸣[(*i*?)]

38 (= 2') *nu* [GIŠ]*la-aḫ-ḫur-nu-uz*[5)]*-zi kat-ta-an*[6)] *iš-pár-ra-an-z*⸤*i nu-uš*⸥*-*[(*ša-an*)[7)]] ⸢UZU⸣Ì NINDA.GU⸢R4⸣.[(RA.ḪI.A URUDU)]

39 (= 3') GÍR!.TUR-*li-i̯a ki-ša-an*(!)[8)] *ḫa-an-da*[9)]*-an-zi n*[(*am-ma IŠ-TU* KAŠ GA)]L.ḪI.A [DUG]GÌ[(R.GÁN)]

40 (= 4') *šu-un-ni-an-zi nam-ma-kán an-da k*⸤*i-i*⸥[(*š-ša-an me-ma-aḫ*)*-ḫ*]*i ka-*⸤*a-š*⸥[*a*(-) . . . ?]

41 (= 5') *ḫu-*[10)]*da-ak ḫa-an-te*!*-ez-zi pal-ši ú-x̣-*[ ]-⸤*x*⸥ [

(Bo 9630 breaks off here; text continues in KUB 9.32+ obv. 42 ff.)

Text-critical notes: [1)] KUB 9.31 III 61 and KUB 41.17 III 10': *ta-ga-a-an.* [2)] KUB 41.17 III 10': *kat-ta ḫa-an-da-an-zi.* [3)] KBo 13.212:7': *pít-tal-ú-ạn*?. [4)] KUB 41.17 III 11' omits *-u̯a-*. [5)] KUB 9.31 III 62 and KUB 41.17 III 11' omit *-uz-*; KBo 13.212:8' omits [GIŠ]. [6)] KUB 41.17 III 11' omits *-an.* [7)] KUB 41.17 III 12': *nu-uš<<-uš>>-ša-an.* [8)] Thus, probably a scribal slip. KUB 41.17 III 12' has correct *kat-*⸤*t*⸥[*a*(-) . . .] instead. [9)] KUB 41.17 III 12': *-ta-*. [10)] KUB 41.17 III 15' adds *-u-*.

Bo 9650 + KUB 8.51

Description: Mythological.

CTH: 341.III.1.C *"Gilgameš. Version hittite"*

Dating and Script: NH/NS.

Remarks: Bo 9650 is a one-sided fragment, and lines 5-6 directly join KUB 8.51 II$^{!}$ 5$^{!}$-6$^{!}$ (in edition volume line numbers appear as 4-5; CTH 341.III.1.C). Duplicate is KUB 8.55(+) II 1'-3' (CTH 341.III.1.B+D).

Bibliography: S. Košak, hethiter.net/: hetkonk (v. 1.91).
http://www.hethport.uni-wuerzburg.de/hetskiz/sk.php?f=Bo%203341

Bo 9650 + KUB 8.51 obv. II (composite image)

Obverse II

(Old line numbers of KUB 8.51 II$^{!}$ are in parentheses)

§ 1 1 (traces)

2 ^{URU}*U*]-*rụ-gạ* URU-*rị*[1)] *x̣*-[

3]-*šị*$^{?}$ [2)] *ḫạ-lu-gạ-aš ịš-x̣-*[3)][

4 *A-NA* ^{f}]*Ša-an-ḫa-du* EGỊ[(R-*pa me-mi-i)š-ki-iz-zi*

5 (= 4)](.)⸤B⸥ÚN-*aš*[4)] *nu* ^{f}*Ša-a*⸢*n-ḫ*⸣[(*a*)-*du-uš*

6 (= 5) EGIR-*pa me*]-*mị-iš-ki-ịz-zi* ^{d}[(GIŠ.GIM).MAŠ

7 (= 6) (traces) [*pé*-(*e-ḫu*)]-*tẹ-iš*[5)]-*kạ́n-z*[(*i* ^{LÚ}GURUŠ-*an-t*)*i*

(Bo 9650 breaks here off; text continues in KUB 8.51 II$^{!}$ 8$^{!}$ ff.)

8$^{!}$]-*an pí-an-zi* [(*nu-u̯a-aš-ši ku-it-ma-an x*$^{?}$)-

9$^{!}$] *mạ-ni-in-ku*[6)]-*u̯a-an* [(*na-a-u̯i*$_{5}$ *pa-iz*)-*zi*]

10$^{!}$ -(*x A-NA*)] $^{d!?}$GIŠ.GIM.MAŠ[7)] ẸGIR-[(*an ar-ḫa x*)-

---

(broken off)

Text-critical notes: [1] This is the revised reading against [*ku-e*(?)]-*ẹl-gạ* in CHDS 2 p. 116. Cf. [^{URU}*U*]-*ra-ga* URU-*ri* but also ^{URU}⌜*U-ru-g*⌝[*a* URU-*ri*] in the same composition KUB 8.57 I 11 // KBo 10.47a I 1'. [2] Alternatively [. . .]-*LỊM* ? [3] To be interpreted as *ḫalugaš* (pl. acc.) *ištamašš*- "to hear the messages" ? Cf. the context of KBo 19.120 II 7-9 from the same composition with mention of the city Uruk. [4] KUB 8.55(+) II 2' has ⌜*ḫa*$^?$-*lu*$^?$-*ga*⌝-*aš*. The equation or even comparation of BÚN (= KA×IM)-*aš* with *ḫalugaš* "message, report", however, would be highly problematic. Moreover, the meaning of BÚN in the Mesopotamian sources is not very clear and varies from "breath, to blow" to "(air) bladder, windpipe$^?$; bellows" or even "rage, revolt, rebellion". Among these only the latter meaning (= *nappaḫtu*) would fit the context here which would express the rage of the citizens of Uruk against the tyrannizing rule of Gilgameš over them; cf. G. Beckman, in: FsHoffner (2003) 45. Consequently, the alternative reading [*ḫa-tu*$^?$]-⌜*ú*$^?$-*ga*⌝-*aš* "[frig]htfully" in KUB 8.55(+) II 2' would make more sense, but even this is not fully satisfactory. [5] KUB 8.55(+) II 4': -*te-eš*. [6] KUB 8.55(+) II 6' adds -*u*-. [7] KUB 8.55(+) II 7': ^{d}GIŠ.GIM.PA$^{(!)}$.

Bo 9705 + KUB 15.1 + Bo 8282

Description: Vow.
CTH: 584.1 "*Songes de la reine.*"
Dating and Script: NH/NS.
Remarks: Bo 9705 is a one-sided fragment, and lines 1'-8' directly join KUB 15.1 II 48-52 and Bo 8282:1'-8'.
Bibliography: S. Košak, hethiter.net/: hetkonk (v. 1.91); J. de Roos, Votive (2007) 93, 101–02 (text edition of KUB 15.1 without joins); I. Taş, DBH 43 (2014) 7 (transliteration of Bo 8282 only).
http://www.hethport.uni-wuerzburg.de/hetskiz/sk.php?f=Bo%202473

Bo 8282 + Bo 9705 obv. II

KUB 15.1 + Bo 9705 + Bo 8282 obv. II (composite image)

Obverse II

(Line numbers of Bo 9705 are in parentheses)

§ 9 48 (= 1') [*Ú-U*]*L ku-ẹ-*[*e*]*z-ka*$_4$ GÙB-*li-iš-zi* ⌜ ⌝(eras.) ⌞^{d}⌟LỤGAL-[*m*]*a*[1] $^{URU.d}$U-*aš-ša-u̯a*

49 (= 2')] Ụ̀-*it u-uḫ-ḫi nu-u̯a A-NA* ^{d}LUGAL-[*m*]*a*[1]

50 (= 3') [I SILA$_4$ ^{NA_4}]ZA.GÌN DÙ-*mi* I Ụ$_4$[1] KÙ.BABBAR I U$_4$[2] GUŠKIN [. . .] KỤ̀.BABBAR

51 (= 4') K]I.LÁ.BI NU.GÁL *ŠA* SỊLA$_4$-*i̯a-u̯a-m*[*a*(-) . . .](-)⌞*x*(-)*ga-an*⌟[3]-[

52 (= 5')](.)x̣.MEŠ ^{d}LUGAL-*ma* DÙ-*mị* [. . . $^{?}$]

(KUB 15.1 breaks here off; text continues in Bo 9705)

53 (= 6')]-*x̣* ŠEŠ ^{d}UTU-*ŠI-u̯a-ra-at ku-it*(-)*x̣*(-)[

---

§ 10 54 (= 7') *še-ḫi-l*]*i-iš-ki-i̯a-aš-šạ*[4] *kụ-iš* GUNNI [. . . $^{?}$]

55 (= 8')]-*x̣* SILA$_4$ *ị-i̯a-mi* [

(broken off)

Text-critical notes: [1] Thus, revise the restoration with ^{d}MUNUS.LUGAL by J. de Roos, Votive (2007) 93 with n. 100. [2] After the direct join the sign in question appears as a clear "*ut* = U$_4$", hence the restoration [MA.N]A posited by J. de Roos, Votive 93 is no longer tenable. With U$_4$ KÙ.BABBAR / GUŠKIN is meant a "day" symbol made of silver or gold. Similar votive objects of precious metals, e. g., GEŠTU "ear", ZI "soul" and URU-*LUM* "town" are found in the same text (II 12, 27, 36, III 3', 20', 25', 30', 52'). [3] These signs may belong to the word (*arḫa*) *ganganumi* "I will weigh out"; cf. KUB 21.27 + III 41'-42'. [4] For restoration see Bo 9577:4' (CHDS 2 p. 44 with n. 3).

Bo 9731

Description: Festival.
CTH: 670.2972.B "Fragments divers."
Dating and Script: NS.
Remarks: Bo 9731 is a one-sided fragment from the top portion (with upper edge) of a tablet, and lines 1-3 duplicate Bo 9083 right column (obv. II?) 1-3 (CTH 670.2972.A) which shows a similar tablet layout as our fragment.
Bibliography: S. Košak, hethiter.net/: hetkonk (v. 1.91).

§ 1 1 [(DUMU.É.GAL LUGAL)]-*ị* ŠỤ.ḪI.A-*aš u̯a-a-tar* [
2 [(*pa-a-i* LUGAL-*uš Q*)]*A-TỊ*-HỊ.Ạ-*ŠỤ a-ar-r*[(*i*)]

---

§ 2 3 [(GAL.DUMU.MEŠ.É.GAL GADA-*an pa*)]-⌞*a-i*⌟ [
(broken off)

APPENDIX 2: CONCORDANCE OF Bo-TEXTS AND CHDS 2–3 NUMBERS

After an agreement with our colleagues in the Akademie der Wissenschaften und der Literatur Mainz (Kommission für den Alten Orient) we decided to number the Bo-texts after their appearance order in each CHDS volume since the latter can be considered now as a regular cuneiform edition. For the convenience for the readers in future, the following concordances provide the Bo-texts and their CHDS numbers as they will appear also at the *Konkordanz der hethitischen Keilschrifttafeln* (http://www.hethport.uni-wuerzburg.de/hetkonk/) under their relevant text categories. For the bibliographic references to the Bo-fragments edited in this series we would suggest the abbreviated citations CHDS 2.1, CHDS 3.1 etc.

CONCORDANCE OF Bo 9536–Bo 9736 AND CHDS 2

Bo	CHDS 2
9536 +	1
9537 +	2
9538	3
9539	4
9541	5
9542 +	6
9543	7
9544	8
9545	9
9547	10
9548	11
9549	12
9550	13
9553	14
9554	15
9555	16
9556	17
9557 +	18
9559	19
9560 +	20
9561	21
9562	22
9563	23
9564	24
9565	25
9566	26
9567	27
9568	28
9569 +	29
9570	30
9571 +	31
9572	32
9573	33
9574	34
9575	35
9576	36
9577	37
9578	38
9579	39
9580	40
9581	41
9582 +	42
9583 +	43
9584	44
9585	45
9586	46
9587 +	47
9588	48
9589	49
9590	50
9591	51
9593	52
9594 +	53
9595	54
9596	55

9701	142
9702	143
9704	144
9705 +	145
9706	146
9708 +	147
9710	148
9711	149
9712 +	150
9713	151
9715	152
9716	153
9719	154
9720	155
9721	156
9722	157
9723	158
9724	159
9725	160
9726	161
9727	162
9728	163
9729	164
9730	165
9731	166
9732	167
9733	168
9734	169
9735	170
9736	171

CONCORDANCE OF Bo 6151–Bo 9535 AND CHDS 3

Bo	**CHDS 3**
6151	1
6207	2
6238	3
6271	4
6370	5
6570	6
6788	7
6810 +	8
6827	9
6909	10
6978	11
7050	12
7103	13
7284	14
7317	15
7444	16
7833	17
7937	18
8029	19
8084	20
8695	21
8696 +	22
8697	23
8698	24
8699	25
8701	26
8703	27
8704 +	28
8706	29
8707	30
8708	31
8709	32
8710 +	33
8712	34
8713	35
8714	36
8716	37
8717	38
8718	39
8719	40
8720	41
8721	42
8722	43
8723	44
8724	45
8725	46
8726	47
8727	48
8729	49

INDEX OF PROPER NAMES

DIVINE NAMES

^{d}Allanni		
^{d}*Al-la-a*⸢*n*⸣-[*ni*$^{?}$]	(dat.)	Bo 6238:14’
^{d}Adamma		
^{d}*A-dam-ma*	(acc.)	Bo 8704 + I 4’
^{d}Āššiya		
[^{d}]*A-aš-ši-i̯a*-[*za*$^{?}$]	(pl. nom. or acc.)	Bo 6271 rt. col. 12’
^{d}Enki		
[^{d}*E*]*n-ki*	(Sumerian)	Bo 9520:4’
^{d}Ḫalipinu		
^{d}*Ḫa-li-pí-i*[*n-nu-*...]	(–)	Bo 8729:4’
^{d}Ḫapantaliya		
^{d}*Ḫa-pa-an-ta-l*[*i-i̯a*]	(dat.)	Bo 6909 obv.$^{?}$ 4
⸤^{d}*Ḫ*⸥*a-pa-an-ta-li-i̯*[*a*$^{?}$]	(–)	Bo 7317:7’
^{d}Ḫaratši		
^{d}*Ḫa-ra-at-š*[*i-in*$^{?}$]	(acc.)	Bo 6151 lt. col. 2’
^{d}*Ḫa-ra-at-ši*	(acc.)	Bo 6207 obv. III 7’
^{d}Ḫašammili		
[^{d}*Ḫ*]*a-ša-am-mi-li*	(dat.)	Bo 6909 obv.$^{?}$ 5
[^{d}*Ḫa-ša*]-*am-me-li*	(dat.)	Bo 6909 rev.$^{?}$ 1’
^{d}Ḫašammiu		
^{d}*Ḫa-ša-am-mi-ú-un*	(acc.)	Bo 7937:7’
^{d}Ḫepat		
⸢^{d}*Ḫé*⸣-[*pát*(?)]	(–)	Bo 8695:1’
^{d}Ḫuwaššanna		
^{d}[*Ḫu-u̯a-aš-ša-an-na-an*]	(acc.)	Bo 9516 + III 4’
^{d}Inar		
^{d}*I-na-a*[*r*(-) . . .]	(–)	Bo 9450:2’

^{d}Išduštaya

[^{d}*I*]*š-du-uš-t*[*a-i̯a*]	(dat.$^{?}$)	Bo 9484:2’

^{d}Kampipuitti

[^{d}*Kam*]*-pí-pu-it-ti*	(dat.)	Bo 6909 obv.$^{?}$ 2

^{d}Kattaḫḫa/i

[^{d}*K*]*a-taḫ-ḫa*	(dat.)	Bo 6909 obv.$^{?}$ 3
^{d}*Ka-at-taḫ-ḫi-in*	(acc.)	Bo 7937:6’

^{d}Kupapa

^{d}*Ku-pa-p*[*a*]	(acc.)	Bo 8704 + I 4’

^{d}Milku

⸤^{d}*Mil*⸥*-ku-uš*	(nom.)	Bo 8787:8’

^{d}Minki

⸢^{d}*Mi*⸣-[*in-ki-iš*]	(nom.)	Bo 8773:2’

^{d}Piḫami

^{d}*Pí-ḫa-mi-i*[*š*]	(nom.)	Bo 8787:8’

^{d}Namšara

[^{d}*Na*]-⸢*am*⸣*-ša-ra-aš*	(nom.)	Bo 8773:2’

^{d}Pappaya

[^{d}*Pa*]-⸢*ap-pa-i̯a*⸣	(dat.$^{?}$)	Bo 9484:1’

^{d}Pirwa

^{d}*Pí-ir-u̯a*	(dat.)	Bo 8721:5’

^{d}Šušumaḫḫi

^{d}*Šu-šu-ma-aḫ-ḫ*[*i-in*]	(acc.)	Bo 7937:9’

^{d}Šuwaliyat(ti)

^{d}*Šu-u̯a-li-i̯*[*a-at-ti*$^{?}$]	(dat.$^{?}$)	Bo 9482:3’

^{d}Telipinu

^{d}*Te-li-pí-nu-un*	(acc.)	Bo 7937:7’
^{d}*Te-*[*li*]*-pí-nu*(-)[. . .]	(acc.)	Bo 8696 + obv.$^{?}$ III 7’

^{d}Wa$_{a}$ḫiši

[(^{d}*Wa*$_{a}$*-a*)*-ḫi-ši-i*]*n*	(acc.)	Bo 9507:7”

^{d}Wa$_{a}$šezzili

[^{d}*W*]*a*$_{a}$*-še-ez-zi-li-i̯a*	(dat.)	Bo 6909 obv.$^{?}$ 6

^{d}Zentuḫi

⸢^{d}*Ze-en-tu-ḫi-x̣*$^{?}$⸣(-)[. . .]	(acc.)	Bo 7284 rt. col. 3’
^{d}*Ze-e*[*n-tu-ḫi-i̯a*]	(gen.)	Bo 7284 rt. col. 4’

^{d}Zitḫariya

^{d}*Zi-it-ḫa-ri-i̯a-a*[*n*]	(acc.)	Bo 6788 I 2
^{d}*Zi-i*⸤*t-ḫa*⸥-[*ri-i̯a*(-) . . .]	(dat.)	Bo 6909 obv.$^{?}$ 1
^{d}*Zi-it-ḫ*[*a-ri-i̯a*]	(dat.)	Bo 6909 obv.$^{?}$ 3

^{d}GIŠ.GIM.MAŠ

^{d}[(GIŠ.GIM).MAŠ]	(—)	Bo 9650 + II 6

^{d}IB

^{d}I[(B)]	(dat.)	Bo 6570 II 22’

^{d}IŠKUR

⸢^{d}⸣IŠKUR	(acc.)	Bo 7937:6’
^{d}IŠKUR (^{URU}*Ariḫazziya*)	(acc.)	Bo 7937:8’

^{d}LAMMA

[^{d}L]AMMA	(dat.)	Bo 9582 + III 24’
^{d}LAMMA	(acc.)	Bo 7937:9’
⸢^{d}LAMM⸣A	(gen.)	Bo 6810 + II 16’
⸤^{d}LAMMA$^{?}$⸥(-)[. . .]	(—)	Bo 6810 + II 25’
^{d}LAMMA-*aš*	(nom. or gen.)	Bo 7833 III 14’
^{d}LAMMA (^{URU}*Ḫatt*[*i*])	(—)	Bo 8779:4’, 5’
[^{d}L]AMMA$^{?}$ (^{KUR}[*L*]*awataš*)	(nom.)	Bo 8787:5’
[^{d}LAMMA] ([^{URU}*Taur*]*iša*)	(acc.)	Bo 6271 rt. col. 10’

^{d}LUGAL-ma

^{d}LUGAL-[*m*]*a*	(dat.)	Bo 9705 + II 49
^{d}LUGAL-*ma*	(gen.)	Bo 9705 + II 52
⸤^{d}⸥LUGAL-[*m*]*a* ($^{URU.d}$U-*ašša*)	(—)	Bo 9705 + II 48

^{d}NIN.URTA

^{d}NIN.URTA	(dat.)	Bo 8783:4’

^{d}NISABA

^{d}NISAB⸢A⸣(-)[. . .]	(—)	Bo 8768 lt. col. 2’

^{d}U

^{d}U	(nom.)	Bo 8787:6’
^{d}U	(dat.$^{?}$)	Bo 9443:5’
^{d}U	(gen.$^{?}$)	Bo 8695:3’
^{d}U	(gen.)	Bo 8785:7’, 9’
⸢^{d}U⸣	(—)	Bo 8768 lt. col. 1’
^{d}U$^{?}$	(dat.)	Bo 9506:11’
^{d}U (^{URU}*Ḫa*[*tti*(?)])	(—)	Bo 9491 rt. col. 5’
^{d}U (^{URU}*Ḫurš*[*a* . . .])	(—)	Bo 8768 lt. col. 3’

^{d}U (^{URU}*Kašda[ma]*)	(nom.)	Bo 8787:7'
[^{d}U] ([^{URU}*N]erikka*)	(nom.)	Bo 8787:7'
^{d}U *ḫu-u-u̯a-ri-i̯a-u̯[a- . . .]*	(nom.)	Bo 8787:6'
^{d}U *mu-u̯a-tal-la-ḫi-ta-aš*	(acc.)	Bo 8710 + rt. col. 14'
^{d}U *pí-ḫa-aš-ša-š[i-iš]*	(acc.)	Bo 8710 + rt. col. 13'
^{d}U *ŠA-ME-E*	(acc.)	Bo 6570 II 5'

^{d}UTU

^{d}UTU-*uš*	(nom.)	Bo 6370 rev. (III$^{?}$) 2, Bo 7833 II 17
^{d}UTU-*i*	(dat.)	Bo 7833 II 5
^{d}UTU-*aš*	(gen.)	Bo 8776:5'
^{d}UTU	(acc.)	Bo 7937:6'
^{d}UTU (^{URU}*[A-ri-in-na]*)	(—)	Bo 9485 rt. col. 2'
[^{d}UTU] ([^{URU}*Ar]inna*)	(dat.)	Bo 8751 upper edge 2
[ták-n]a-aš ^{d}UTU-*aš*	(gen.)	Bo 6207 rev. IV 6'

^{d}IŠTAR

^{d}*IŠTAR*	(dat.)	Bo 8789:2

^{d}ZABA$_4$BA$_4$

^{d}*ZA-BA$_4$-BA$_4$*	(acc.)	Bo 7937:9'
[^{d}Z]*A-BA$_4$-BA$_4$*	(dat.$^{?}$)	Bo 8698:4'

INCOMPLETE DIVINE NAMES

^{d}*Iš$^{?}$-[. . .]*	(dat.)	Bo 8726:5'
^{d}*Ka-pa$^{?}$-[. . .]*	(acc.)	Bo 7937:8'
$^{d?}$*Ma-[. . .]*	(—)	Bo 8706 rev.$^{?}$ 5'
^{d}*T[e$^{?}$- . . .]*	(—)	Bo 8708 obv.$^{?}$ rt. col. 2'
^{d}*Za$^{?}$-[. . .]*	(—)	Bo 9498: 8'
^{d}*Z[i- . . .]*	(dat.)	Bo 6909 obv.$^{?}$ 2
[. . . $^{?}$]⌞x$^{?}$.x⌟.GAL (^{URU}*Ḫatt[i]*)	(—)	Bo 8779:6'
^{d}⌞*x-x$^{?}$*⌟(-)[. . .]	(dat.)	Bo 9525:4'
^{d}*x-[. . .]*	(acc.)	Bo 7937:6'
^{d}x(.)[. . .]	(—)	Bo 8787:3'
^{d}x(./-)[. . .]	(—)	Bo 7833 III 3'
^{d}x	(—)	Bo 8787:3' (2x)
^{d}[. . .]	(dat.)	Bo 8726:4'
⌞$^{d?}$⌟[. . .]	(—)	Bo 9487:7'

PERSONAL NAMES

^{m}Eḫeya

^{m}*E-ḫé-i̯a*	(–)	Bo 9490 + obv. 3’
$^{m⸢}$*E*⸣-[*ḫé-i̯a*]	(gen.)	Bo 9490 + obv. 6’

^{m}Ḫattušili

[(^{m})]⸤*Ḫa*⸥-*at-tu-ši*-DINGIR-*LIM-iš*	(nom.)	Bo 6570 II 18’

^{m}Ḫimuili

[^{m}*Ḫi*$^{?}$]-*i-mu*-DINGIR-*L*[*IM*(-) . . .]	(–)	Bo 8765:3’

^{m}Kalimuna

^{m}*Ka-li-mu-na*	(gen.)	Bo 8742 + rev. 7

^{f}Šanḫadu

^{f}*Ša-a*⸢*n-ḫ*⸣[(*a*)-*du-uš*]	(nom.)	Bo 9650 + II 5

^{m}Šunaili

^{m}*Šu-na-i*-[*li*(-)...]	(–)	Bo 8766 rt. col. 2’

^{m}Ušapa

^{m}*Ú-ša-a-pa*	(gen.)	Bo 8742 + rev. 6, 9, 11

$^{m.d}$AMAR.UTU.LÚ

$^{m.d}$AMAR.[UTU.LÚ(?)(-)...]	(–)	Bo 8084:3’

^{m}UR.MAḪ.LÚ

^{m}UR.MAḪ.LÚ-*iš*	(nom.)	Bo 6238:11’

INCOMPLETE PERSONAL NAMES

[^{m}...]-*i-li-i*[*š*(-)...]	(nom.)	Bo 8765:2’
$^{⸢m}$U⸣[R. ...]	(–)	Bo 8734:1’
$^{m?}$*x*-[...]	(–)	Bo 8769:1’

GEOGRAPHICAL NAMES

^{URU}Apzuwa

$^{[UR]U}$*Ap-zu-u-i*	(dat.-loc.)	Bo 9582 + III 28’

^{URU}Ariḫazziya

^{URU}*A-ri-ḫa-az-zi-i̯a*	(gen.)	Bo 7937:8’

^{URU}Arinna

[^{URU}*A-ri*]-⸤*in*⸥-*na*	(gen.)	Bo 8751 upper edge 2
$^{UR⸢U⸣}$[*A-ri-in-na*]	(gen.)	Bo 9485 rt. col. 2’

^{URU}Arzauwa

^{URU}*Ar za u u̯a*	(gen.)	Bo 8752 + I 1

^{URU}Ḫanḫana

^{URU}*Ḫa-an-ḫa-na*	(gen.)	Bo 7937:14’

^{URU}Ḫatti

^{URU}*Ḫa-at-t*[*i*]	(gen.)	Bo 8779:4’, 5’, 6’
^{URU}*Ḫa-a*[*t*$^?$*-ti*$^?$]	(gen.)	Bo 9491 rt. col. 5’

^{URU}Ḫattuša

$^{[U]RU}$*Ḫa-at-tu-š*[*a*(-) . . .]	(—)	Bo 8734:2’
$^{U[(R)]U}$*Ḫa-at-tu-ši*	(dat.)	Bo 9511 + rev. 30’

^{URU}Kaneš

^{URU}*Ka-né-eš*	(gen.)	Bo 6570 II 6’

^{URU}Kašdama

^{URU}*Kaš-da-*[*ma*]	(gen.)	Bo 8787:7’

^{URU}Gašduḫa

[^{URU}*G*]*a-aš-du-ḫa*	(—)	Bo 9502:3’

^{KUR}Lawata

^{KUR}[*L*]*a-u̯a-ta-aš*	(gen.)	Bo 8787:5’

^{URU}Nerik(a)

[^{URU}*N*]*e-ri-ik*	(—)	Bo 9470 obv.$^?$ 6’
[^{URU}*N*]*e-ri-i*[*k*(-) . . .]	(—)	Bo 9514 + II 13’
[^{URU}*N*]*e-ri-ik-ka*$_4$	(gen.)	Bo 8787:7’
[^{URU}*N*]*e-ri-ik*	(—)	Bo 8708 rev.$^?$ lt. col. 3

^{URU}Tauriša

[^{URU}*Ta-ú-r*]⸤*i*⸥*-ša*	(gen.)	Bo 6271 rt. col. 10’

^{URU}Uruga

[^{URU}*U*]*-ru-ga*	(dat.-loc.)	Bo 9650 + II 2

^{URU}KÁ.DINGIR.RA

[^{URU}K]Á.DINGIR.RA-*x*(-)[. . .]	(—)	Bo 8761:2’

$^{URU.d}$U-aššša

$^{URU.d}$U*-aš-ša-u̯a*	(gen. + ≠*wa*)	Bo 9705 + II 48

INCOMPLETE GEOGRAPHICAL NAMES

^{URU}*Ḫa-*[. . .]	(abl.)	Bo 9488:3’
^{URU}*Ḫa-a*[*t*$^?$- . . .]	(—)	Bo 8763 rt. col. 3’
^{URU}*Ḫur-š*[*a*$^?$- . . .]	(gen.)	Bo 8768 lt. col. 3’

URU*Ša-aḫ-mi-*[. . .]	(nom.)	Bo 8797:3'
URU*Ta-a-x-*[. . .]	(gen.)	Bo 7937:11'
URU*Ta-ḫ*[*a-na*?- . . .]	(–)	Bo 8766 rt. col. 3', 4'
URU*Tu-u-m*[*a*?- . . .]	(nom.)	Bo 8797:2'
[URU . . .]-⌊*x*⌋-*aš*	(nom.)	Bo 8797:3'
[URU . . .]-*ra-aš*	(nom.)	Bo 8797:2'
[URU . . .]-*x-ua-aš-na-aš-ša*(-)[. . .]	(nom.?)	Bo 8797:4'
⌊URU?⌋-[. . .]	(–)	Bo 8763 rt. col. 5'

MOUNTAIN NAMES

ḪUR.SAGḪaḫaya

[ḪUR.SAG*Ḫ*]*a-a-ḫa-a-i*[*a*(-) . . .]	(–)	Bo 8716:3'

ḪUR.SAGNašalma

[ḪUR.S]AG*Na-ša-al-ma*	(–)	Bo 9582 + III 27'

ḪUR.SAGDaḫa

ḪUR.SAG[(*Da-a-ḫa-pát*)]	(gen. + =*pat*)	Bo 9538:5'

SPRING NAME

TÚLKalimma

TÚL*Ka-li-i*[*m-ma-an*]	(acc.)	Bo 6271 rt. col. 10'

SELECT LEXICAL ENTRIES FROM Bo 6151–Bo 9535

This section is dedicated to select lexemes and does not claim to be a complete word list of the fragments Bo 6151 - Bo 9535. It should mainly focus on *hapax legomena*, rare forms and spellings, and those words that are now in their corrected and completed forms as one can determine from the recent (direct) joins and duplicates. Although their number is small, these occurrences will be useful for future lexical studies. For reasons of space, the occurrences are cited with Bo-numbers only, and line numberings are always in accordance with those given in the transliteration section.

SYLLABIC WORDS

a-ịš-šir	Bo 9478:3’ **pret. pl. 3** → *aiš(š)-* (verb, mng. unkn.)
ᴱ́ar-ga-i-ú-ta	Bo 6827:5’ **pl. nom.-acc. neut.** (Luw.) → *ᴱ́arkiu-* (a building or room)
ᴱ́ar-ki-u̯i₅(-i̯a)	Bo 6151 lt. col. 3’ **sg. dat.-loc.** → *ᴱ́arkiu-* (a building or room)
an-nạ-ạl-[li(-) . . .]	Bo 7103 III 8’ (–) → *annalla/i-* “earlier, former”
[a]n-na-aš-šar	Bo 9450:3’ **sg. nom.-acc. neut.** → *annaššar* (noun, mng. unkn.)
a-ar-aš-kán-d[(u)]	Bo 7103 III 15’ **iter. imp. pl. 3** → *ar-* “to reach, arrive at”
ar-za-na-aš pár-na	Bo 7937:11’ **sg. all. com.** → *arzanaš parn-* “hostel”
ạr-za-nạ-aš Ẹ́-[. . .]	Bo 7937:15’ (–) → *arzanaš parn-*
ᴱ́aš-ta-tu-ụ-i	Bo 7284 rt. col. 6’ **sg. dat.-loc.** → *ᴱ́aštatu(wa)-* (a building or room)
⸤e?⸥-pa-an-du	Bo 9493 I? and II? 4’ (–) → *epantu-* (noun, mng. unkn.)

e-eš-ti	Bo 6238:10’ **pres. sg. 2** → *eš-* “to be”
ẹ-eš-šu-u-an (with following *te-eḫ-ḫi*)	Bo 6238:15’ **sup.** → *eššа-* “to perform, fulfill”
ẹ-za-az-zi	Bo 7937:4’ **pres. sg. 3** → *ezza-* “to eat”
^{É}*ḫạ-le-en-ti-u-az*	Bo 7937:10’ **sg. abl. neut.** → ^{É}*ḫalentuwa-* “palace-complex”
^{É}*ḫa-le-en-tu-u-i*	Bo 6271 rt. col. 7’ **sg. dat.-loc. neut.** → ^{É}*ḫalentuwa-* “palace-complex”
$^{\text{URU(!)}}$*ḫa-le-en-tu-u-u̯a-aš*	Bo 6570 II 7’ **pl. dat.-loc. neut.** → ^{É}*ḫalentuwa-* “palace-complex”
ḫạ-lu-gạ-aš	Bo 9650 + II 3 **pl. acc. com.**$^{?}$ → *ḫaluga-* “message, report”
^{DUG}*ḫal-u̯a-tal-la*	Bo 6570 II 15’ **sg. nom.-acc. neut.** → ^{DUG}*ḫalwatalla-* (a container)
ḫa-an-ta-an-za	Bo 6570 II 14’ **sg. nom. com.** → *ḫandant-* “checked; true”
[(*ḫa-a*)]*n-te-ez*$^{!}$*-zum-ni*	Bo 6810 + II 17’ **sg. dat.-loc. com.** → *ḫantezumna-* “entrance hall$^{?}$, front court$^{?}$”
⸢*ḫar-ra‹-nu›-u*⸣*š-kán*$^{!}$*-du*	Bo 9560 + II 2’ **iter. imp. pl. 3** → *ḫarranu-* “to break up”
‹*ḫa-*›*a-ri-i̯a-an-zi*	Bo 9449 + IV 10’ **pres. pl. 3** → *ḫariya-* “to bury”
⸤*ḫa*⸥*-tu-kán*	Bo 6370 III$^{?}$ 10 **sg. nom.-acc.** → *ḫatuka-* “terrifying”

ḫa-az-zi-u̯i$_5$	Bo 6238:15’ **sg. nom.-acc. neut.** → *ḫazziwi-* “rite, cult act”
[$^{\text{LÚ.MEŠ}}$*ḫé-eš*]*-tu-um-né-eš*	Bo 9477:3’ **pl. nom. com.** → ^{LÚ}*ḫeštumna-* “functionary of *ḫešta*-house”
^{É}*ḫi-i-li-i̯a-aš*	Bo 6810 + II 20’ **pl.? dat.-loc. com.** → ^{É}*ḫila/i*$^{?}$*-* “courtyard”
ḫi-in-‹ik-›zi	Bo 6810 + II 20’ **pres. sg. 3** → *ḫink-* “to do reverence”
⌞$^{\text{NA4}}$*ḫu-u*⌟*-ḫa̩-an*	Bo 9526 + II 23’ **sg. acc. com.** → $^{\text{NA4}}$*ḫuḫa-* (a valuable stone or object)
ḫu-i-da-a-a[*r*]	Bo 8773:4’ **pl. nom.-acc. neut.** → *ḫuitar* “(wild) animals”
ḫu-u-ke-eš-šar	Bo 6909 obv.? 9 **sg. nom.-acc. neut.** → *ḫukeššar* “slaughter (ration)”
[(*ḫur-l*)]*a-ti-iš*	Bo 6978:12’ **pl. nom. com.** → *ḫurlati-* (an ingredient of porridge)
^{TÚG}*ḫu-u-u̯a-al-ta̩-az*	Bo 9594 + I 11’ **sg. abl.** → ^{TÚG}*ḫuwalta-* (a linen or cloth)
in-na-ra-u̯a-aš (with following ^{d}LA̩MMA-*aš*)	Bo 7833 III 14’ **sg. gen.** → *innarawa* “vigorous”
in-na-ra-u̯a-an	Bo 7833 II 15, III 15’ **sg. nom.-acc. neut.** → *innarawa* “strong”
⌜*iš-ḫu-u-u̯a-u-u̯a-aš*⌝ (with preceding *kat-ta-an*)	Bo 6570 II 4’ **verbal subst. gen.** → *išḫuwa-* “to pour, scatter”
i̩š-ki-i̯a-az-z[*i*]	Bo 8785:4’ **pres. sg. 3** → *iškiya-* “to anoint, smear”

^{DUG}*iš-nu-u-ri*	Bo 8726:3’ **sg. dat.-loc. com.** → ^{DUG}*išnura/i-* “dough bin”
iš-pa-an-ṭa-[a]z	Bo 7833 III 9’ **sg. abl. com.** → *išpant-* “night”
ka-la-ak-tar	Bo 7833 II 18 **sg. nom.-acc. neut.** → *galaktar* (a substance for relief)
^{É}*k⸢a⸣-ri̥-im-ma-na-aš*	Bo 9514 + II 17’ **pl. dat.-loc. com.** → ^{É}*karimmana-* “temple”
[g]a-ri̥-ra-pí	Bo 9529:4’ **pres. sg. 3** → *karirap-* “to eat, devour”
kar-di̥-i̥t	Bo 6370 III$^{?}$ 4 **sg. inst. neut.** → *kard-* “heart, inside”
ku-ga-ni-ẹ-[(e)š$^{?}$]	Bo 6978:12’ **pl. nom. com.** → *kugani-* (an ingredient of porridge)
[gul$^{?}$]-lạ-ak-ku-an	Bo 9529:3’ **sg. nom.-acc. neut.** → *gullakuwan* “scandal, shame”
[^{GI}]$^{\mathrm{Š.ḪUR}}$*gul-za-tar*	Bo 7103 III 5’ **sg. nom.-acc. neut.** → $^{\mathrm{GIŠ.ḪUR}}$*gulzatar* “wooden tablet”
^{GIŠ}*ku-ra-ak-ki*	Bo 6909 obv.$^{?}$ 11 **sg. dat.-loc. com.** → ^{GIŠ}*kurakki-* “pillar, column”
[(la-a)]-ḫu-u̯a-a-an-du	Bo 7050 lt. col. 11’ **imp. pl. 3** → *laḫuwai-* “to pour (out)”
la-a-ú (with preceding *[ar-ḫ]a*)	Bo 8729:3’ **imp. sg. 3** → *la-* “to loose”
[(l)]a-lu-uk-ki-u$^{!}$-u̯a-an-t[(e-eš)]	Bo 8778 II$^{?}$ 2’ **pl. nom. com.** → *lalukkiwant-* “luminous, shining”

la-at-ta-al-li̯(-)[. . .]
Bo 7833 II 9
(—)

la-at-ta-al-l[*i*(-) . . .]
Bo 7833 II 13
(—)
→ *lattalli*$^{?}$(-)[. . .] (an object or a tool used in ritual)

ma-an-ni-in-ni̯-uš(*-u̯a-mu*)
Bo 6238:17'
pl. nom. or **acc. com.**
→ *maninni-* "necklace"

ma-ni-in-ku-u̯a-nu-ut
Bo 6238:7'
pret. sg. 3
→ *maninkuwanu-* "to make near / short$^{?}$"

[*m*]*e-mi-i̯a-nu-u*[*š*]
Bo 8741:6'
pl. acc. com.
→ *memiya*(*n*)- "word"

me-mi-iš-ki-ši
Bo 6238:6'
iter. pres. sg. 2
→ *mema-* "to speak"

[(*m*)]⸢*i-iš-ri*⸣-[*u*-(*u̯*)]*a-a*⸢*n-z*⸣[(*a*)]
Bo 8778 II$^{?}$ 1'
sg. nom. com.
→ *mišriwant-* "splendid, beautiful"

[(*mu-g*)]*a-a-u-u̯a-aš*
Bo 9479:3'
sg. gen. neut.
→ *mugawar* "evocation ritual"

^{GIŠ}*mu-kar*
Bo 9514 + II 18'
sg. nom.-acc. neut.
→ ^{GIŠ}*mukar* (a noise-making implement)

mu̯-u̯a-tal-la-ḫi-ta-aš (with preceding ^{d}U̯)
Bo 8710 + rt. col. 14'
sg. gen.
→ *muwatallaḫit-* "ability to inspire awe$^{?}$"

na-aḫ-ši-i[*š*]
Bo 8784:2'
sg. nom. com.
→ *naḫši-* (a measurement)

ne-eḫ-ḫi
Bo 9457:7'
pres. sg. 1
→ *nai-* "to turn"

$^{\text{EZEN}_4}$*nu-un-tar-aš-ḫa-aš*
Bo 6570 II 12', 14'
sg. nom. com.
→ $^{\text{EZEN}_4}$*nuntarašḫaš* "festival of haste"

pa-ra-a-aš-ši-i̯[(*a-an-na-aš*)] (with preceding [Z]Ì.DA) | Bo 6978:14'
sg. gen.
→ *parā(-)šiyannaš* "... of sprouting forth"

p̣a?-*ạš-pa-na-a-aš* | Bo 8773:5'
sg. nom. com.
→ *pašpana-* (an insect)

pé-eš-ši-iš-ki-iz-zi (with preceding *an-da*) | Bo 7833 III 12'
pres. sg. 3
→ *peššiya-* "to throw"

p̣í-i-e-et | Bo 9529:5'
pret. sg. 3
→ *piya-* "to send"

pí-iḫ-ḫu-un(-*u̯a-aš-ši*) | Bo 6238:13'
pret. sg. 1
→ *pai-* "to give"

pí-ḫa-aš-ša-š[*i-iš*] (with preceding dỤ) | Bo 8710 + rt. col. 13'
sg. nom. com.
→ *piḫaššašši-* (epithet of a stormgod; "lightning")

[*pé-*(*e-ḫu*)]-*tẹ-iš-ḳán-z*[(*i*)] | Bo 9650 + II 7
iter. pres. pl. 3
→ *peḫute-* "to bring there"

pé-e-da‹-*an*› (with preceding *da-a-an*) | Bo 6978:9'
sg. nom.-acc. neut.
→ *peda-* "place, position"

⌜*pí*?-*d*⌝*a-ụ́* | Bo 9457:1'
imp. sg. 3
→ *peda-* "to carry (somewhere)"

ša-ḫu-i̯a-an-ti | Bo 9502:8'
(–)
→ **šaḫui-* or **šaḫuyant-* (mng. unkn.)

ši-i-e-ez-zi | Bo 9516 + III 3'
pres. sg. 3
→ *šai-* / *šiya-* "to hurl"

GIŠ*ša-i̯a-an* | Bo 8029:4'
sg. nom.-acc. neut.?
→ GIŠ*šaya*(*n*)- (a wood or wooden object)

ša-li-ga-ri | Bo 9478:6'
mid. pres. sg. 3
→ *šalik-* "to touch"

ša-li-ga-˻r˼[i]	Bo 9478:7' **mid. pres. sg. 3** → *šalik-* "to touch"
[še-ḫi-l]i-iš-ki-i̯a-aš(-šạ)	Bo 9705 + II 54 **sg. gen. com.** → *šeḫiliški-* "purification ritual / offering"
[še]-iš-kị-iš-kị-[(u-u̯a-an)] (with following *[(d)]⸢a-a-iš⸣*)	Bo 9441 + III 16 **double iter. sup.** → *šeš-* "to sleep (for incubation)"
da-a	Bo 6370 III$^{?}$ 3,Bo 8729:7' **imp. sg. 2** → *da-* "to take"
[tá]k$^{?}$-ši-iš-šar	Bo 9442:3 **sg. nom.-acc. neut.** → *takšeššar* "assemblage (of foodstuffs)"
ták-ku	Bo 9478:5' → *takku* "if"
da-la-a-aḫ-ḫ[u-un] (with preceding *[a]r-ḫa*)	Bo 8729:6' **pret. sg. 1** → *dala-* "to leave (alone)"
[d]a-a-la-i	Bo 9526 + III 15' **pres. sg. 3** → *dala-* "to leave (alone)"
tal-la-i̤$^{?}$	Bo 9485 rt. col. 3' **pres. sg. 3$^{?}$** → **tallai-* "to evoke (a deity)$^{?}$"
ta-lu̯-ri-i$^{!}$	Bo 8796 + IV 12 (–) → *taluri-* (mng. unkn.)
ta-me-ek-˻ta˼	Bo 9457:8' **pret. sg. 3** → *dame(n)k-* "to join oneself to"
[(d)]ạ-ạ-rị-nu-ut	Bo 9441 + III 17 **mid. pret. sg. 3** → *dariyanu-* "to let someone implore"
[d]ạ-a-ri-nu-ut	Bo 9441 + III 14 **mid. imp. sg. 2** → *dariyanu-* "to let someone implore"

[*t*]*ar-na-an* (with following *ḫar-tén*)	Bo 9494:3’ **part. sg. nom.-acc. neut.** → *tarna-* “to let”
tar-na-aš	Bo 9478:4’ **pret. sg. 3** → *tarna-* “to let”
tar-ni-iš-kán-zi	Bo 6207 obv. III 12’ **iter. pres. pl. 3** → *tarna-* “to let”
tar-pa-li-[*uš*(-) . . .]	Bo 9519:7’ **pl. acc. com.** → *tarpalli-* “substitute”
t[*i-i*]*ḫ-ḫi* (with preceding E̥GIR-*an*)	Bo 9582 + III 29’ **pres. sg. 1** → *dai-* / *tiya-* “to place, put”
ti-i̯a-ti-i̥š?	Bo 6978:12’ **pl. nom. com.** → *tiyati-* “asafoetida?”
[*ti*]-⌞*i*⌟*t-ta-nu-mi*	Bo 9519:8’ **pres. sg. 1** → *tittanu-* “to set, place”
du-uš-ga-ra-at-ta-an	Bo 6370 III? 6 **sg. acc. com.** → *dušgaratt-* “entertainment”
u-un-na-aḫ-ḫ[*u-un*]	Bo 8729:5’ **pret. sg. 1** → *unna-* “to drive here”
up-pa-an-za	Bo 8772:4’ **part. sg. nom. com.** → *uppa-* “to send here”
ụ́-tạḫ-ḫụ-ụn	Bo 9504:2’ **pret. sg. 1** → *uda-* “to bring here”
u̯a-aḫ-nu-ši	Bo 6238:16’ **pres. sg. 2** → *waḫnu-* “to turn”
u̯a-al-ḫạ-an-ni-an-⌞*zi*⌟ (with preceding EGIR-*an*)	Bo 7937:13’ **pres. pl. 3** → *walḫanniya-* “to keep striking / playing”

ú-el-lu-u̯a
Bo 9478:4'
sg. all.
→ *wellu-* "meadow"

ú-ẹ-eš
Bo 6827:4'
→ *weš* "wir"

ú-e-te-mi
Bo 8743:7'
pres. sg. 1
→ *wete-* "to build"

ụ́-e-ed-du
Bo 9488:5'
imp. sg. 3
→ *uwa-* "to come"

ú-i-te-na-aš
Bo 7833 II 4
sg. gen. neut.
→ *watar* / *weten-* "water"

^{GIŠ}*ú-⌞i-du-l⌟[i-i̯a*$^{?}$]
Bo 6827:7'
sg. dat.-loc.$^{?}$ com.
→ ^{GIŠ}*widuli-* "fence, screen$^{?}$"

[^{GIŠ}*ú*]*-ị-du-le-e-eš*
Bo 6827:6'
pl. nom. com.
→ ^{GIŠ}*widuli-* "fence, screen$^{?}$"

^{NINDA}*zi-i⌞p-p⌟u-lạ-aš-ši-in*
Bo 8696 + obv.$^{?}$ III 11'
sg. acc. com.
→ ^{NINDA}*zippulašši-* (a kind of bread)

INCOMPLETE SYLLABIC WORDS

x̣-an-ku-ut-ti — Bo 8796 + IV 13

ar-lụ-u̯a-x̣(-)[. . .] — Bo 9518 + I 5'

[. . . (-)*m*]*i-nụ-ma-aš* — Bo 9488:6'

zị-nu-pí(-)[. . .] — Bo 9514 + II 12'

^{TÚG}*zi-iz-z*[*i*$^{?}$- . . .] — Bo 8781 rt. col. 5'

LOGOGRAMS AND AKKADOGRAMS

[. . .](.)⌞B⌟ÚN-*aš*
Bo 9650 + II 5
(–)
→ BÚN "rage, revolt$^{?}$"

^{DUG}DÍLIM.GAL
Bo 8726:1'
→ ^{DUG}DÍLIM.GAL "bowl"

DINGIR.MẸŠ-*eš*	Bo 9492:1' **pl. nom. com.** → DINGIR / *šiu*(*n*)- "god"
⌞DUḪ⌟.LÀL	Bo 9479:9' → DUḪ.LÀL "wax"
⌞DUMU.L⌟Ú.U$_{19}$.LU	Bo 9478:8' → DUMU.LÚ.U$_{19}$.LU "human"
DUMU.LÚ.U$_{19}$.LU-*ỤT*$^?$-[*TI*$^?$]	Bo 9519:6' (–) → DUMU.LÚ.U$_{19}$.LU-*UTTU* "population"
[^{TÚG}]Ẹ.ÍB	Bo 8739:3' → ^{TÚG}E.ÍB "sash"
[EZEN$_4$] ⌞NÍG⌟.MỤNUS.ÚS.SÁ	Bo 9515:3'
[EZEN$_4$ NÍG.M]UNUS.ÚS.SÁ	Bo 9515:5' → EZEN$_4$ NÍG.MUNUS.ÚS.SÁ "festival of brideprice"
[EZEN$_4$] Ụ.BAR$_8$(-*i̯a-k*[*án*])	Bo 9487:6' → EZEN$_4$ Ú.BAR° "festival of spring"
$^{\text{TÚG?}}$GADA.GAL	Bo 6978:2' → ^{TÚG}GADA.GAL "large cloth$^?$"
⌜GIŠ⌝.ḪI.A-*ru*	Bo 8709:3' **pl. nom.-acc. neut.** → GIŠ / *taru*- "wood, tree"
GIŠ.KÍN	Bo 9446:3' → GIŠ.KÍN "tree fruit"
GÚ.GÍD.DA	Bo 6570 II 16' → GÚ.GÍD.DA "(with) long neck"
GU$_4$.LÍL	Bo 8803:6' → GU$_4$.LÍL "ox of the steppe"
GU$_4$.NIGA	Bo 8803:5' → GU$_4$.NIGA "fattened ox"
[(IGI-*u̯a*)]-⌞*an*$^?$-*ta*$^?$-*ri*$^?$-*nu-u*⌟*š-kán*-[(*zi*)]	Bo 7103 III 16' **iter. pres. pl. 3** → IGI-*wantari*(*ya*)*nu*- / *šakuwantari*(*ya*)*nu*- "to neglect"
NAM.LÚ.Ụ$_{19}$.LU(-*i̯a*)	Bo 7833 II 3 → NAM.LÚ.U$_{19}$.LU "mankind, humanity"
[^{TÚG}NÍG].⌜LÁM⌝.ḪI.⌜A⌝	Bo 9493 I$^?$ / II$^?$ 1' **pl. nom.** or **acc.** → ^{TÚG}NÍG.LÁM "sumptuous garment"
NINDA.ZI.SIG	Bo 8746:3' → NINDA.ZI.SIG (a kind of bread)

^{GIŠ}SAG.KUL-*aš* GIŠ-*r*[*u-i*]	Bo 6909 rev.$^{?}$ 5' **sg. dat.-loc. neut.** → ^{GIŠ}SAG.KUL-*aš* GIŠ-*ru* / *Ḫattalwaš taru-* "doorBolt"
SIG$_{5}$-*ta-ti*	Bo 9478:5' **mid. pret. sg. 3** → SIG$_{5}$ / *lazziya-* "to be good, get well"
SUR$_{7}$	Bo 8697:1' → SUR$_{7}$ "mound"
ŠÀ-*ịt*	Bo 6370 III$^{?}$ 8 **sg. inst. neut.** → ŠÀ / *kard-* "heart, inside"
^{GIŠ}U$_{4}$.Ḫ[I.IN]	Bo 9446:6' → ^{GIŠ}U$_{4}$.ḪI.IN "unripe date"
U$_{4}$.SAKAR	Bo 8803:4' → U$_{4}$.SAKAR "crescent"
$^{LÚ.MEŠ}$UKU.UŠ	Bo 8029:8' **pl. nom.$^{?}$** → ^{LÚ}UKU.UŠ "warrior"
URU.DIDLI.ḪI.A	Bo 8742 + rev. 10 **pl. acc.** → URU "city"
^{LÚ}*ḪA-ZA-NU*	Bo 6151 lt. col. 4' **sg. nom.** → ^{LÚ}*ḪAZANNU* "mayor"
MAŠ-LU	Bo 8739:3' → *MAŠLU* "trimmed"
[(*NA-A*)]*K-TÁM-ŠU*$^{(!)}$	Bo 9479:5' → *NAKTAMU* "lid"

NUMERALS

IV-*na*	Bo 9478:7'
⸤IX⸥-*an*	Bo 8796 + IV 12

AKKADIAN WORDS

pa-ni-iš	Bo 9490 + obv. 4'
^{LÚ}*mu-un-na-ab-tu$_{4}$*	Bo 9490 + obv. 9'
ul-lu-ú	Bo 9490 + obv. 10'

HURRIAN WORD

[at-t]⌞a⌟-[ni-u̯i̯-na]	Bo 8704 + I 7'

SUMERIAN WORDS

á-gál	Bo 9520:3'
ḫé-éb-ba?*-an-sụm(-)*	Bo 9520:5'
lugal-ab-zu-ke$_4$	Bo 9520:4'
nạm-tar?	Bo 9520:3'
nu-gạ́l?	Bo 9520:3'

LEXICAL CITATIONS

In the following list are the words, compounds and expressions from the treated Bo-texts and related lexical entries from the Hittite lexicon. There are no detailed discussions, but rather brief remarks which are necessary for some lexical topics.

HITTITE

aiš(š)- (verb)	Bo 9478 n. 1
annašnant-	Bo 9450 n. 1
an-na-aš-šar	Bo 9450 n. 1
**an-na-aš*^{SAR}	Bo 9450 n. 1
(IX-*an*) *x̣-an-ku-ut-ti*	Bo 8796 + n. 4 and 5
araḫza gimri	Bo 9525 n. 1
$^{\text{(É)}}$*argawi-* / $^{\text{(É)}}$*arkiwi-*	Bo 6827 n. 3
ar-lụ-u̯a-x̣(-)[. . .]	Bo 9518 + n. 1
arzili-	Bo 9450 n. 1
**ạ-ši-iš-šar* (= *ašeššar*)	Bo 9442 n. 1
^{É}*aš-ta-tu-ụ́-i*	Bo 7284 n. 4
e-pa-an-d[*u*?]	Bo 9493 n. 3
ḫaluga-	Bo 9650 + n. 3, 4
ḫarranušk-	Bo 9560 + n. 2
ḫa-at-ta-lu-u̯a-aš	Bo 7937 n. 1
$^{\text{LÚ.MEŠ}}$*ḫé-eš-tu-u-um-né-eš*	Bo 9477 n. 1
$^{\text{NA4}}$*ḫūḫa-*	Bo 9526 + n. 2
anda ḫulaliya-	Bo 8759 n. 1
$^{\text{(TÚG)}}$*ḫupita-*	Bo 8739 n. 2
ḫurlatiš	Bo 6978 n. 8
ḫurt-	Bo 9459 n. 2
ḫurtai-	Bo 9459 n. 2
^{TÚG}*ḫu(wa)lta-*	Bo 9594 + n. 2
ḫu-u-u̯a-ri-i̯a-u̯[*a-*...]	Bo 8787 n. 4
i-pa-an-du/tu	Bo 9493 n. 3
iškiya-	Bo 8785 n. 1
^{DUG}*išnura-*	Bo 8726 n. 1
iš-da-ra-u-u̯a-a⸢*n-za*⸣	Bo 9459 n. 1

˻iš˼-ta-ra-a-u-u̯a-an-za	Bo 9459 n. 1
(*arḫa*) *ganganumi*	Bo 9705 + n. 3
(*arḫa*) *karira-*	Bo 9529 n. 2
^{TÚG}*kariulli*	Bo 9493 n. 2
$^{\text{(DUG)}}$*kattakurant-*	Bo 8736 n. 1
kinupi-	Bo 9514 + n. 2
kuganeš	Bo 6978 n. 8 and 10
gullakkuwa-	Bo 9529 n. 1
ku-ul-la-ak-ku-u̯a-an	Bo 9529 n. 1
$^{\text{GIŠ.ḪUR}}$*gulzatar*	Bo 7103 n. 2
ku-ra-ak-ki-iš	Bo 6909 n. 2
ar-ḫa la-a-ú	Bo 8729 n. 1
†[*la-l*]*a-me-eš*	Bo 9466 n. 1
l[*alawešaš*]	Bo 8773 n. 3
lattalli(-)[. . .]	Bo 7833 n. 1
la-at-ti-in	Bo 6978 n. 8
maniyaḫḫai-	Bo 8730 n. 1
maršaštarri-	Bo 8721 n. 3
memiyanzi	Bo 8735 n. 1
(𒑱)*mulatar*	Bo 9488 n. 1
[*mušgall*]*aš*	Bo 8773 n. 3
mu̯-u̯a-tal-la-ḫi-ta-aš	Bo 8710 + n. 1-2
na-aḫ-ḫa-ši-iš	Bo 8784 n. 1
^{LÚ}*pal-u̯a-tal-la«tal-la-»-aš*	Bo 9507 n. 1
parāšiyannaš	→ ŠE *parāšiyannaš*
parāššiyannaš	→ ZÌ.DA *parāššiyannaš*
parašnauaš⸗kan ^{LÚ}SAGI.A-*aš uizzi*	Bo 9507 n. 2
parkui	Bo 6788 n. 1
paršulli	Bo 8792 n. 1
pašpana-	Bo 8773 n. 3
putalliya-	Bo 8734 n. 3
^{GIŠ}*šaya*(*n*)-	Bo 8029 n. 2
šakuwal-	Bo 9526 + n. 3
ši-mu-uš / DINGIR-*mu-uš*	Bo 8796 + n. 1

(SEMI-)LOGOGRAPHIC WORDS AND AKKADOGRAMS

EZEN$_4$ *kušata-*	Bo 9515 n. 3
EZEN$_4$ x-*ŠU ḫapušanzi*	Bo 9515 n. 2
EZEN$_4$ NÍG.MUNUS.ÚS(.SÁ)	Bo 9515 n. 3
GAL.GAL	Bo 6151 n. 1
(IX-*an*) "GAŠAN"-*ti* (or "GAŠAN+TI")	Bo 8796 + n. 5
GIŠ.KÍN *karš*[*iyan*(*t*)-]	Bo 9446 n. 1
GIŠ.KÍN.ḪI.A *duwarnanda*	Bo 9446 n. 1
GU$_4$.LÍL	Bo 8803 n. 2
GU$_4$.MAḪ.LÍL	Bo 8803 n. 2
^{UDU}GUK[KAL$^?$+KUN]	Bo 8803 n. 3
$^{\text{LÚ.MEŠ}}$ḪUB.BÍ *tarkuwanzi*	Bo 9507 n. 2
"KA×IM"	→ BÚN
"KI.GAG"	→ SUR$_7$
KÙ.GA	Bo 9506 n. 1
†NAGGA-*aš-šar*	Bo 9450 n. 1
^{TÚG}NÍG.LÁM.MEŠ	Bo 9493 n. 1
NÍG.MUNUS.ÚS(.SÁ)	Bo 9515 n. 3
NINDA.GUR$_4$.RA.KU$_7$	Bo 8726 n. 1
NINDA."ZI".ḪAR.ḪAR	Bo 8746 n. 1
NINDA."ZI".SIG	Bo 8746 n. 1
^{GIŠ}SAG.KUL-*aš* GIŠ-*i*	Bo 6909 n. 4
^{LÚ}SIPA.UDU	Bo 9513 n. 2
SUR$_7$	Bo 8697 n. 2
ŠE *parāšiyannaš*	Bo 6978 n. 12
ŠID-*eššar* (= *kappueššar*)	Bo 8753 n. 2 and 3
^{MUNUS}ŠU.GI	Bo 9497 n. 2
UGULA $^{\text{LÚ.MEŠ}}$MUḪALDIM	Bo 8736 n. 1
^{LÚ}UKU.UŠ	Bo 8029 n. 3
ZÌ.DA *parāššiyannaš*	Bo 6978 n. 12
ZÌ.DA.DUR$_5$	Bo 9447 n. 1; Bo 9506 n. 1
ZÌ.DA.ḪÁD.DU.A	Bo 9447 n. 1
[*A-ZA*]-*AN-NU*	Bo 6978 n. 7
^{LÚ}*ḪAZANNU*	Bo 6151 n. 3
$^{\text{(GIŠ)}}$*ḪURPALÛ*	Bo 6238 n. 1

HATTIAN

HURRIAN

LUWIAN

CITATIONS FROM OTHER BOĞAZKÖY TEXTS

The citations from other Boğazköy texts that concern lexical and textual details are listed here under the related Bo- and "text-critical notes" numbers. The duplicate text entries as part of *textual apparatus* are not included.

Bo 3245:7'	Bo 8084 n. 2
Bo 3396 $I^{?}$ 10'	Bo 9605 + n. 1
Bo 9577:4'	Bo 9705 + n. 4
FHL 17:2'-3'	Bo 8739 n. 2
HHT 73 I 10'	Bo 7937 n. 1
IBoT 1.3 I 1-2	Bo 6570 n. 10
IBoT 2.79:8'-9'	Bo 8751 n. 1
IBoT 2.131 rev. 24, 26	Bo 8084 n. 2
IBoT 3.1 obv. 16'	Bo 6151 n. 4
IBoT 3.1 rev. 46'-47'	Bo 6909 n. 3
IBoT 4.48 obv. 2' ff.	Bo 8721 n. 1
IBoT 4.48 obv. 2'	Bo 8721 n. 2
IBoT 4.48 obv. 4'-5'	Bo 8721 n. 3
KBo 2.1 II 32	Bo 8768 n. 1
KBo 2.6 + KUB 18.51 II 16-18	Bo 9515 n. 2
KBo 2.7 obv. 18-20'	Bo 8768 n. 1
KBo 3.22 rev. 58	Bo 9504 n. 1
KBo 5.2 I 38	Bo 6978 n. 12
KBo 5.5 I 10'	Bo 6978 n. 12
KBo 5.5 IV 4'	Bo 8803 n. 2
KBo 9.106 II 52	Bo 7833 n. 3
KBo 10.20 III 45	Bo 8768 n. 1
KBo 10.25 VI 4'-5' // KBo 30.14 V 8'	Bo 8773 n. 2
KBo 10.26 I 10	Bo 8776 n. 2
KBo 10.34 I 24	Bo 9446 n. 1
KBo 10.39:12'	Bo 8796 + n. 5
KBo 11.24 + 23 I 7	Bo 8784 n. 1
KBo 11.43 I 15	Bo 8737 n. 3
KBo 11.49 VI 4'	Bo 6207 n. 2
KBo 12.8 IV 24'	Bo 9535 n. 2

KBo 25.171 II? 7'	Bo 9477 n. 1
KBo 26.151 I 6'	Bo 8716 n. 1
KBo 26.190 II 5'	Bo 9487 n. 3
KBo 26.191:16'	Bo 8716 n. 2
KBo 27.42 II 32	Bo 6151 n. 4
KBo 28.108:17'	Bo 9490 + n. 2
KBo 29.72 + KBo 14.96 II 7', 13'	Bo 9516 + n. 1
KBo 29.72 + KBo 14.96 II 9'	Bo 9516 + n. 2
KBo 29.72 + KBo 14.96 II 11'	Bo 9516 + n. 3
KBo 29.203 rev. 4'	Bo 9525 n. 1
KBo 30.13 rev. 11'	Bo 8776 n. 2
KBo 30.37 I 5'-6'	Bo 9486 n. 1
KBo 30.61 obv.? 10'	Bo 8790 n. 1
KBo 30.69 III 5'-9'	Bo 8722 n. 2
KBo 34.106 I 2	Bo 8716 n. 2
KBo 38.36:2'-6'	Bo 9486 n. 1
KBo 38.80 obv. 7	Bo 8803 n. 1
KBo 38.120 + KBo 30.92 rev. 1-2	Bo 9482 n. 2
KBo 39.83 rev. 2'	Bo 8708 n. 4
KBo 40.372:3', 11'	Bo 9459 n. 1
KBo 41.94 I 8'-9'	Bo 7284 n. 2
KBo 44.98 + III 5'	Bo 8695 n. 3
KBo 44.170:5'	Bo 6207 n. 1
KBo 45.5:3'	Bo 8767 n. 2
KBo 45.254 I 10'-14'	Bo 8704 + n. 1
KBo 48.71:14' // KUB 40.110 rev. 6'	Bo 6978 n. 2
KBo 49.89 + obv. III 15'-20'	Bo 8722 n. 2
KBo 50.30 + KUB 14.17 II 8', 13'	Bo 9498 n. 2
KBo 55.94 II 2	Bo 9446 n. 1
KBo 55.94 II 7	Bo 9446 n. 3
KBo 55.94 II 8	Bo 9446 n. 4
KBo 55.94 II 14	Bo 9447 n. 1
KBo 55.199:3'	Bo 9605 + n. 1
KUB 2.6 IV 19	Bo 8736 n. 1

KUB 17.35 I 33', IV 32	Bo 8716 n. 1
KUB 18.32:5'	Bo 9605 + n. 2
KUB 19.55 + rev. 42'	Bo 9582 + n. 1
KUB 20.1 III 15-16	Bo 9497 n. 2
KUB 21.27 + III 41'-42'	Bo 9705 + n. 3
KUB 25.3 III 26	Bo 8786 n. 1
KUB 25.3 IV 34'-40'	Bo 8767 n. 1
KUB 25.9 IV 31-33	Bo 8767 n. 1
KUB 25.16 I 5	Bo 8737 n. 2
KUB 25.22 III 2, 17	Bo 8716 n. 2
KUB 25.23 I 22'	Bo 8029 n. 1
KUB 25.44 II$^{?}$ 25'	Bo 8748 n. 1
KUB 26.81 IV 2	Bo 9535 n. 5
KUB 26.81 IV 7	Bo 9535 n. 4
KUB 27.16 III 2, 7	Bo 8790 n. 1
KUB 30.41 (+) I 21'-24'	Bo 9482 n. 3
KUB 30.49 + IV$^{?}$ 24'	Bo 9529 n. 2
KUB 31.53 + 1320/u obv. 10	Bo 8753 n. 2
KUB 31.53 + 1320/u obv. 11	Bo 8753 n. 3
KUB 31.82:3'	Bo 9490 + n. 1
KUB 31.82:7'	Bo 9490 + n. 3
KUB 32.82 rt. col. 8	Bo 8751 n. 1
KUB 32.112 IV$^{?}$ 3'	Bo 8759 n. 1
KUB 32.112 IV$^{?}$ 4'	Bo 8759 n. 2
KUB 32.133 I 9	Bo 8781 n. 1
KUB 32.133 I 14	Bo 8784 n. 1
KUB 33.68 II 10	Bo 6370 n. 1
KUB 34.125 lt. col. 11'	Bo 8748 n. 1
KUB 35.34:2'-7'	Bo 9497 n. 2
KUB 35.136 + I 4', 7'	Bo 9525 n. 1
KUB 35.142 IV 12'	Bo 6978 n. 11
KUB 38.1 IV 28'-29'	Bo 9583 + n. 1
KUB 38.6 I 9', 13', 17', 21', 33'	Bo 8787 n. 1
KUB 38.6 I 24', 30'	Bo 8787 n. 3

KUB 60.1 + rev. III$^{?}$ 19’	Bo 9480 n. 1
KUB 60.161 II 7	Bo 9494 n. 1
KUB 60.161 II 8	Bo 9519 n. 4
KUB 60.161 II 13-15	Bo 9497 n. 2
KuT 49 obv. 2	Bo 6151 n. 3
RŠ 25.421 obv. 28’	Bo 6909 n. 2
VS 28.1 obv. 6’	Bo 6788 n. 2
VS 28.13 III 16”	Bo 8708 n. 4
VS 28.14 obv. 10	Bo 9442 n. 1
VS 28.30 IV 28	Bo 8796 + n. 4
VS 28.126:3’	Bo 8730 n. 3
VS 28.126:10’, 11’	Bo 8730 n. 1
VS 28.126:13’	Bo 8730 n. 2

CONCORDANCE OF THE CTH NUMBERS OF Bo 6151–Bo 9535 ACCORDING TO CHDS 3 AND *KONKORDANZ*

Bo	*CHDS 3*	*Konkordanz (as of 31.12.2015)*
6151	670	670.2461
6207	635	635
6238	590	832
6271	617	617.?
6370	323	470.459
6570	626	626
6788	625	670.2599
6810 +	682.1.C	670.2611
6827	470 or 670	670.2615
6909	670	670.2627
6978	448	670.2632
7050	594.N	594
7103	261	832
7284	666	666
7317	670	670.2690
7444	832	670.2714
7833	470	470.620
7937	668	668
8029	530	470.631
8084	530	670.2792
8695	470 or 670	500.486
8696 +	626	626
8697	832	832
8698	530 or 670	832
8699	470 or 670	832
8701	670	832
8703	832	832
8704 +	706	706
8706	670	670.2901
8707	832	832

Bo	CHDS 3	Konkordanz (as of 31.12.2015)
8708	647	832
8709	832	832
8710 +	656.4	656.4
8712	670	670.3484
8713	832	832
8714	832	825
8716	530	670.2902
8717	831	790
8718	470 or 670	832
8719	832	832
8720	670	670.2903
8721	582	582
8722	670	670.2904
8723	591.I.b.M	591
8724	670	832
8725	832	832
8726	500 or 670	670.2905
8727	530 or 670	530
8729	370 or 458	470.731
8730	212 or 275	832
8731	832	832
8732	470 or 670	470.732
8734	215	832
8735	470 or 670	470.733
8736	670	670.2906
8737	670	670.2907
8738	832	832
8739	243 or 470	470.734
8741	470 or 670	670.2908
8742 +	146	146
8743	215, 389 or 590	215.?
8744	832	832
8746	670	670.2909
8748	470 or 670	832

Bo	CHDS 3	Konkordanz (as of 31.12.2015)
8749	530	832
8750	832	832
8751	670	470.735
8752 +	402.G	402.G
8753	590	832
8754	670	470.736
8757	40	40
8758	670	832
8759	470	832
8760	670	470.737
8761	832	832
8762	470	470.738
8763	832	670.2910
8764	832	470.739
8765	832	470.740
8766	234	140
8767	670	670.2911
8768	530 or 670	670.2912
8769	832	215.?
8770	832	832
8771	832	832
8772	832	670.2913
8773	449	448
8774	470 or 670	470.741
8776	670	670.2914
8777	831	215.?
8778	385	212.159
8779	685	685
8780	613	670.2915
8781	470	832
8782	530	670.2916
8783	670	670.2917
8784	470 or 670	470.742
8785	670	670.2918

Bo	CHDS 3	Konkordanz (as of 31.12.2015)
8786	594 or 634	670.2919
8787	510	530
8788	832	832
8789	720	470.743
8790	670	670.2920
8791	670	832
8792	670	832
8794	670	670.2921
8795	832	470.744
8796 +	591.I.b.A	591.I.b.A
8797	832	832
8799	670	670.2923
8800	627	670.2924
8801	791	791
8802	470 or 670	470.745
8803	530	460
9441 +	311.2.B	311.2.B
9442	670	670.3415
9443	470 or 670	470.2184
9444	791	831
9445	832	832
9446	470	460
9447	470	832
9448	670	832
9449 +	400.A	400.A
9450	39 or 832	670.3416
9457	832	832
9459	470	470.2186
9460	470	470.2187
9461	470 or 670	832
9462	670	670.3417
9463	832	832
9464	670	670.3418
9465 (+$^{?}$)	744.11	670.2996

Bo	*CHDS 3*	*Konkordanz (as of 31.12.2015)*
9466	3.2	250.?
9470	670	670.3420
9471	832	215.?
9472	670	647
9474	275	832
9476	670	670.?
9477	670	670.2997
9478	457	370
9479	323.1.C	323.1.C
9480	242	470.2188
9482	660, 669 or 670	470.2189
9483	670	832
9484	670	832
9485	670	832
9486	670	832
9487	530	832
9488	470	832
9489	212	832
9490 +	29.A	29.A
9491	670	832
9492	832	832
9493	460	832
9494	470	832
9495	670	832
9497	409 or 448	832
9498	832	832
9500	832	832
9501	832	832
9502	530 or 670	832
9503	215	832
9504	215	832
9505	582	832
9506	530	832
9507	626	832

Bo	CHDS 3	Konkordanz (as of 31.12.2015)
9508	670	832
9509	470	832
9511 +	3.1.B	3.1.B
9512	470 or 670	832
9513	832	832
9514 +	674	674
9515	568	832
9516 +	691.2	691.2
9517	500 or 670	832
9518 +	255.2.E	255.2.E
9519	470	832
9520	819	832
9522	831	832
9523	832	832
9524	470 or 670	832
9525	470 or 670	832
9526 +	292.II.b.A	292.II.b.A
9527	470 or 670	832
9528	832	832
9529	832	832
9530	832	832
9531	832	832
9532	832	832
9534	832	832
9535	215 or 275	832